# MCSE Core Four Practice Tests

Ed Tittel
James Michael Stewart
Gary Novosel

## MCSE Core Four Practice Tests Exam Cram

© 1999 The Coriolis Group. All Rights Reserved.

This book may not be duplicated in any way without the express written consent of the publisher, except in the form of brief excerpts or quotations for the purposes of review. The information contained herein is for the personal use of the reader and may not be incorporated in any commercial programs, other books, databases, or any kind of software without written consent of the publisher. Making copies of this book or any portion for any purpose other than your own is a violation of United States copyright laws.

### Limits Of Liability And Disclaimer Of Warranty

The author and publisher of this book have used their best efforts in preparing the book and the programs contained in it. These efforts include the development, research, and testing of the theories and programs to determine their effectiveness. The author and publisher make no warranty of any kind, expressed or implied, with regard to these programs or the documentation contained in this book.

The author and publisher shall not be liable in the event of incidental or consequential damages in connection with, or arising out of, the furnishing, performance, or use of the programs, associated instructions, and/or claims of productivity gains.

### Trademarks

Trademarked names appear throughout this book. Rather than list the names and entities that own the trademarks or insert a trademark symbol with each mention of the trademarked name, the publisher states that it is using the names for editorial purposes only and to the benefit of the trademark owner, with no intention of infringing upon that trademark.

The Coriolis Group, LLC
14455 N. Hayden Road, Suite 220
Scottsdale, Arizona 85260

480/483-0192
FAX 480/483-0193
http://www.coriolis.com

Library of Congress Cataloging-in-Publication Data
Tittel, Ed
    MCSE core four practice tests exam cram / by Ed Tittel, James Michael Stewart, and Gary Novosel.
        p.   cm.
    ISBN 1-57610-475-3
    1. Electronic data processing personnel--Certification.
2. Microsoft software--Examinations Study guides.   I. Stewart, James Michael.   II. Novosel, Gary.   III. Title.
QA76.3.T573657   1999
005.4'4769--dc21                                        99-24319
                                                        CIP

Printed in the United States of America
10 9 8 7 6 5 4 3 2 1

**Publisher**
Keith Weiskamp

**Acquisitions Editor**
Shari Jo Hehr

**Marketing Specialist**
Cynthia Caldwell

**Project Editor**
Sharon Sanchez McCarson

**Production Coordinator**
Wendy Littley

**Cover Design**
Jody Winkler

**Layout Design**
April Nielsen

**CD-ROM Developer**
Robert Clarfield

 CORIOLIS

**⊘ CORIOLIS**

14455 North Hayden Road, Suite 220 • Scottsdale, Arizona 85260

# Coriolis: The Training And Certification Destination ™

Thank you for purchasing one of our innovative certification study guides, just one of the many members of the Coriolis family of certification products.

Certification Insider Press™ has long believed that achieving your IT certification is more of a road trip than anything else. This is why most of our readers consider us their *Training And Certification Destination*. By providing a one-stop shop for the most innovative and unique training materials, our readers know we are the first place to look when it comes to achieving their certification. As one reader put it, "I plan on using your books for all of the exams I take."

To help you reach your goals, we've listened to others like you, and we've designed our entire product line around you and the way you like to study, learn, and master challenging subjects. Our approach is *The Smartest Way To Get Certified™*.

In addition to our highly popular *Exam Cram* and *Exam Prep* guides, we have a number of new products. We recently launched Exam Cram Live!, two-day seminars based on *Exam Cram* material. We've also developed a new series of books and study aides—*Practice Tests Exam Crams* and *Exam Cram Flash Cards*—designed to make your studying fun as well as productive.

Our commitment to being the *Training And Certification Destination* does not stop there. We just introduced *Exam Cram Insider*, a biweekly newsletter containing the latest in certification news, study tips, and announcements from Certification Insider Press. (To subscribe, send an email to **eci@coriolis.com** and type "subscribe insider" in the body of the email.) We also recently announced the launch of the Certified Crammer Society and the Coriolis Help Center—two new additions to the Certification Insider Press family.

We'd like to hear from you. Help us continue to provide the very best certification study materials possible. Write us or email us at **cipq@coriolis.com** and let us know how our books have helped you study, or tell us about new features that you'd like us to add. If you send us a story about how we've helped you, and we use it in one of our books, we'll send you an official Coriolis shirt for your efforts.

Good luck with your certification exam and your career. Thank you for allowing us to help you achieve your goals.

Keith Weiskamp
Publisher, Certification Insider Press

# About The Authors

## Ed Tittel

**Ed Tittel** is the Series Editor for the Certification Insider Press *Exam Cram* series, and has personally contributed to nearly half the titles currently available in that series. A contributor to over 90 computer-related books, Ed has written on subjects as diverse as *Stupid PC Tricks* (Addison-Wesley, 1991) and study guides on Windows NT Workstation and Networking Essentials.

Ed is also a member of the faculties for NetWorld+Interop, and for The Internet Security Conference (TISC), where he teaches classes with James Michael Stewart on Windows NT security and performance issues. In a past life, Ed worked for Novell, Inc., where his final job was Director of Technical Marketing. In that position, he oversaw technical content for trade shows and the BrainShare developer's conference, prior to his departure in 1994. Since then, Ed has presided over LANWrights, Inc., a small training and research consultancy, and spends his time writing, teaching, and researching networking topics.

In his spare time, Ed is a devoted, if indifferent, pool player, and likes to cook (especially homemade stock, and all the good things that come from it). Ed and his trusty and frenetic Labrador retriever, Blackie, make their home in Austin, Texas.

You can reach Ed via email at **etittel@lanw.com,** or at his Web site at **http://www.lanw.com.**

## James Michael Stewart

**James Michael Stewart** is a full-time writer focusing on Windows NT and Internet topics. Most recently he has worked on several titles in the *Exam Cram* and *Exam Prep* series, including *NT Server 4, NT Workstation 4, NT Server 4 in the Enterprise, Windows 98, IIS 4.0, Proxy 2.0, and FrontPage 98.* Michael has written articles for numerous print and online publications, including C|Net, *Computer Currents, InfoWorld, Windows NT Magazine,* and *Datamation.* He is also a regular speaker at Networld+Interop, and has taught at TISC, WNTIS, and NT SANS.

Michael has been developing Windows NT 4 MCSE-level courseware and training materials for several years, including both print and online publications, as well as classroom presentation of NT training materials. He has been an MCSE since 1997, with a focus on Windows NT 4.0.

Despite his degree in philosophy, his computer knowledge is self-acquired, based on almost 14 years of hands-on experience. Michael has been active on the Internet for quite some time, where most people know him by his "nomme de wire" as McIntyre.

You can reach Michael by email at **michael@lanw.com**, or through his Web page at **http://www.lanw.com/jmsbio.htm**.

# Gary Novosel

**Gary Novosel** is an MCSE, MCP+ Internet, and MCT. He is currently employed as an IM Project Manager with Compaq Computer Corporation in northwest Houston, TX. He started building PCs and networks in 1983, has expertise in Unix as well as Windows NT, and is an expert in distributed document management. Gary graduated summa cum laude from the University of the State of New York with a Bachelor's degree in Computer Information Systems. He has consulted for General Electric, the Department of Defense, the Department of Energy, and several commercial nuclear power plants. Gary served nine years in the nuclear Navy in both submarines and nuclear instructor service.

In his spare time, he enjoys taking perfectly good pieces of wood and attempting to turn them into recognizable objects other than sawdust. Gary also spends much of his off time with his wife Yvete, daughter Jamie, grandson Matthew, and pet dog-humans Lady and Chancey. You can contact Gary by email at **gnovosel@swbell.net**.

# Acknowledgments

## Ed Tittel

To begin with, I'd like to thank the many authors who contributed one or more practice tests to this book or to the Web site, including Bill Peeples, Craig Epstein, James Michael Stewart, Pete Cramer, and Gary Novosel. Without their expert help and knowledge of the tests and their underlying concepts, terms, and technologies, this book wouldn't be half as good as it has turned out. Next, I'd like to thank the crew at LANWrights who worked on this book, including Dawn Rader, my project manager, friend, and helpmeet; and also Kathleen Scanlon, Kyle Findlay, and Louise Leahy, for their editing services and insights. You guys help us keep things turned in on time, and we're grateful to each and every one of you!

Then, too, there's the crew at Coriolis who made this whole adventure possible. Starting at the top, thanks to Keith Weiskamp yet again for his vision, marketing genius, and his unwillingness to take "no" for an answer. After that, our doughty acquisitions gang, which now includes both Shari Jo Hehr and Jeff Kellum, deserves more than just a pat on the back. On the editing and production sides of the house, we want to thank Sandra Lassiter and Paula Kmetz, managers extraordinaire, plus Sharon McCarson, our wonderful project editor. Then, too, the production coordinator, Wendy Littley, the cover designer, Jody Winkler, and April Nielsen, the layout designer, all deserve their share of kudos. Please accept our fervent thanks for your help with this book.

Finally, I'd like to thank my family and my friends for making this whole mad adventure possible. First, to my parents, Al and Ceil (happy 80th birthday, Mom!), thanks for helping me appreciate the value of lifelong learning. To my sister, Kathi, her husband, Mike, and the offspring, Helen and Colin: Thanks for helping me relearn the value of family, patience, and laughter. Finally, to Robert Wiggins, my best friend (and sometime co-author): Thanks for listening to me rant when I needed to, and for following up with advice that was both humorous and effective when the ranting was over. You're the best!

## James Michael Stewart

Thanks to my boss and co-author, Ed Tittel, for including me in this book series. To my parents, Dave and Sue, thanks for your love and consistent support. To Mark, I count the days until…well, I've been counting for so long I don't remember anymore. To HERbert, everyone knows what type of pet you are because you've marked everything I own with cat fur. And finally, as always, to Elvis—every time I sing in the shower, I have to fish the glue-on, lamb-chop sideburns out of the drain.

## Gary Novosel

There are a few times in one's life when you know you were in the right place at the right time. This happened for me when I was introduced to the staff at LANWrights. From the beginning, Ed, Mary, Dawn, and Kyle continue to bend over backwards to make my life easier and the efforts of writing less painful. Thanks to all of you.

For my wife, Yvete, I know you have tolerated me more than everybody else has in my life. I have always loved you and couldn't imagine my server room without you. For my daughter, Jamie, I am very proud of your accomplishments and will continue to be there for you at every turn. To my grandson, Matthew, at one year old I realize that eating this book is more of a possibility for you than reading it; however, I'll get you a copy anyway. If there was ever someone that motivated me to be successful and loving in my life, it would be you.

Finally, to my Mom. Although you probably don't understand what's in this book, you can now show everybody what I do for a living. Thanks for being my Mom.

# Table Of Contents

# Introduction

## You Spoke

Welcome to *MCSE Core Four Practice Tests Exam Cram*! A recent survey of Coriolis readers showed us how important practice questions are in your efforts to prepare to take and pass certification exams. You asked us to give you more practice tests on a variety of certification topics, including MCSE Core Four, MCSE+I, A+, Network+, and others.

## We Responded

The *Practice Tests Exam Cram* series is our answer to your requests, and provides you with entirely new practice tests for many certification topics. Each practice test appears in its own chapter, followed by a corresponding answer and explanation chapter, in the same format as the Sample Test and Answer Key chapters at the end of each of our *Exam Cram* books. We not only tell you which answers are correct, but we also explain why the right answers are right and why the wrong answers are wrong. That's because we're convinced that you can learn as much from understanding the wrong answers as you can from knowing the right ones!

This book makes a perfect companion to any study material you may own that covers the exam subject matter. For those of you who already own the *MCSE Core Four Exam Cram* books, we have included a time-saving study feature. At the end of each answer, you will find a reference to the corresponding *Exam Cram* book or to another valuable resource in which that topic is more thoroughly explained. That way, if you want to review the material on which the question is based in more depth, you will be able to quickly locate that information.

## But Wait, There's More!

This book also includes a CD-ROM that contains four more exams, one on each of the Core Four topics. These additional exams are built using an interactive adaptive format that allows you to practice in an exam environment similar to Microsoft's own testing formats.

Thus, this book gives you access to a pool of 200 questions for each of the Core Four exam topics. Thorough review of these materials should provide you with a reasonably complete view of the numerous topics and types of questions you're likely to see on a real Microsoft exam. Because questions come and go on Microsoft exams pretty regularly, we can't claim total coverage, but we have designed these question pools to deal with the topics and concepts that are most likely to appear on a real exam in some form or fashion.

# Using This Book To Prepare For An Exam

You should begin your preparation process by working through the materials in the book to guide your studies. As you discover topics or concepts that may be unfamiliar or unclear, be sure to consult additional study materials to increase your knowledge and familiarity with the materials involved. In fact, you should employ this particular technique on any practice test questions you come across that may expose areas in your knowledge base that may need further development or elaboration.

To help you increase your knowledge base, we suggest that you work with whatever materials you have at hand. Certainly, we can't help but recommend our own *Exam Cram* and *Exam Prep* books, but you will find that the *Exam Crams* also cite numerous other sources of information as well.

Among those tools, some other materials worth obtaining include any Resource Kits available from Microsoft Press for software under discussion. For this book, that clearly means the *Windows NT 4.0 Workstation Resource Kit* and the *Windows NT 4.0 Server Resource Kit* (don't forget the three supplements to the latter that are now also available as well). Microsoft's TechNet CD (which includes electronic copies of all Resource Kits and their supplements), plus copies of the Knowledge Base, product manuals, Technical Notes, and training materials, is a pricey (a subscription costs $299 per year) but valuable source of information. You can learn more about this invaluable tool online at **http:// www.microsoft.com/technet**. Finally, for the Networking Essentials exam, Microsoft also offers a Self-Study Kit on that topic, currently available in a second edition. It too, is a worthwhile resource (as is our own *MCSE Networking Essentials Exam Prep*).

Once you've worked your way through the text-based practice tests in the book, use the interactive adaptive exams on the CD to assess your test readiness. That way, you can build confidence in your ability to sit for and pass these exams, as you master the subject material for each one.

We recommend you shoot for a passing result when you take the practice tests. If you don't make the grade, you should probably take some other practice exams—possibly from one or more of the vendors shown below, all of whom offer practice exams for under $100 (in most cases, well under $100). The following are some vendors of practice exams and their corresponding URLs:

➤ CramSession     **http://www.cramsession.com/**

➤ Hardcore MCSE   **http://www.hardcoremcse.com/**

➤ LANWrights     **http://www.lanw.com/books/examcram/order.htm**

➤ MeasureUp      **http://www.measureup.com/**

Use these practice exams to increase your knowledge, familiarity, and understanding of the materials involved in the topic area, rather than spending the money on a Microsoft test that you may not pass. Because each Microsoft exam costs $100, we think you're better off spending some of that money on more preparation, and saving what you can to help pay for the exam when you're really ready to pass it!

# Tell Us What You Think

Feel free to share your feedback on the book with us. We'll carefully consider your comments. Please be sure to include the title of the book in your message; otherwise, we'll be forced to guess which book you are writing about. Please send your comments and questions to us at **cipq@coriolis.com**.

Visit our Web site at **www.certificationinsider.com** for the latest on what's happening in the world of certification, updates, and new *Exam Prep* and *Exam Cram* titles. For the latest information on Microsoft certification exams, visit Microsoft's Web site at **www.microsoft.com/train_cert**. Good luck with your exams!

# Networking Essentials Practice Test #1

## Question 1

Your Windows NT Workstation computer has a serial mouse on COM1, an external modem on COM2, and a laser printer on LPT1. The ports for these devices are using their standard default IRQs. You add a 3Com NIC to the system with an IRQ setting of 3. Which of the following ports is in conflict with the new NIC?

○ a.  LPT1

○ b.  COM1

○ c.  COM2

○ d.  LPT2

## Question 2

Bridges are used to connect to networks, and are often referred to as Media Access Control (MAC) *bridges* because they operate at this level of the OSI model. In the OSI model, which of the seven layers contains the Media Access Control (MAC) sublayer?

○ a.  Physical layer

○ b.  Application layer

○ c.  Network layer

○ d.  Data Link layer

○ e.  Transport layer

○ f.  Session layer

# Question 3

Two wires are placed close together in a wiring rack. A signal is passed through one wire. Some of the same signal is detected in the other wire. What is this occurrence called?

○ a. Bleeding

○ b. Broadcast storm

○ c. Attentuation

○ d. Beaconing

○ e. Crosstalk

# Question 4

A subnet mask is a TCP/IP bit pattern used for what purpose?

○ a. To mask a portion of an IP address to distinguish the network ID from the host ID

○ b. To mask a portion of an IP address to distinguish the DHCP server address from the DNS server address

○ c. To mask a portion of an IP address to distinguish the NetBIOS name from the DNS name

○ d. To mask a portion of an IP address to distinguish the default gateway address from the router address

# Question 5

Which of the following is the naming scheme used by Windows NT to identify network members via human-friendly names?

○ a. DNS

○ b. NWLink

○ c. NetBIOS

○ d. AppleTalk

○ e. DHCP

# Question 6

As the length of cable increases, the amount of _____ also increases.

○ a.  Nodes

○ b.  Terminators

○ c.  Attenuation

○ d.  Chatter

○ e.  Crosstalk

# Question 7

Two networks, both using IPX/SPX, need to be connected. However, one employs token ring technology and the other is an Ethernet network. Which device can be used to connect these two networks?

○ a.  Hub

○ b.  Router

○ c.  Transceiver

○ d.  Repeater

# Question 8

Which network cabling type can be used to connect nodes separated by no more than 185 meters due to attenuation?

○ a.  Fiber-optic

○ b.  10Base2 (Thinnet coaxial)

○ c.  10BaseT (twisted-pair)

○ d.  10Base5 (Thicknet coaxial)

# Question 9

You must select a naming convention and resolution system for a TCP/IP-based Windows NT network.

Required result:

- Resources must be accessible across the network through standard browse lists (that is, Network Neighborhood and Windows NT Explorer). Note that the network employs several routers.

Optional desired results:

- Network settings for each client must be dynamically assigned to eliminate manual configuration hassles.

- Internet information services must be accessible using either FQDN or 15-character device names.

Proposed solution:

- Implement both a HOSTS file and an LMHOSTS file on each client workstation.

Which results does the proposed solution produce?

- ○ a. The proposed solution produces the required result and both the optional desired results.

- ○ b. The proposed solution produces the required result and only one of the optional desired results.

- ○ c. The proposed solution produces the required result but does not produce either of the optional desired results.

- ○ d. The proposed solution does not produce the required result.

# Question 10

You're having difficulty getting a client to communicate with the rest of the network. It's connected to the network via twisted-pair cable to a hub. Using a volt-ohm meter (VOM), you test the wires in the twisted-pair cable. To detect whether there's a break in the wire, what should you set the VOM to read?

- ○ a. Impedance measured in ohms

- ○ b. Resistance measured in ohms

- ○ c. Voltage measured in volts

- ○ d. Current measured in amps

# Question 11

Which networking protocol supported by Windows NT Server can be used to communicate with Macintosh computers?

- ○ a.  AppleTalk
- ○ b.  TCP/IP
- ○ c.  DLC
- ○ d.  NetBEUI
- ○ e.  NWLink

# Question 12

You need to connect a network that is spread over three dozen locations. You decide to employ a networking service that can provide high bandwidth at each location. Users will have a periodic need for significant bandwidth; however, you don't want to pay for a large pipeline when it's not in use. What's the best WAN technology you can lease for this situation?

- ○ a.  X.25
- ○ b.  T3
- ○ c.  Frame relay
- ○ d.  ISDN
- ○ e.  T1

# Question 13

What is a broadcast storm?

- ○ a.  A kind of interference where signals traveling on one set of wires can impose on another set running in parallel (often within the same cable bundle).
- ○ b.  When the number of wide-distribution messages overwhelms a network's carrying capacity.
- ○ c.  The effects of impedance on signal strength in cables (that is, the further the signals must travel, the weaker they become).
- ○ d.  The technique used to elect a ring monitor on a token ring network whenever a new node enters the ring (or when the current ring monitor exits the ring).

# Question 14

In order for routers to search through multiple paths and decide which path is the most expedient delivery direction for each packet, which network topology do you need to deploy?

○ a. Ring

○ b. Bus-star

○ c. Mesh

○ d. Star

# Question 15

Which network device reduces broadcast storms on a network by simply not forwarding the broadcasts?

○ a. Router

○ b. Repeater

○ c. Hub

○ d. Bridge

# Question 16

Which troubleshooting or detection device can be used to view collisions and frame counts on network segments?

○ a. Time-domain reflectometer (TDR)

○ b. Oscilloscope

○ c. Advanced cable tester

○ d. Volt-ohm meter (VOM)

# Question 17

Which of the following statements are true about peer-to-peer or workgroup networking? [Check all correct answers]

❑ a. When a server goes offline, it can prevent new users from logging on.

❑ b. Groups are used to grant or restrict access across the network.

❑ c. The host of a resource may experience a performance degradation if many users access the resource at the same time.

❑ d. No specialized or advanced hardware is required to maintain the network.

❑ e. A central repository of usernames and passwords is maintained.

❑ f. Logging into a network station does not grant you immediate access to all network resources.

# Question 18

Why is the cabling type CAT5 UTP the most susceptible to crosstalk?

○ a. It uses signals of light.

○ b. It has a large diameter.

○ c. It isn't shielded.

○ d. It supports only a short cable-segment lengths.

# Question 19

A gateway is used to perform what action or function?

○ a. To connect two networks that use different topologies (for example, token ring, bus, and star)

○ b. To connect two networks that use different protocols

○ c. To strengthen the signal strength of transmissions

○ d. To connect two networks that use different cable types

○ e. To connect two or more network segments

# Question 20

What's the maximum throughput possible when four 56K modems are combined in a multiplexer link?

○ a. 56Kbps

○ b. 128Kbps

○ c. 224Kbps

○ d. 1.54Mbps

# Question 21

Which of the following actions will result in a faster network by reducing the number of network reads and writes?

○ a. Changing the TCP window size to a smaller setting

○ b. Deploying an Ethernet network instead of a token ring network

○ c. Using TCP/IP as the primary protocol instead of NetBEUI

○ d. Increasing the size of network packets

# Question 22

To implement user-level security on a peer-to-peer network with Windows 95 clients, which component needs to be added?

○ a. WINS server

○ b. DHCP server

○ c. DLC

○ d. Windows NT Server

# Question 23

Which process is used by a token ring network to resume communications after an interruption?

○ a. Attenuation

○ b. Broadcasting

○ c. Beaconing

○ d. Flux identification

# Question 24

The process of repackaging data bits into data frames is the responsibility of which layer of the OSI model?

○ a.  Session layer

○ b.  Presentation layer

○ c.  Data Link layer

○ d.  Network layer

# Question 25

Your organization runs a NetBEUI network. It comprises two segments, each on different floors, that are connected by a bridge. After 15 new clients are added to the network, there's too much traffic, resulting in numerous collisions, session timeouts, and failed communications.

Required result:

- Reduce network traffic to restore a more stable environment.

Optional desired results:

- Keep costs low.

- Do not deploy another protocol.

Proposed solution:

- Replace the bridge with an Ethernet switching hub.

Which results does the proposed solution produce?

○ a.  The proposed solution produces the required result and both the optional desired results.

○ b.  The proposed solution produces the required result and only one of the optional desired results.

○ c.  The proposed solution produces the required result but does not produce either of the optional desired results.

○ d.  The proposed solution does not produce the required result.

# Question 26

Your organization has leased additional office space in a building that's one-quarter mile down the street. The workers in the new space need access to the LAN. You've been given permission by the city to run network cabling from the original building to the new building using the existing telephone poles.

Required result:

- Establish a network link between the two buildings.

Optional desired results:

- Keep costs low.
- Keep interference to a minimum.

Proposed solution:

- Run UTP wire between the two buildings.

Which results does the proposed solution produce?

- ○ a. The proposed solution produces the required result and both the optional desired results.

- ○ b. The proposed solution produces the required result and only one of the optional desired results.

- ○ c. The proposed solution produces the required result but does not produce either of the optional desired results.

- ○ d. The proposed solution does not produce the required result.

# Question 27

Which of the following standard cable types can be used to connect network segments separated by a distance of 150 meters or more without a repeater or amplifier? [Check all correct answers]

- ❑ a. Thinnet
- ❑ b. UTP
- ❑ c. FDDI
- ❑ d. Thicknet

# Question 28

Your network employs the TCP/IP protocol. The size of your network is growing quickly. You need to deploy name resolution services that can resolve a name into an IP address. Which of the following Windows NT Server services or capabilities cannot be used to resolve names? [Check all correct answers]

❏ a.  DNS

❏ b.  DHCP

❏ c.  OSPF

❏ d.  HOSTS

❏ e.  WINS

❏ f.  RAS

❏ g.  PPTP

# Question 29

You're custom building all the cables to be used to connect your clients, servers, and network devices. If you're using 10Base2 cabling, which connector type should you use?

○ a.  RJ-11

○ b.  RJ-45

○ c.  BNC

○ d.  AUI

# Question 30

Which category of cable is rated for use as a voice communications carrier only?

○ a.  CAT1

○ b.  CAT2

○ c.  CAT3

○ d.  CAT4

# Question 31

Which of the following are not advantages of the Network Driver Interface Specification (NDIS)? [Check all correct answers]

❑ a. NDIS binds a protocol stack to a network card.

❑ b. NDIS allows you to bind multiple protocols to a single network card.

❑ c. NDIS allows you to bind multiple network cards to a single protocol.

❑ d. NDIS can use ODI.

# Question 32

On Windows NT networks, what's the maximum character length of a NetBIOS name?

○ a. 8

○ b. 255

○ c. 15

○ d. 16

# Question 33

You're wiring a 10Base2 network. Using a digital volt-ohm meter, you test the resistance of your cabling and connection components. Which of the following measurements indicate a faulty part? [Check all correct answers]

❑ a. Terminators reading 50 ohms

❑ b. T-connectors reading 1,000 ohms

❑ c. Cabling reading 0 ohms

❑ d. Barrel connectors reading 50 ohms

# Question 34

Which of the following items functions in the Network layer of the OSI model?

○ a. Software

○ b. A router

○ c. An Ethernet switching hub

○ d. A terminator

# Question 35

Which type of disk configuration is rated as RAID 5?

○ a.  Expanding volume set

○ b.  Disk duplexing

○ c.  Disk mirroring

○ d.  Disk striping with parity

# Question 36

Which device can be used to measure the length of a cable segment?

○ a.  A gateway

○ b.  A volt-ohm meter

○ c.  A time-domain reflectometer

○ d.  A protocol analyzer

# Question 37

After installing several new segments of 10Base2 cabling, you realize you forgot to terminate several sections of cable. If you do not install the 50-ohm terminators, what will occur on the network?

○ a.  Attenuation

○ b.  Amplification

○ c.  Signal bounce

○ d.  Crosstalk

○ e.  Broadcast storm

# Question 38

Which device can be added to an IPX/SPX-only network to grant clients access to the Internet without adding another protocol?

○ a.  A bridge

○ b.  A router

○ c.  A gateway

○ d.  A hub

# Question 39

Which of the following statements about CSMA/CD is true?

○ a. It's a network access method that expects data transmission collisions on the network and expects hosts to resend data when it collides.

○ b. It resolves beaconing through multiple timed broadcasts over restricted segments.

○ c. It announces to the network its intention to transmit data over the network media.

○ d. It reduces attenuation by increasing the output gain on NICs.

# Question 40

You're the systems administrator of a network that serves five floors of your office building. Recently, due to an increased need to access files and re-sources on various floors and the Internet, traffic has greatly increased, causing an overall degradation in network performance.

Required result:

• Increase network performance by reducing unnecessary network traffic.

Optional desired results:

• Reduce the amount of broadcast traffic.

• Sort or filter packets to reduce the traffic transmitted between floors (that is, segments).

Proposed solution:

• Install a bridge between each floor.

Which results does the proposed solution produce?

○ a. The proposed solution produces the required result and both the optional desired results.

○ b. The proposed solution produces the required result and only one of the optional desired results.

○ c. The proposed solution produces the required result but does not produce either of the optional desired results.

○ d. The proposed solution does not produce the required result.

# Question 41

Which device in the following list does not have the capability to sort or filter packets?

○ a. A router

○ b. A gateway

○ c. A bridge

○ d. A repeater

○ e. A brouter

# Question 42

A PS/2 mouse typically uses which IRQ?

○ a. 3

○ b. 4

○ c. 5

○ d. 7

○ e. 9

○ f. 12

# Question 43

Which of the following operating systems can employ share-level security? [Check all correct answers]

❑ a. Windows 95

❑ b. Windows NT Workstation

❑ c. Windows For Workgroups 3.11

❑ d. Windows NT Server

# Question 44

A router can be used on networks that employ which of the following protocols? [Check all correct answers]

❑ a.  AppleTalk

❑ b.  NetBEUI

❑ c.  IPX/SPX

❑ d.  TCP/IP

# Question 45

A BNC barrel connector is used to perform what function?

○ a.  It's used to connect a piece of cable to a repeater.

○ b.  It's used to connect cable to a network client.

○ c.  It's used to connect two pieces of cable in a linear bus topology.

○ d.  It absorbs signals to prevent signal bounce.

# Question 46

What is NetBIOS?

○ a.  A protocol used on all Unix networks

○ b.  A nonroutable protocol used by Microsoft networks

○ c.  A small, fast, and efficient Transport layer protocol

○ d.  A software interface and naming convention

# Question 47

Which of the following network scenarios is most secure?

○ a.  A network of Windows 95 computers

○ b.  A standalone Windows For Workgroups 3.11 system

○ c.  A peer-to-peer network of Windows NT Workstation computers

○ d.  A Windows NT Server-hosted domain

# Question 48

The ability to bind multiple protocols to a single NIC or a single protocol to multiple NICs is afforded a network server or client by which of the following networking standards? [Check all correct answers]

❏  a.  IEEE 802

❏  b.  NDIS

❏  c.  FDDI

❏  d.  Ethernet

❏  e.  SONET

❏  f.  ODI

# Question 49

The principle of "the device that holds the electronic voucher is allowed to transmit data onto the network" is true of which one of the following items?

○  a.  CSMA/CD

○  b.  A router

○  c.  Token ring

○  d.  A gateway

# Question 50

Which WAN technology was developed to replace analog phone lines, but has been deployed most often to support data transmissions in the U.S.?

○  a.  Frame relay

○  b.  SONET

○  c.  ATM

○  d.  ISDN

○  e.  DSL

# Question 51

Which packet-switching technology transmits variable-length frames at the Data Link layer through the most cost-effective path?

○ a. FDDI

○ b. SMDS

○ c. Frame relay

○ d. ATM

# Question 52

Which of the following protocols are not transport protocols? [Check all correct answers]

❑ a. NetBEUI

❑ b. TCP

❑ c. IP

❑ d. IPX

❑ e. SPX

❑ f. PPP

❑ g. AppleTalk

# Question 53

You send a TCP/IP packet with a destination address of 172.16.1.54. Your Windows NT Server system's TCP/IP settings are as follows:

- IP address: 172.16.1.5
- Subnet mask: 255.255.0.0
- Gateway: 172.16.1.10

What destination will receive this packet?

○ a. The device with a host ID of 16.1.54 and a network ID of 172

○ b. The device with a host ID of 1.54 and a network ID of 172.16

○ c. The device with a host ID of 172.16 and a network ID of 1.54

○ d. The device with a host ID of 54 and a network ID of 172.16.1

# Question 54

RG-62 A/U coaxial is the standard cable type used on which type of network?

○  a.  FDDI

○  b.  ATM

○  c.  ARCNet

○  d.  Ethernet

# Question 55

Which connection technologies rely on line of sight? [Check all correct answers]

❏  a.  Microwave

❏  b.  Radio wave

❏  c.  Infrared

❏  d.  Fiber-optic

# Networking Essentials Answer Key #1

**2**

| | | | |
|---|---|---|---|
| 1. c | 15. a | 29. c | 43. a, c |
| 2. d | 16. c | 30. a | 44. a, c, d |
| 3. e | 17. c, d, f | 31. a, d | 45. c |
| 4. a | 18. c | 32. c | 46. d |
| 5. c | 19. b | 33. b, d | 47. d |
| 6. c | 20. c | 34. b | 48. b, f |
| 7. b | 21. d | 35. d | 49. c |
| 8. b | 22. d | 36. c | 50. d |
| 9. b | 23. c | 37. c | 51. c |
| 10. b | 24. c | 38. c | 52. c, d, f, g |
| 11. a | 25. a | 39. a | 53. b |
| 12. c | 26. d | 40. b | 54. c |
| 13. b | 27. a, c, d | 41. d | 55. a, c |
| 14. c | 28. b, c, f, g | 42. f | |

## Question 1

Answer c is correct. COM2 and COM4 typically use IRQ 3. Therefore, the NIC is in conflict with COM2. LPT1 typically uses IRQ 7. Therefore, answer a is incorrect. COM1 and COM3 typically use IRQ 4. Therefore, answer b is incorrect. LPT2 typically uses IRQ 5. Therefore, answer d is incorrect.

For more information, see Chapter 5 of *MCSE Networking Essentials Exam Cram*.

## Question 2

Answer d is correct. The MAC sublayer is contained by the Data Link layer. The Data Link layer is also the home of the Logical Link Control (LLC) sublayer. Therefore, answers a, b, c, e, and f are incorrect.

For more information, see Chapter 3 of *MCSE Networking Essentials Exam Cram*.

## Question 3

Answer e is correct. When a signal from one wire bleeds into another, it's called crosstalk. Therefore, answers a, b, c, and d are incorrect.

For more information, see Chapter 4 of *MCSE Networking Essentials Exam Cram*.

## Question 4

Answer a is correct. A subnet mask is used to mask a portion of an IP address to distinguish the network ID from the host ID. Therefore, answers b, c, and d are incorrect.

For more information, see Chapter 5 of *MCSE TCP/IP Exam Cram*.

## Question 5

Answer c is correct. NetBIOS is the naming scheme and software interface used by Windows NT to identify network members by 15-character names. DNS is a name resolution service associating FQDN with IP addresses. Therefore, answer a is incorrect. NWLink is a networking protocol. Therefore, answer b is incorrect. AppleTalk is a networking protocol that's supported to allow for Macintosh client communications. Therefore, answer d is incorrect. DHCP is a dynamic IP addressing tool for client configuration. Therefore, answer e is incorrect.

For more information, see Chapter 9 of *MCSE Networking Essentials Exam Cram*.

## Question 6

Answer c is correct. As the length of a cable increases, the amount of attenuation also increases. Nodes are connection points on a network and are not associated with cable length. Therefore, answer a is incorrect. Terminators appear only on the ends of certain cable types. Therefore, answer b is incorrect. Chatter is another term for network traffic and is not associated with cable length. Therefore, answer d is incorrect. Crosstalk occurs when signals from one wire are picked up by another wire. Therefore, answer e is incorrect.

For more information, see Chapter 4 of *MCSE Networking Essentials Exam Cram*.

## Question 7

Answer b is correct. A router can be used to connect two networks that use the same protocol but have different networking topologies. A hub is little more than a repeater that connects segments of a network employing the same technology. Therefore, answer a is incorrect. A transceiver is the connection point on network devices that sends and receives signals. Therefore, answer c is incorrect. A repeater is a device used to strengthen signals. It does not connect networks that use different technologies. Therefore, answer d is incorrect.

For more information, see Chapter 5 of *MCSE Networking Essentials Exam Cram*.

## Question 8

Answer b is correct. 10Base2 cabling has a maximum use limit of 185 meters. Fiber-optic cable has a limitation of 2 kilometers. Therefore, answer a is incorrect. 10BaseT cannot be used over 100 meters. Therefore, answer c is incorrect. 10Base5 can be used up to 500 meters. Therefore, answer d is incorrect.

For more information, see Chapter 4 of *MCSE Networking Essentials Exam Cram*.

## Question 9

Answer b is correct. The proposed solution produces the required result and only one of the optional desired results. Windows NT uses NetBIOS as its base naming convention. Its base resolution method is via NetBIOS broadcasts, which are not transferred over routers. Therefore, the HOSTS and LMHOSTS files will provide resolution no matter where a client or resource is located. However, without DHCP, DNS, and WINS, clients are not dynamically configured. Plus, the HOSTS and LMHOSTS files demand a high level of management to remain current.

For more information, see chapters 3 and 9 of *MCSE Networking Essentials Exam Cram*.

## Question 10

Answer b is correct. Short circuits are most easily detected by measuring resistance, in ohms, between two conductors. VOMs do not usually test for impedance. Therefore, answer a is incorrect. The wire will not have a voltage or a current, so measuring these will be inconclusive. Therefore, answers c and d are incorrect.

For more information, see Chapter 11 of *MCSE Networking Essentials Exam Cram*.

## Question 11

Answer a is correct. AppleTalk is used to communicate with Macintosh computers. TCP/IP, DLC, NetBEUI, and NWLink cannot be used to communicate with IBM mainframes. Therefore, answers b, c, d, and e are incorrect.

For more information, see Chapter 3 of *MCSE Networking Essentials Exam Cram*.

## Question 12

Answer c is correct. Frame relay is the only listed technology that offers a variable bandwidth and a pay-for-what-you-use plan (provided by a service company). X.25 has a low-bandwidth ceiling. Therefore, answer a is incorrect. T3, ISDN, and T1 are all high-bandwidth technologies, but they do not have variable bandwidth options. Therefore, answers b, d, and e are incorrect.

For more information, see Chapter 10 of *MCSE Networking Essentials Exam Cram*.

## Question 13

Answer b is correct. A broadcast storm occurs when the number of wide-distribution messages overwhelms a network's carrying capacity. Crosstalk refers to the kind of interference that signals traveling on one set of wires can impose on another set running in parallel. Therefore, answer a is incorrect. Attenuation describes the effects of impedance on signal strength in cables. Therefore, answer c is incorrect. Beaconing is the technique used to elect a ring monitor on a token ring network whenever a new node enters the ring (or when the current ring monitor exits the ring). Therefore, answer d is incorrect.

For more information, see chapters 6 and 11 of *MCSE Networking Essentials Exam Cram.*

## Question 14

Answer c is correct. A mesh topology is the only listed topology that provides multiple paths between sender and receiver. Ring, bus-star, and star all provide only a single path between sender and receiver. Therefore, answers a, b, and d are incorrect.

For more information, see Chapter 5 of *MCSE Networking Essentials Exam Cram.*

## Question 15

Answer a is correct. A router reduces broadcast storms on a network by simply not forwarding the broadcasts. Repeaters, hubs, and bridges all pass broadcast messages. Therefore, answers b, c, and d are incorrect.

For more information, see chapters 6 and 11 of *MCSE Networking Essentials Exam Cram.*

## Question 16

Answer c is correct. Advanced cable testers are able to display frame counts and collisions. TDRs are used to check for cable faults or measure cable lengths. Therefore, answer a is incorrect. Oscilloscopes can only measure and monitor waveforms. Therefore, answer b is incorrect. VOMs can only measure voltage, current, and basic electrical activity. Therefore, answer d is incorrect.

For more information, see Chapter 11 of *MCSE Networking Essentials Exam Cram.*

# Question 17

Answers c, d, and f are correct. The statements "The host of a resource may experience a performance degradation if many users access the resource at the same time," "No specialized or advanced hardware is required to maintain the network," and "Logging into a network station does not grant you immediate access to all network resources" are all true. Peer-to-peer networks do not have servers. Therefore, answer a is incorrect. Groups are not used to grant access across a peer-to-peer network. Therefore, answer b is incorrect. A central control system is not found in a peer-to-peer network. Therefore, answer e is incorrect.

For more information, see Chapter 2 of *MCSE Networking Essentials Exam Cram*.

# Question 18

Answer c is correct. CAT5 UTP is susceptible to crosstalk because it lacks shielding. The use of light, such as by fiber-optic cable, would prevent crosstalk. Therefore, answer a is incorrect. The diameter of a cable does not prevent or enable crosstalk. Therefore, answer b is incorrect. The length of a cable does not prevent or enable crosstalk. Therefore, answer d is incorrect.

For more information, see Chapter 4 of *MCSE Networking Essentials Exam Cram*.

# Question 19

Answer b is correct. A gateway connects two networks that use different protocols. A router connects two networks that use different topologies. Therefore, answer a is incorrect. A repeater or amplifier is used to strengthen the signal strength of transmissions. Therefore, answer c is incorrect. A bridge is used to connect two networks that use different cable types. Therefore, answer d is incorrect. A hub is used to connect two or more network segments. Therefore, answer e is incorrect.

For more information, see Chapter 5 of *MCSE Networking Essentials Exam Cram*.

# Question 20

Answer c is correct. Four modems used in a multiplexer link create the maximum bandwidth of all their individual throughputs aggregated into a whole—or in this situation, 224Kbps. Therefore, answers a, b, and d are incorrect.

For more information, see Chapter 15 of *MCSE TCP/IP Exam Cram*.

## Question 21

Answer d is correct. Increasing the size of the network packets is the only action in this list that results in a faster network. A smaller TCP window size will increase network reads and writes, thus slowing down the network. Therefore, answer a is incorrect. Token ring uses fewer network reads and writes due to its 4 and 16KB packets, whereas Ethernet uses a 1,564-byte packet. Therefore, answer b is incorrect. TCP/IP requires more system overhead and is slower in operation than NetBEUI. Therefore, answer c is incorrect.

For more information, see Chapter 3 of *MCSE Networking Essentials Exam Cram.*

## Question 22

Answer d is correct. A Windows NT Server added to a peer-to-peer network transforms the network into a domain that uses user-level security. A WINS server is a name resolution service that associates NetBIOS names with IP addresses. Therefore, answer a is incorrect. A DHCP server is a dynamic IP addressing tool for client configuration. Therefore, answer b is incorrect. DLC is a protocol used to communicate with mainframes and network-attached printers. Therefore, answer c is incorrect.

For more information, see Chapter 2 of *MCSE Networking Essentials Exam Cram.*

## Question 23

Answer c is correct. Beaconing is the communication-recovery process used by token ring. Attenuation is the loss of signal strength over a long cable. Therefore, answer a is incorrect. Broadcasting is sending out signals to all recipients at the same time. Therefore, answer b is incorrect. Flux identification is a fictitious process. Therefore, answer d is incorrect.

For more information, see Chapter 5 of *MCSE Networking Essentials Exam Cram.*

## Question 24

Answer c is correct. The Data Link layer is responsible for repackaging data bits into data frames. The Session layer is responsible for maintaining communications between different systems. Therefore, answer a is incorrect. The Presentation layer is responsible for translating information from generic formats to platform or application formats, and vice versa. Therefore, answer b is incorrect. The Network layer is responsible for addressing and routing. There-fore, answer d is incorrect.

For more information, see Chapter 3 of *MCSE Networking Essentials Exam Cram*.

## Question 25

Answer a is correct. The proposed solution produces the required result and both the optional desired results. An Ethernet switching hub works at the Media Access Control (MAC) sublayer to reduce traffic from one segment to the next. No additional protocols are required, and it's a moderately inexpen-sive solution. Therefore, answers b, c, and d are incorrect.

For more information, see Chapter 5 of *MCSE Networking Essentials Exam Cram*.

## Question 26

Answer d is correct. The proposed solution does not produce the required re-sult. UTP has a length limitation of 100 meters. One-quarter of a mile is over 400 meters. The cable would not support the network traffic. Therefore, no network link would be established. Although costs are kept low, interference is *not* kept to a minimum because UTP is unshielded. Therefore, answers a, b, and c are incorrect.

For more information, see Chapter 4 of *MCSE Networking Essentials Exam Cram*.

## Question 27

Answers a, c, and d are correct. Thinnet, FDDI, and Thicknet all have a dis-tance capability of over 100 meters. UTP has a distance limit of 100 meters. Therefore, answer b is incorrect.

For more information, see Chapter 4 of *MCSE Networking Essentials Exam Cram*.

## Question 28

Answers b, c, f, and g are correct. DHCP, OSPF, RAS, and PPTP are not name resolution services. However, DNS, HOSTS, and WINS *are* name reso-lution services. Therefore, answers a, d, and e are incorrect.

For more information, see chapters 3 and 9 of *MCSE Networking Essentials Exam Cram.*

## Question 29

Answer c is correct. 10Base2 is Thinnet cabling, which uses BNC connectors. RJ-11 is used for telephone wire. Therefore, answer a is incorrect. RJ-45 is used for 10BaseT networks. Therefore, answer b is incorrect. Attachment Unit Interface (AUI) connectors are used for 10Base5 (Thicknet) networks. Therefore, answer d is incorrect.

For more information, see Chapter 4 of *MCSE Networking Essentials Exam Cram.*

## Question 30

Answer a is correct. CAT1 cabling is rated for voice communications only. CAT2, CAT3, and CAT4 are rated as data carriers at 4, 10, and 16Mbps, respectively. Therefore, answers b, c, and d are incorrect.

For more information, see Chapter 4 of *MCSE Networking Essentials Exam Cram.*

## Question 31

Answers a and d are correct. NDIS cannot bind a protocol stack to a network card, and it cannot use ODI; ODI is used only by NetWare networks, NDIS is used by Microsoft networks. NDIS allows multiple protocols to be bound to a single NIC, or a single protocol to multiple NICs. Therefore, answers b and c are incorrect.

For more information, see Chapter 4 of *MCSE Networking Essentials Exam Cram.*

## Question 32

Answer c is correct. The maximum length is 15 characters. A character length of 8 is the name limitation for files on an MS-DOS-based FAT partition. Therefore, answer a is incorrect. A character length of 255 is the name limitation for files on a Windows NT FAT or NTFS partition. Therefore, answer b is incorrect. The actual NetBIOS name, as maintained by the system, is 16 characters long, but the last character is reserved for system use to define the type of object the name refers to. Therefore, answer d is incorrect.

For more information, see Chapter 9 of *MCSE Networking Essentials Exam Cram.*

## Question 33

Answers b and d are correct. T-connectors and barrel connectors should not offer any resistance (0 ohms). Terminators should offer 50 ohms of resistance. Therefore, answer a is incorrect. Cabling should offer 0 ohms of resistance. Therefore, answer c is incorrect.

For more information, see Chapter 11 of *MCSE Networking Essentials Exam Cram.*

## Question 34

Answer b is correct. A router operates at the Network layer of the OSI model. Software operates above the Application layer. Therefore, answer a is incorrect. An Ethernet switching hub operates at the Data Link layer. Therefore, answer c is incorrect. A terminator operates below the Physical layer. Therefore, answer d is incorrect.

For more information, see Chapter 3 of *MCSE Networking Essentials Exam Cram.*

## Question 35

Answer d is correct. Disk striping with parity is RAID 5. A volume set is RAID 0. Therefore, answer a is incorrect. Disk duplexing and disk mirroring are RAID 1. Therefore, answers b and c are incorrect.

For more information, see Chapter 9 of *MCSE Networking Essentials Exam Cram.*

## Question 36

Answer c is correct. A time-domain reflectometer is used to measure the length of a cable. A gateway is used to translate between protocols from one network to another. Therefore, answer a is incorrect. A volt-ohm meter is used to check resistance on cable segments, connectors, and terminators. Therefore, answer b is incorrect. A protocol analyzer has the ability to collect network statistics as well as examine individual data packets transmitted over a network wire. Therefore, answer d is incorrect.

For more information, see Chapter 11 of *MCSE Networking Essentials Exam Cram.*

# Question 37

Answer c is correct. The absence of terminators results in signal bounce. Attenuation is signal degradation caused by lengthy cable segments, and it's reduced by an amplification device. Therefore, answers a and b are incorrect. Crosstalk occurs when signals from one wire are picked up by another adjacent wire. Therefore, answer d is incorrect. A broadcast storm occurs when one or more machines send out signals to multiple destinations to the extent that no other traffic can occur over the network. Therefore, answer e is incorrect.

For more information, see chapters 4 and 5 of *MCSE Networking Essentials Exam Cram.*

# Question 38

Answer c is correct. A gateway is the only device that has the ability to translate between one protocol and another, as would be needed to grant IPX/SPX clients access to TCP/IP-based Internet resources. Bridges, routers, and hubs do not have translation capabilities. Therefore, answers a, b, and d are incorrect.

For more information, see Chapter 5 of *MCSE Networking Essentials Exam Cram.*

# Question 39

Answer a is correct. Carrier Sense Multiple Access with Collision Detection, or CSMA/CD, is a network access method that expects data transmission collisions on the network, and expects hosts to resend data when it collides. The statement in answer b is a fictitious construct. Therefore, answer b is incorrect. Carrier Sense Multiple Access with Collision *Avoidance*, or CSMA/CA, announces to the network its intention to transmit data over the network media. Therefore, answer c is incorrect. The statement in answer d is a fictitious construct. Therefore, answer d is incorrect.

For more information, see Chapter 5 of *MCSE Networking Essentials Exam Cram.*

# Question 40

Answer b is correct. Installing a bridge will reduce network traffic by sorting frames based on the MAC address of their destination, thus satisfying the primary requirement and one of the optional requirements. However, a bridge will not restrict broadcast traffic between segments. Therefore, answers a, c, and d are incorrect.

For more information, see Chapter 5 of *MCSE Networking Essentials Exam Cram.*

## Question 41

Answer d is correct. A repeater does not sort or filter packets. Routers, gateways, bridges, and brouters all include varying levels of packet sorting and filtering. Therefore, answers a, b, c, and e are incorrect.

For more information, see Chapter 5 of *MCSE Networking Essentials Exam Cram.*

## Question 42

Answer f is correct. IRQ 12 is typically used by a PS/2 mouse. IRQ 3 is used by COM2 or COM4. IRQ 4 is used by COM1 or COM3. IRQ 5 is often used by sound cards or LPT2. IRQ 7 is used by LPT1. IRQ 9 is a cascading IRQ. Therefore, answers a, b, c, d, and e are all incorrect.

For more information, see Chapter 5 of *MCSE Networking Essentials Exam Cram.*

## Question 43

Answers a and c are correct. Windows 95 and WFW 3.11 support share-level security. Windows NT does not support share-level security. Therefore, answers b and d are incorrect.

For more information, see chapters 2 and 9 of *MCSE Networking Essentials Exam Cram.*

## Question 44

Answers a, c, and d are correct. AppleTalk, IPX/SPX, and TCP/IP are routable protocols. NetBEUI is not routable. Therefore, answer b is incorrect.

For more information, see Chapter 3 of *MCSE Networking Essentials Exam Cram.*

## Question 45

Answer c is correct. A BNC barrel connector is used to connect two pieces of cable in a linear bus topology. An RJ-45 is used to connect UTP or STP cable to a repeater. Therefore, answer a is incorrect. A NIC is used to connect a network client to a cable. Therefore, answer b is incorrect. A terminator absorbs signals to prevent signal bounce. Therefore, answer d is incorrect.

For more information, see Chapter 4 of *MCSE Networking Essentials Exam Cram.*

## Question 46

Answer d is correct. NetBIOS is a software interface and naming convention. TCP/IP is a protocol used on all Unix networks. Therefore, answer a is incorrect. NetBEUI is a nonroutable protocol used by Microsoft networks, and it's a small, fast, and efficient Transport layer protocol. Therefore, answers b and c are incorrect.

For more information, see Chapter 3 of *MCSE Networking Essentials Exam Cram.*

## Question 47

Answer d is correct. A Windows NT Server-hosted domain is the most secure network environment in this list. Workgroups, standalone systems, and peer-to-peer networks do not offer client/server authentication and secure password databases, which both provide for a secure environment. Therefore, answers a, b, and c are incorrect.

For more information, see Chapter 2 of *MCSE Networking Essentials Exam Cram.*

## Question 48

Answers b and f are correct. NDIS and ODI are networking standards that grant the ability to bind multiple protocols to a single NIC, or a single protocol to multiple NICs. This is afforded a network server or client for Microsoft and Novell networks, respectively. IEEE 802 defines various network topologies, interfaces, and connections. Therefore, answer a is incorrect. FDDI is a fiber-optic, token-passing, networking technology. Therefore, answer c is incorrect. Ethernet is a networking technology defined by IEEE 802.3. Therefore, answer d is incorrect. SONET is a high-speed network connection. Therefore, answer e is incorrect.

For more information, see Chapter 4 of *MCSE Networking Essentials Exam Cram.*

# Question 49

Answer c is correct. "The device that holds the electronic voucher is allowed to transmit data onto the network" is the principle of token ring. Carrier Sense Multiple Access with Collision Detection (CSMA/CD) is a network access method that expects data transmission collisions on the network, and expects hosts to resend the data when collisions occur. Therefore, answer a is incorrect. A router connects two or more networks and allows data to pass between the networks. Therefore, answer b is incorrect. A gateway translates packets from one protocol to another. Therefore, answer d is incorrect.

For more information, see Chapter 5 of *MCSE Networking Essentials Exam Cram.*

# Question 50

Answer d is correct. ISDN (Integrated Services Digital Network) is a WAN technology originally developed to replace analog telephone lines and is most often deployed to support data transmissions in the U.S. Frame relay, SONET, and ATM are all WAN technologies, but they are not intended to replace analog phone lines. Therefore, answers a, b, and c are incorrect. DSL is a connection technology that employs analog telephone lines. Therefore, answer e is incorrect.

For more information, see Chapter 10 of *MCSE Networking Essentials Exam Cram.*

# Question 51

Answer c is correct. Frame relay is a packet-switching technology that transmits variable-length frames at the Data Link layer through the most cost-effective path. FDDI, SMDS, and ATM use a fixed-width cell (frame) technology. Therefore, answers a, b, and d are incorrect.

For more information, see Chapter 10 of *MCSE Networking Essentials Exam Cram.*

# Question 52

Answers c, d, f, and g are correct. IP and IPX are Network layer protocols. PPP is an encapsulation Data Link layer protocol. AppleTalk is a Presentation layer protocol. NetBEUI, TCP, and SPX are all Transport layer protocols. Therefore, answers a, b, and e are incorrect.

For more information, see Chapter 3 of *MCSE Networking Essentials Exam Cram.*

# Question 53

Answer b is correct. The device with a host ID of 1.54 and a network ID of 172.16 will receive this packet. Therefore, answers a, c, and d are incorrect.

For more information, see Chapter 4 of *MCSE TCP/IP Exam Cram.*

# Question 54

Answer c is correct. RG-62 A/U coaxial is the standard cable type used on ARCNet networks. FDDI networks use fiber-optic cable. Therefore, answer a is incorrect. ATM is a packet-switching technology, not a network topology. This type of technology can be hosted by networks using nearly any type of cabling. Therefore, answer b is incorrect. Ethernet networks typically use UTP or STP cabling. Therefore, answer d is incorrect.

For more information, see Chapter 4 of *MCSE Networking Essentials Exam Cram.*

# Question 55

Answers a and c are correct. Microwave and infrared rely on line of sight. Radio wave and fiber-optic do not. Therefore, answers b and d are incorrect. Note that fiber-optic is a type of cable that channels light flashes from sender to receiver; however, light communications without channeling media would be line of sight dependant.

For more information, see Chapter 4 of *MCSE Networking Essentials Exam Cram.*

# Networking Essentials Practice Test #2

## Question 1

Which of the following employs two or more drives in combination for fault tolerance and performance?

○ a. Redundant Array of Independent Drivers

○ b. Repetitive Array of Inexpensive Disks

○ c. Redundant Array of Inexpensive Disks

○ d. Redundant Amount of Inexpensive Drives

## Question 2

Which network diagnostic device can determine the length of a cable and locate breaks in a cable within a few feet using sonar pulses?

○ a. Time-domain reflectometer

○ b. Digital volt-ohm meter

○ c. Oscilloscope

○ d. Protocol analyzer

# Question 3

What's the default IRQ setting for the math coprocessor?

○ a.  IRQ 2(9)

○ b.  IRQ 13

○ c.  IRQ 12

○ d.  IRQ 7

# Question 4

You're designing a peer-to-peer network for a small office that consists of four Microsoft Windows 95 computers. Which protocol should you use to get the workstations connected with very little configuration?

○ a.  TCP/IP

○ b.  AppleTalk

○ c.  NWLink/IPX

○ d.  DLC

# Question 5

What do the NDIS and ODI networking standards enable?

○ a.  They allow multiple protocols to bind to a single network adapter.

○ b.  They allow any network adapter to be used in any NDIS/ODI computer.

○ c.  They allow for universal communication over any medium.

○ d.  They allow for remote accessibility to any server.

# Question 6

Which type of cable is the most resistant to crosstalk?

○ a.  Thicknet

○ b.  Fiber optic

○ c.  Coaxial

○ d.  Thinnet

# Question 7

Which type of signal transmission uses analog signaling over a range of frequencies and uses amplifiers for signal regeneration?

○ a.  Channel transmission

○ b.  Baseband transmission

○ c.  Multiplexed transmission

○ d.  Broadband transmission

# Question 8

Which type of cabling uses BNC connectors?

○ a.  10Base5 (thicknet)

○ b.  10Base2 (thinnet coaxial)

○ c.  10Base-T (twisted-pair)

○ d.  None of the above

# Question 9

Which of the following describes a network in which each workstation has equal capabilities and responsibilities?

○ a.  Client/server

○ b.  File and print server

○ c.  Peer-to-peer

○ d.  Application server

# Question 10

Reagan recently purchased a second network card for his server and is concerned about running out of resources. He presently has a UPS on COM1, a modem on COM2, a network card on IRQ 5, a hardware RAID controller on IRQ 11, and a second SCSI controller on IRQ 10. He has no intention of adding any additional devices in the future other than what's mentioned here. Which remaining resources are available for Reagan to use? [Check all correct answers]

❏ a. IRQ 8

❏ b. IRQ 1

❏ c. IRQ 15

❏ d. IRQ 7

# Question 11

PPP supports which of the following protocols? [Check all correct answers]

❏ a. DLC

❏ b. TCP/IP

❏ c. IPX/SPX compatible

❏ d. NetBEUI

❏ e. AppleTalk

# Question 12

Which of the following files contains mappings between NetBIOS computer names and their IP addresses?

○ a. DNS

○ b. HOSTS

○ c. LMHOSTS

○ d. CSMA/CD

# Question 13

What's the maximum recommended length for RG-11 cable segments?

○ a.  100 meters

○ b.  185 meters

○ c.  20 kilometers

○ d.  500 meters

# Question 14

Which device regenerates an analog data signal so it can travel longer distances without attenuating?

○ a.  Passive hub

○ b.  Router

○ c.  Repeater

○ d.  Bridge

# Question 15

Which network topology provides the highest level of fault tolerance?

○ a.  Ring

○ b.  Bus

○ c.  Star

○ d.  Mesh

# Question 16

Your LAN is running Cat 3 UTP cable to your 10/100 autosensing hub, and every computer in your office has a combo network card. You've been asked to upgrade the LAN to 100Mbps. What must be done to accomplish 100Mbps speeds?

○ a. Upgrade the cabling to Cat 5, upgrade the hub to 100Mbps, and upgrade the NICs to 10/100Mbps cards.

○ b. Upgrade the cabling to Cat 5 and upgrade the NICs to 10/100Mbps cards.

○ c. Upgrade the hub to full duplex and upgrade the NICs to 10/100Mbps cards.

○ d. None of the above will accomplish 100Mbps speeds.

# Question 17

Which of the following protocols uses routing tables to find the most efficient route from point to point?

○ a. WINS

○ b. DNS

○ c. ARP

○ d. RIP

# Question 18

Which of the following IP addresses are Class B addresses? [Check all correct answers]

❏ a. 192.168.100.1

❏ b. 143.122.86.2

❏ c. 88.55.22.1

❏ d. 191.224.100.2

# Question 19

Which protocol does SLIP support?

- ○ a.  NWLink/IPX
- ○ b.  NetBEUI
- ○ c.  NetBIOS
- ○ d.  TCP/IP

# Question 20

At which layers of the OSI model does a gateway work? [Check all correct answers]

- ❏ a.  Presentation
- ❏ b.  Session
- ❏ c.  Transport
- ❏ d.  Application

# Question 21

What does DHCP do for Windows NT Server?

- ○ a.  It configures your NetBIOS naming scheme.
- ○ b.  It assigns dynamic IP addresses to devices on the network.
- ○ c.  It configures the corporate firewall for intranet use.
- ○ d.  None of the above.

# Question 22

Which of the following is a hybrid device that can perform both routing and bridging on the same network?

- ○ a.  Router
- ○ b.  Repeater
- ○ c.  Bridge
- ○ d.  Brouter

# Question 23

You've been contracted to network an office campus. This campus consists of six individual buildings. The buildings are about 300 feet from each other. After talking with the project leader, you're given the OK to connect the buildings however you see fit, but you must keep the costs as low as possible.

Required result:

- Network all the buildings together.

Optional desired results:

- Have the network run at 100Mbps.

- Keep costs as low as possible.

Proposed solution:

- Install fiber-optic cable to connect the buildings.

Which results does the proposed solution produce?

- ○ a. The proposed solution produces the required result and both the optional desired results.

- ○ b. The proposed solution produces the required result and only one of the optional desired results.

- ○ c. The proposed solution produces the required result but does not produce either of the optional desired results.

- ○ d. The proposed solution does not produce the required result.

# Question 24

Which layer of the OSI model is responsible for packet handling, error-free delivery, and error handling?

- ○ a. Data Link layer

- ○ b. Transport layer

- ○ c. Session layer

- ○ d. Presentation layer

# Question 25

After adding 20 new clients to your network, you're getting numerous colli-sions and session timeouts. Your office is running a NetBEUI protocol across three segments connected by a bridge.

Required result:

- Reduce network traffic to restore a more stable environment.

Optional desired results:

- Keep costs low.

- Do not deploy another protocol.

Proposed solution:

- Replace the bridge with a router.

Which results does the proposed solution produce?

○ a.  The proposed solution produces the required result and both the optional desired results.

○ b.  The proposed solution produces the required result and only one of the optional desired results.

○ c.  The proposed solution produces the required result but does not produce either of the optional desired results.

○ d.  The proposed solution does not produce the required result.

# Question 26

Your organization has opened a branch office on the other side of town. This branch office needs access to the corporate domain.

Required result:

- Establish a network link between the two buildings.

Optional desired results:

- Have data transmission speeds up to 1.54Mbps.

- Keep costs to a minimum.

Proposed solution:

- Lease a T3 line from the phone company to connect to the branch office.

Which results does the proposed solution produce?

- ○ a. The proposed solution produces the required result and both the optional desired results.

- ○ b. The proposed solution produces the required result and only one of the optional desired results.

- ○ c. The proposed solution produces the required result but does not produce either of the optional desired results.

- ○ d. The proposed solution does not produce the required result.

# Question 27

Which of the following cable types can be used to connect network segments separated by 450 feet or more without an amplifier or a repeater? [Check all correct answers]

- ❑ a. 10Base-T

- ❑ b. 10Base2

- ❑ c. FDDI

- ❑ d. 10Base5

# Question 28

Which of the following can divide transmissions into two or more channels on a single medium?

○ a.  Repeater

○ b.  Multiplexer

○ c.  Router

○ d.  Gateway

# Question 29

Which of the following protocols are routable? [Check all correct answers]

❏ a.  TCP/IP

❏ b.  NetBEUI

❏ c.  DLC

❏ d.  AppleTalk

❏ e.  DECnet

❏ f.  LAT

❏ g.  NWLink/IPX

# Question 30

Which of the following is a type of packet-switching technology that was originally designed to connect remote terminals to mainframe host systems?

○ a.  ATM

○ b.  ISDN

○ c.  Frame relay

○ d.  X.25

# Question 31

Which dial-up protocol provides dynamic IP addressing, multiprotocol support, and a password login?

○ a. SLIP

○ b. NetBEUI

○ c. PPP

○ d. NDIS

# Question 32

Which network diagnostic tool would you use to determine bottlenecks, connection errors, and traffic problems?

○ a. DHCP

○ b. A protocol analyzer

○ c. Performance Monitor

○ d. ATM

# Question 33

Which of the following RAID levels are supported by Windows NT? [Check all correct answers]

❑ a. Disk striping with parity

❑ b. Disk striping with large blocks

❑ c. Disk mirroring

❑ d. Disk striping

# Question 34

Which of the following protocols reside at the Transport layer of the OSI model? [Check all correct answers]

❑ a. IP

❑ b. TCP

❑ c. IPX

❑ d. SPX

❑ e. DLC

# Question 35

A user in your office is having problems connecting to the network. The only protocol he's using is TCP/IP. Looking at the following information, determine what this user's problem is.

User's TCP/IP configuration:

- IP Address: 192.168.100.5

- Subnet Mask: 255.255.0.0

- Network Address: 192.168.100.0

- Subnet Mask: 255.255.255.0

○ a. An incorrect IP address is being used.

○ b. WINS is not configured correctly.

○ c. An incorrect subnet mask is being used.

○ d. An incorrect IP address and subnet mask are being used.

# Question 36

Which protocols do not guarantee delivery of data? [Check all correct answers]

❑ a. TCP

❑ b. SPX

❑ c. IP

❑ d. IPX

# Question 37

Which of the following WAN technologies offers packet switching and speeds upward of 100Mbps, and is ideal for teleconferencing?

○ a. X.25

○ b. ATM

○ c. ISDN

○ d. T1

# Question 38

You're putting together a peer-to-peer network in your home office. You have three Windows 95 machines. Which protocol should you use to connect your machines?

○ a. NWLink/IPX

○ b. AppleTalk

○ c. DLC

○ d. ATM

# Question 39

Which of the following statements about CSMA/CA is true?

○ a. CSMA/CA is a network access method that expects data transmission collisions on the network and expects hosts to resend data when it collides.

○ b. CSMA/CA sends data across the network at scheduled intervals.

○ c. CSMA/CA announces to the network its intention to transmit data over the network media.

○ d. CSMA/CA reduces attenuation by increasing the output gain on NICs.

# Question 40

The VP of your company would like you to increase the performance of the company's network. She has noticed that Internet access and her connection to a shared database on the network have slowed within the last couple of weeks. She assumes that because she's noticing the problem, other users on the network are as well. After some initial troubleshooting, you notice a high level of broadcast traffic on your network. You notice that the engineering, sales, and manufacturing departments, all in opposite parts of the buildings, are causing almost all the broadcast traffic.

Required result:

- Increase the performance of the company's network.

Optional desired results:

- Reduce the amount of broadcast traffic across the entire network.

- Divide the network to keep broadcasts contained to their own segments.

Proposed solution:

- Install routers between departments.

Which results does the proposed solution produce?

- ○ a. The proposed solution produces the required result and both the optional desired results.

- ○ b. The proposed solution produces the required result and only one of the optional results.

- ○ c. The proposed solution produces the required result but does not produce either of the optional desired results.

- ○ d. The proposed solution does not produce the required result.

# Question 41

Which of the following is a hardware address that uniquely identifies a node on the network?

- ○ a. IP address
- ○ b. Default gateway
- ○ c. ARP
- ○ d. MAC address

# Question 42

Which IRQ is normally reserved for the keyboard?

○ a. 3

○ b. 1

○ c. 5

○ d. 7

○ e. 9

○ f. 12

# Question 43

How many ohms must the cable terminator read on the end of a coaxial cable?

○ a. 75 ohms

○ b. 55 ohms

○ c. 50 ohms

○ d. 0 ohms

# Question 44

Which categories of cable can sustain transmission rates of up to 16Mbps? [Check all correct answers]

❑ a. Cat 5

❑ b. Cat 2

❑ c. Cat 3

❑ d. Cat 4

# Question 45

What does WINS do?

- ○ a.  It resolves host names to IP addresses.
- ○ b.  It maintains and distributes IP addresses to clients.
- ○ c.  It maintains domain name registrations.
- ○ d.  It resolves NetBIOS names to IP addresses.

# Question 46

What's the Application layer of the OSI model responsible for?

- ○ a.  Preparing data to be delivered or translated into generic or platform-specific formats.
- ○ b.  Providing network services that support applications, error recovery, and flow control.
- ○ c.  Setting up and terminating lines of communication across a network.
- ○ d.  Breaking data down into manageable chunks to be sent over the network.

# Question 47

Which protocols reside in the Physical layer of the OSI model? [Check all correct answers]

- ❑ a.  TCP
- ❑ b.  SPX
- ❑ c.  IP
- ❑ d.  IPX
- ❑ e.  None of the above

# Question 48

Which of the following WAN technologies allows for bandwidth on demand?

○ a. X.25

○ b. ISDN

○ c. Frame relay

○ d. FDDI

# Question 49

Which choices are associated with share-level security? [Check all correct answers]

❑ a. Windows 95

❑ b. A high level of security

❑ c. Passwords can be given to resources on a network

❑ d. Windows NT

# Question 50

Which layer of the OSI model does the IEEE 8.02 standard deal with?

○ a. Application

○ b. Data Link

○ c. Presentation

○ d. Network

# Question 51

Which of the following is a TCP/IP protocol that provides remote terminal emulation?

○ a. FTP

○ b. HTTP

○ c. Telnet

○ d. SNMP

# Question 52

Which of the following protocols are connection-oriented protocols? [Check all correct answers]

❑ a.  NetBEUI

❑ b.  TCP

❑ c.  IP

❑ d.  IPX

❑ e.  SPX

❑ f.  X.25

❑ g.  UDP

# Question 53

You send a TCP/IP packet with a destination address of 192.168.100.54. Your Windows NT Server system's TCP/IP settings are as follows:

- IP address: 192.168.100.5

- Subnet mask: 255.255.255.0

- Default gateway: 192.168.100.1

Which destination will receive this packet?

○ a.  The device with a host ID of 168.100.54 and a network ID of 192

○ b.  The device with a host ID of 100.54 and a network ID of 192.168

○ c.  The device with a host ID of 192.168 and a network ID of 100.54

○ d.  The device with a host ID of 54 and a network ID of 192.168.100

# Question 54

You plan on using RAID 5 on your server. What's the minimum number of hard drives you'll need?

○ a.  2

○ b.  1

○ c.  6

○ d.  3

# Question 55

Which type of connector is used by Thicknet?

○ a.  BNC

○ b.  RJ-45

○ c.  AUI

○ d.  RJ-11

# Networking Essentials
# Answer Key #2

| | | | |
|---|---|---|---|
| 1. c | 15. d | 29. a, d, e, g | 43. c |
| 2. a | 16. b | 30. d | 44. a, d |
| 3. b | 17. d | 31. c | 45. d |
| 4. c | 18. b, d | 32. b | 46. b |
| 5. a | 19. d | 33. a, c, d | 47. e |
| 6. b | 20. a, b, c, d | 34. b, d | 48. c |
| 7. d | 21. b | 35. c | 49. a, c |
| 8. b | 22. d | 36. c, d | 50. b |
| 9. c | 23. b | 37. b | 51. c |
| 10. c, d | 24. b | 38. a | 52. b, e, f |
| 11. b, c, d | 25. d | 39. c | 53. d |
| 12. c | 26. b | 40. a | 54. d |
| 13. d | 27. b, c, d | 41. d | 55. c |
| 14. c | 28. b | 42. b | |

# Question 1

Answer c is correct. Redundant Array of Inexpensive Disks (RAID) is a category of disk drives that employ two or more drives in combination for fault tolerance and performance. Answers a, b, and d are incorrect—these are not valid expansions of RAID.

For more information, see Chapter 9 of *MCSE Networking Essentials Exam Cram*.

# Question 2

Answer a is correct. A time-domain reflectometer (TDR) sends sonar-like pulses to look for crimps, breaks, and shorts in a cable. A TDR is also able to determine the length of a cable run and whether it's longer than specifications require. A digital volt-ohm meter (DVM) measures resistance on a cable. Therefore, answer b is incorrect. Oscilloscopes measure signal voltage over time. Therefore, answer c is incorrect. A protocol analyzer monitors all traffic sent over the network. Therefore, answer d is incorrect.

For more information, see Chapter 11 of *MCSE Networking Essentials Exam Cram*.

# Question 3

Answer b is correct. The default IRQ for the math coprocessor is 13. IRQ 2(9) is used by the video card. IRQ 12 is for a PS/2 mouse, and IRQ 7 is reserved for LPT1. Therefore, answers a, c, and d are incorrect.

For more information, see Chapter 5 of *MCSE Networking Essentials Exam Cram*.

# Question 4

Answer c is correct. The easiest protocol to install for this situation is NWLink/IPX. Although TCP/IP is a viable option for connecting the workstations, it's not the best option in this case. The question asked for a connection with very little configuration needed. DLC and AppleTalk would not work for this scenario. Therefore, answers a, b, and d are incorrect.

For more information, see Chapter 3 of *MCSE Networking Essentials Exam Cram*.

## Question 5

Answer a is correct. The Network Device Interface Specification (NDIS) and Open Data Interconnect (ODI) standards are Microsoft's and NetWare's (respectively) methods for enabling the binding of multiple protocols to a single network adapter. Answers b, c, and d do not accurately describe NDIS and ODI. Therefore, answers b, c and d are incorrect.

For more information, see Chapter 4 of *MCSE Networking Essentials Exam Cram.*

## Question 6

Answer b is correct. Crosstalk is when a signal from one wire is picked up by another wire. Fiber-optic cable is the most resistant cable to crosstalk because the physical signal is being passed over the cable as light, which is not as susceptible to this problem as are electronic signals. Thicknet, coaxial, and thinnet cables are all less resistant to crosstalk than fiber optic. Therefore, answers a, c, and d are incorrect.

For more information, see Chapter 4 of *MCSE Networking Essentials Exam Cram.*

## Question 7

Answer d is correct. Broadband transmission uses several different frequencies or channels for transmission over a single medium. It also uses amplifiers for signal regeneration. None of the other options signal over a range of frequencies and use amplifiers. Therefore, answers a, b, and c are incorrect.

For more information, see Chapter 5 of *MCSE Networking Essentials Exam Cram.*

## Question 8

Answer b is correct. 10Base2 cables use BNC (British Naval Connector) for connecting coax cable. AUI connectors are associated with 10Base5 cable. Therefore, answer a is incorrect. 10Base-T uses RJ-45 connectors. Therefore, answer c is incorrect. Because answer b is correct, answer d is incorrect.

For more information, see Chapter 4 of *MCSE Networking Essentials Exam Cram.*

# Question 9

Answer c is correct. Peer-to-peer networking has no hierarchy among computers, and each computer is responsible for sharing its own resources. Peer-to-peer networking is generally simpler and less expensive but does not offer the same performance under heavy loads. Client/server networking is an architecture in which some computers are dedicated to serve other computers. Therefore, answer a is incorrect. File and print servers are dedicated to file and print sharing. Therefore, answer b is incorrect. Application servers are used to provide application services to clients. Therefore, answer d is incorrect.

For more information, see Chapter 2 of *MCSE Networking Essentials Exam Cram.*

# Question 10

Answers c and d are correct. Answer c is correct because IRQ 15 is usually available, so Reagan would be able to use it for his second network card. Answer d is correct because there's no mention of a printer, and Reagan has no intention of adding any more devices, so IRQ 7 would also be available to use. IRQ 8 is for the server's realtime clock. Therefore, answer a is incorrect. The keyboard uses IRQ 1. Therefore, answer b is incorrect.

For more information, see Chapter 5 of *MCSE Networking Essentials Exam Cram.*

# Question 11

Answers b, c, and d are correct. PPP (Point-to-Point Protocol) includes support for TCP/IP, IPX/SPX, and NetBEUI. It does not include support for DLC and AppleTalk. Therefore, answers a and e are incorrect.

For more information, see Chapter 3 of *MCSE Networking Essentials Exam Cram.*

# Question 12

Answer c is correct. The LMHOSTS file contains mappings between NetBIOS names and their IP addresses. NetBIOS name resolution involves checking the NetBIOS name mapping tables in various places until an entry is found that maps the NetBIOS name to the IP address. The DNS (Domain Name Service) database resolves hostnames to IP addresses. The HOSTS file is a text file that contains hostname-to-IP address mappings. CSMA/CD is a network access method and does not apply in this scenario. Therefore, answers a, b, and d are incorrect.

For more information, see Chapter 11 of *MCSE Networking Essentials Exam Cram.*

## Question 13

Answer d is correct. RG-11 cable (a.k.a. 10Base5) is limited to a maximum of 500 meters. UTP and STP are limited to 100 meters. Therefore, answer a is incorrect. Thinnet (RG-58) is limited to 185 meters. Therefore, answer b is incorrect. Answer c is incorrect because 20 kilometers is the limitation for fiber-optic cable.

For more information, see Chapter 4 of *MCSE Networking Essentials Exam Cram.*

## Question 14

Answer c is correct. A repeater is a network device that amplifies network signals to extend the distance they can travel without losing signal strength. Answer a is incorrect; passive hubs merely connect multiple segments of a network. Routers are devices that use addressing to route data to its appropriate destination and have nothing to do with the re-amplification of a signal. Therefore, answer b is incorrect. A bridge is used to address filter network traffic and has nothing to do with the regeneration of a data signal. Therefore, answer d is incorrect.

For more information, see Chapter 5 of *MCSE Networking Essentials Exam Cram.*

## Question 15

Answer d is correct. The mesh topology provides the highest level of fault tolerance due to the number of redundant links between computers. Ring topologies have no fault tolerance due to the lack of redundant links. Therefore, answer a is incorrect. Answer b is incorrect because if a cable segment breaks or becomes unterminated in a bus topology, network activity stops. Answer c is incorrect because if the hub in a star topology fails, the network goes down.

For more information, see Chapter 5 of *MCSE Networking Essentials Exam Cram.*

# Question 16

Answer b is correct. Upgrading the cable to Cat 5 and the NICs to 10/100Mbps will accomplish 100Mbps speeds. Answer a is incorrect; the hub does not need to be upgraded because it's an autosensing hub that can already achieve 100Mbps. Cat 3 can only support 10Mbps. Upgrading the hub to full duplex and the NICs to 10/100Mbps still does not fix the fact that Cat 3 can only support 10Mbps. Therefore, answer c is incorrect. Because answer b is correct, answer d is incorrect.

For more information, see Chapter 4 of *MCSE Networking Essentials Exam Cram*.

# Question 17

Answer d is correct. RIP (Routing Information Protocol) is a distance vector routing protocol that's concerned with not only finding a method for moving information from point a to point b, but also with how many hops it takes to connect to a remote host. Answers a, b, and c are not routing protocols and are therefore incorrect.

For more information, see Chapter 3 of *MCSE Networking Essentials Exam Cram*.

# Question 18

Answers b and d are correct. 143-122 and 128-191 in the first octet define a Class B address. Answer a is incorrect; 192-224 in the first octet of an IP address defines a Class C address. Answer c is incorrect; 0-126 in the first octet of an IP address defines a Class A address.

For more information, see Chapter 4 of *MCSE TCP/IP Exam Cram*.

# Question 19

Answer d is correct. SLIP (Serial Line Internet Protocol) is an older dial-up protocol that uses TCP/IP only. SLIP does not support NWLink/IPX, NetBEUI, or NetBIOS. Therefore, answers a, b, and c are incorrect.

For more information, see Chapter 6 of *MCSE NT Server 4 Exam Cram*.

# Question 20

Answers a, b, c, and d are correct. A gateway can work at all these layers.

For more information, see Chapter 5 of *MCSE Networking Essentials Exam Cram*.

## Question 21

Answer b is correct. DHCP (Dynamic Host Configuration Protocol) dynamically assigns IP addresses across the network. It also makes network administration much easier, because it can automatically assign IP addresses to computers logging into the network. Answers a, c, and d are incorrect—these are not functions of DHCP.

For more information, see Chapter 3 of *MCSE Networking Essentials Exam Cram*.

## Question 22

Answer d is correct. A brouter knows how to route specific protocols (router) and forward other types of packets onto other networks (bridge). None of the other answers are able to perform both routing and bridging. Therefore, answers a, b, and c are incorrect.

For more information, see Chapter 5 of *MCSE Networking Essentials Exam Cram*.

## Question 23

Answer b is correct. The proposed solution produces the required result and only one of the optional desired results. By using fiber-optic cable, you can connect the buildings together at 100Mbps, thus fulfilling both the required and one of the optional desired results. However, you won't keep costs as low as possible. Note that Cat 5 cable will accomplish the job as well and is much less expensive than fiber-optic cable.

For more information, see Chapter 4 of *MCSE Networking Essentials Exam Cram*.

## Question 24

Answer b is correct. The Transport layer is responsible for packet handling, error-free delivery, and error handling. The Data Link layer is responsible for managing the Physical layer communications between connecting computers. Therefore, answer a is incorrect. The Session layer is responsible for providing synchronization between connecting computers. Therefore, answer c is incorrect. The Presentation layer is responsible for translating information from generic formats to platform or application formats, and vice versa. Therefore, answer d is incorrect.

For more information, see Chapter 3 of *MCSE Networking Essentials Exam Cram*.

## Question 25

Answer d is correct. The proposed solution does not produce the required result—NetBEUI is not a routable protocol.

For more information, see Chapter 5 of *MCSE Networking Essentials Exam Cram*.

## Question 26

Answer b is correct. The proposed solution produces the required result and only one of the optional results. Although a leased T3 line will connect the branch office with the corporate domain at sustained speeds of 1.54Mbps, it's not as cost-effective as leasing a T1 line.

For more information, see Chapter 4 of *MCSE Networking Essentials Exam Cram*.

## Question 27

Answers b, c, and d are correct. 10Base2, FDDI, and 10Base5 all are able to carry data over 450 feet (150m). 10Base-T is only able to carry data up to 328 feet (100m). Therefore, answer a is incorrect.

For more information, see Chapter 4 of *MCSE Networking Essentials Exam Cram*.

## Question 28

Answer b is correct. A multiplexer can divide transmissions into multiple channels on a single medium. Repeaters, routers, and gateways are unable to divide transmissions into two or more channels on a single medium. Therefore answers a, c, and d are incorrect.

For more information, see Chapter 6 of *MCSE Networking Essentials Exam Cram*.

## Question 29

Answers a, d, e, and g are correct. TCP/IP, AppleTalk, DECnet, and NWLink/ IPX are all routable. NetBEUI, DLC, and LAT are nonroutable. Therefore, answers b, c, and f are incorrect.

For more information, see Chapter 5 of *MCSE Networking Essentials Exam Cram*.

# Question 30

Answer d is correct. X.25 was the first packet-switching standard. It uses virtual circuit packet switching with error control to reach supported speeds of up to 64Kbps. ATM, ISDN, and frame relay are considerably faster than X.25. Therefore, answers a, b, and c are incorrect.

For more information, see Chapter 10 of *MCSE Networking Essentials Exam Cram*.

# Question 31

Answer c is correct. Only PPP (Point-to-Point Protocol) allows for IP address negotiation. SLIP, NetBEUI, and NDIS do not allow for such negotiation. Therefore, answers a, b, and d are incorrect.

For more information, see Chapter 3 of *MCSE Networking Essentials Exam Cram*.

# Question 32

Answer b is correct. Protocol analyzers can look inside packets and can give insight into connection errors, bottlenecks, and even traffic problems. DHCP and ATM are not network diagnostic tools. Therefore, answers a and d are incorrect. Performance Monitor is not able to determine the scenarios described in the question. Therefore, answer c is incorrect.

For more information, see Chapter 11 of *MCSE Networking Essentials Exam Cram*.

# Question 33

Answers a, c, and d are correct. RAID 5 (disk striping with parity), RAID 1 (disk mirroring), and RAID 0 (disk striping) are all supported under Windows NT. Disk striping with large blocks is RAID 4, which is not supported. Therefore, answer b is incorrect.

For more information, see Chapter 9 of *MCSE Networking Essentials Exam Cram*.

## Question 34

Answers b and d are correct. TCP and SPX reside at the Transport layer. IP, DLC, and IPX reside at the Network layer of the OSI model. Therefore, answers a, c, and e are incorrect.

For more information, see Chapter 3 of *MCSE Networking Essentials Exam Cram.*

## Question 35

Answer c is correct. The user is using the wrong subnet mask. He'll need to change it to 255.255.255.0 to be able to get on the network where everyone else is. Answers a, b, and d do not apply and are therefore incorrect.

For more information, see Chapter 5 of *MCSE TCP/IP Exam Cram.*

## Question 36

Answers c and d are correct. IP and IPX are connectionless protocols that do not guarantee delivery of messages. TCP and SPX are connection-oriented protocols, which means they can guarantee delivery of messages. Therefore, answers a and b are incorrect.

For more information, see chapters 2 and 3 of *MCSE Networking Essentials Exam Cram.*

## Question 37

Answer b is correct. ATM (Asynchronous Transfer Mode) uses fixed-length cells to transfer data. This ensures that no one data stream uses all the bandwidth. This is also the reason why this WAN technology can reach transmission speeds as high as it does. X.25, ISDN, and T1 do not meet the standards of ATM. Therefore, answers a, c, and d are incorrect.

For more information, see Chapter 10 of *MCSE Networking Essentials Exam Cram.*

## Question 38

Answer a is correct. NWLink/IPX is the recommended protocol to use out of the available choices. It's very easy to install and needs very little configuration, if any. Answers b, c, and d are incorrect because Windows 95 machines do not support any of those protocols.

For more information, see Chapter 3 of *MCSE Networking Essentials Exam Cram.*

## Question 39

Answer c is correct. CSMA/CA (Carrier Sense Multiple Access with Collision Avoidance) transmits a signal to the network notifying it that data is about to be sent. Answer a has to do with CSMA/CD (Carrier Sense Multiple Access with Collision Detection). Therefore, answer a is incorrect. Answers b and d are incorrect because they do not relate to CSMA/CA.

For more information, see Chapter 5 of *MCSE Networking Essentials Exam Cram.*

## Question 40

Answer a is correct. Installing a router will reduce network traffic by sorting frames based on the IP addresses, thus satisfying the primary requirement and both the optional requirements.

For more information, see Chapter 5 of *MCSE Networking Essentials Exam Cram.*

## Question 41

Answer d is correct. A Media Access Control (MAC ) address is a hardware address that uniquely identifies a node on a network. Answers a, b, and c are incorrect because they have no relevance to a hardware MAC address.

For more information, see Chapter 9 of *MCSE Networking Essentials Exam Cram.*

## Question 42

Answer b is correct. IRQ 1 is normally used for the keyboard. COM2 or COM4 uses IRQ 3. IRQ 5 can be used by LPT2 or sound cards, or it can be available. IRQ 7 is for LPT1, and IRQ 9 is the cascading IRQ. IRQ 12 is normally for the PS/2 mouse. Therefore, answers a, c, d, e, and f are incorrect.

For more information, see Chapter 5 of *MCSE Networking Essentials Exam Cram.*

## Question 43

Answer c is correct. In a coax bus configuration, each end of the cable must have 50-ohm terminators to avoid the signal being bounced around. Answers a, b, and d are incorrect.

For more information, see Chapter 4 of *MCSE Networking Essentials Exam Cram*.

## Question 44

Answers a and d are correct. Category 4 and 5 can carry data at speeds of up to 16Mbps and 100Mbps, respectively. Category 2 can support up to 4Mbps. Category 3 can only support up to 10Mbps. Therefore, answers b and c are incorrect.

For more information, see Chapter 4 of *MCSE Networking Essentials Exam Cram*.

## Question 45

Answer d is correct. WINS (Windows Internet Name Service) is a NetBIOS name service that resolves NetBIOS names to IP addresses. Resolving host names to IP addresses is a function of DNS. Therefore, answer a is incorrect. Maintaining and distributing IP addresses to clients is a function of DHCP. Therefore, answer b is incorrect. Maintaining domain name registrations is a function of InterNIC. Therefore, answer c is incorrect.

For more information, see Chapter 9 of *MCSE Networking Essentials Exam Cram*.

## Question 46

Answer b is correct. The Application layer provides network services that support applications, error recovery, and flow control. Preparing data to be delivered and translated into generic or platform-specific formats is the responsibility of the Presentation layer. Therefore, answer a is incorrect. Setting up and terminating lines of communication across the network is the responsibility of the Session layer. Therefore, answer c is incorrect. Breaking data down into manageable pieces to be sent across a network is the responsibility of the Transport layer. Therefore, answer d is incorrect.

For more information, see Chapter 3 of *MCSE Networking Essentials Exam Cram*.

## Question 47

Answer e is correct. No protocols reside in the Physical layer of the OSI model. Answers a and b are incorrect because TCP and SPX both reside in the Transport layer. IP and IPX reside in the Network layer. Therefore, answers c and d are incorrect.

For more information, see Chapter 3 of *MCSE Networking Essentials Exam Cram*.

## Question 48

Answer c is correct. Frame relay is a WAN technology developed from X.25 and ISDN, and it allows for bandwidth as needed. Answers a, b, and d are incorrect. Although they are all WAN technologies, they do not allow for bandwidth on demand.

For more information, see Chapter 10 of *MCSE Networking Essentials Exam Cram*.

## Question 49

Answers a and c are correct. Answer a is correct because Windows 95 used in a peer-to-peer network can only support share-level security. Answer c is correct because passwords can be given to shared resources. Answer b is incorrect because share-level security is very insecure. Any individual with the password for a particular device has full control of the contents of that particular device. Answer d is incorrect because Windows NT uses user-level security.

For more information, see chapters 2 and 9 of *MCSE Networking Essentials Exam Cram*.

## Question 50

Answer b is correct. The IEEE 8.02 standard deals with the Data Link layer of the OSI model. The IEEE divides this layer into two sublayers: the Data Link Control (DLC) sublayer and the Media Access Control (MAC) sublayer. Answers a, c, and d are not a part of the IEEE standards and are therefore incorrect.

For more information, see Chapter 3 of *MCSE Networking Essentials Exam Cram*.

## Question 51

Answer c is correct. Telnet allows users to remotely control a server over a network or the Internet. The File Transfer Protocol (FTP) is used for just that, transferring files across a network or the Internet. Therefore, answer a is incorrect. Answer b is incorrect because the Hypertext Transfer Protocol (HTTP) defines how Web servers and browsers should respond to various commands. Answer d is incorrect because the Simple Network Management Protocol (SNMP) is used for the management of networks.

For more information, see Chapter 3 of *MCSE Networking Essentials Exam Cram.*

## Question 52

Answers b, e, and f are correct. TCP, SPX, and X.25 are all examples of connection-oriented protocols. Connection-oriented protocols are responsible for guaranteeing the delivery of messages. NetBEUI is a nonroutable protocol for small networks. IP, IPX, and UDP are examples of connectionless protocols. Therefore, answers a, c, d, and g are incorrect.

For more information, see Chapter 3 of *MCSE Networking Essentials Exam Cram.*

## Question 53

Answer d is correct. The device with a host ID of 54 and a network ID of 192.168.100 will receive this packet. 192.168.100.54 is on the same subnet as 192.168.100.5, so the packet will be received without going through the default gateway. Therefore, answers a, b, and c are incorrect.

For more information, see Chapter 4 of *MCSE TCP/IP Exam Cram.*

## Question 54

Answer d is correct. The minimum number of drives necessary for a RAID 5 configuration is three. Two drives are necessary for a RAID 1 (mirror) configuration. One drive can be used in a RAID 0 configuration, and six drives can be used in any RAID configuration (0, 1, and 5). Therefore, answers a, b, and c are incorrect.

For more information, see Chapter 9 of *MCSE Networking Essentials Exam Cram.*

## Question 55

Answer c is correct. Thicknet uses AUI connectors. BNC connectors are used by Thinnet. Therefore, answer a is incorrect. Twisted-pair cable uses RJ-45 and RJ-11 connectors. Therefore, answers b and d are incorrect.

For more information, see Chapter 4 of *MCSE Networking Essentials Exam Cram*.

# Windows NT Server 4 Practice Test #1

## Question 1

Your domain is spread over three cities. The PDC is housed in the central office with a BDC in each of the other cities' portions of the network. You create and deploy a system policy on the PDC. Users in other cities complain that their old settings are still present. Why?

- ○ a. System policies must be enabled through the User Manager For Domains.
- ○ b. System policies only apply to computers.
- ○ c. The system policies have not been duplicated to the BDCs.
- ○ d. The system policies must be placed in each profile directory.

# Question 2

A NetWare 3.11 network is being migrated to Windows NT. Several new Windows NT Server systems that host important resources have been added to the network. How can the clients from the NetWare 3.11 network gain access to the Windows NT Server-hosted resources without changing the clients?

○ a. Install Client Services for NetWare (CSNW) on the Windows NT Server machines.

○ b. Install Gateway Service for NetWare (GSNW) on the Windows NT Server machines.

○ c. Install File and Print Services for NetWare (FPNW) on the Windows NT Server machines.

○ d. Install NetWare Gateway Services for Microsoft (NGSM) on the NetWare server.

# Question 3

Your network is spread across two buildings. You log into the network in BLDG1, where the PDC resides. You change your password. A manager in BLDG2 calls asking for help with an application. You log out and walk over to BLDG2. There you attempt to log on but your new password does not work. What should you do to solve this problem?

○ a. Log on with your old password and then change it again.

○ b. Force a domain synchronization.

○ c. Reboot the BDC in BLDG2.

○ d. Return to BLDG1 and change your password again.

# Question 4

Your Windows NT Server computer is the host of the five-drive RAID array that hosts the network's data files. The drive configuration is a stripe set with parity. A power glitch causes one of the drives in the configuration to fail. How can you restore access to the files?

○ a. Reboot Windows NT Server.

○ b. Break the set and then re-create it with just the four drives.

○ c. Restore the data from backup tapes to another volume.

○ d. Nothing. Windows NT Server automatically compensates for the failed drive.

# Question 5

The custom applications deployed on your Windows NT Server machine require a special file backup process before powering down. You have a UPS attached to this machine. If the power remains off for a significant amount of time, the UPS applet will shut the system down. Which configuration setting in the UPS applet can be used to ensure your custom applications are terminated properly?

○ a.  Execute Command File

○ b.  Shut Down Command

○ c.  Remote Execute File

○ d.  Remote UPS Shutdown

# Question 6

Which priority level on Windows NT Server is considered "realtime"?

○ a.  4

○ b.  8

○ c.  13

○ d.  24

# Question 7

You suspect your computer is experiencing excessive paging. Which counters can you watch through Performance Monitor to determine whether this is actually occurring?

○ a.  Memory: Pages/Second

○ b.  Memory: Transition Faults/Second

○ c.  Physical Disk: Average Disk Queue Length

○ d.  Physical Disk: Average Disk Sec/Transfer

# Question 8

Your network is migrating from Unix to Windows NT. The dial-in server has been hosting both PPP and SLIP sessions for remote dial-up users. When you deploy Windows NT Server, what must be done to allow RAS to support these clients?

○ a. Nothing. RAS natively supports SLIP and PPP on inbound connections.

○ b. Install the SLIP Services tool from the Resource Kit.

○ c. Set the RAS authentication to accept anything, including clear text.

○ d. The clients must switch to PPP because RAS does not support inbound SLIP.

# Question 9

Your computer has three EIDE hard drives installed on two drive controllers—two drives on the first controller and the third drive on the second controller. It's also a multiboot system that hosts Windows 95, Windows NT Workstation, and Windows NT Server. The hard drives are partitioned as follows:

- Drive 1:

  1GB; hosts Windows 95

  3 GB; FAT data drive

- Drive 2:

  2 GB; hosts Windows NT Workstation

  4 GB; NTFS data drive

- Drive 3:

  4 GB; NTFS data drive

  2 GB; hosts Windows NT Server

What's the ARC name of the Windows NT Server boot partition?

○ a. scsi(1)disk(0)rdisk(0)partition(2)

○ b. multi(1)disk(0)rdisk(0)partition(2)

○ c. multi(0)disk(0)rdisk(2)partition(2)

○ d. multi(1)disk(0)rdisk(0)partition(1)

○ e. multi(1)disk(1)rdisk(0)partition(2)

# Question 10

The last person to log into the Windows NT Server system changed the video driver. You notice the logon prompt is illegible when you attempt to log in. What can you do to restore the system to normal operation with the least effort?

- ○ a.  Go to a similar system, memorize the keyboard strokes for changing the display driver, and execute them on the troubled system.
- ○ b.  Reinstall Windows NT.
- ○ c.  Use the ERD repair process.
- ○ d.  Use the Last Known Good Configuration (LKGC).

# Question 11

Which one of the following files appears in the system partition of Windows NT Server host systems when non-BIOS enabled SCSI drive controllers are used?

- ○ a.  Scsiboot.sys
- ○ b.  Ntbootdd.sys
- ○ c.  Boot.sys
- ○ d.  Ntldr.sys

# Question 12

Several users complain that their print jobs are not being printed by the print device, and the print jobs listed in the print queue cannot be deleted. What caused this problem?

- ○ a.  The printer's access time has expired.
- ○ b.  The logical printer employed by the users has a low priority setting.
- ○ c.  The printer driver is corrupt.
- ○ d.  The print spooler is hung.

# Question 13

Using your notebook computer, you access several documents on the office LAN over a RAS connection. After travelling to a new location, you attempt to access the same documents again. What happens?

○ a. They are pulled from the RAS cache.

○ b. RAS automatically reestablishes the connection with the office LAN.

○ c. The file with the closest matching file name is loaded from your local hard drive.

○ d. An error message is displayed stating the resource is no longer available.

# Question 14

Your network has a PDC and one BDC. You take the PDC offline to perform hardware replacements but realize several users need to change their passwords the next time they log on. Therefore, you promote the BDC to a PDC. After the repairs are complete, you reboot the old PDC. Now, two PDCs are present on your network. Which step should you take to restore the network to its condition before the repair?

○ a. Demote the new PDC through the Network applet.

○ b. Reinstall Windows NT Server on the old PDC.

○ c. Reboot the new PDC.

○ d. Demote the new PDC through Server Manager.

# Question 15

A system administrator has left your organization. The replacement worker needs the same access as the old employee. What's the Microsoft recommended method for granting this new worker access?

○ a. Give the new worker the username and password used by the old system admin.

○ b. Create a new account from scratch.

○ c. Rename the old account and change the password for the new worker.

○ d. Disable the old account.

# Question 16

A new computer lab has opened at a college. What can you do as system administrator to ensure that the users maintain their own layout and desktop settings no matter which station they log into?

- ○ a.  Change the USER.DAT file to USER.MAN in the Default User profile.
- ○ b.  Configure all user accounts to use the CompLabUser profile.
- ○ c.  Copy all profiles to a network share and delete them from their original locations.
- ○ d.  Create roaming profiles.

# Question 17

Inbound RAS connections can use which networking protocol(s)?

- ○ a.  NWLink and TCP/IP
- ○ b.  TCP/IP and NetBEUI
- ○ c.  NWLink and NetBEUI
- ○ d.  Just TCP/IP
- ○ e.  TCP/IP, NWLink, and NetBEUI

# Question 18

Your computer has an IDE interface for its CD-ROM drive. You previously installed Windows 95 from the CD-ROM without any difficulty. However, the CD-ROM interface is not supported by Windows NT. How can you install Windows NT Server on this machine?

- ○ a.  Use the three setup floppies to initiate installation.
- ○ b.  Launch the installation routine from Windows 95.
- ○ c.  Format the hard drive and then copy the Windows NT Server CD-ROM to the hard drive.
- ○ d.  Reboot the system using the CD-ROM as the boot drive.

# Question 19

On a drive hosted by a Windows NT Server computer, you create a 100MB partition. This partition will be used exclusively by the Marketing department to store image files for projects. What's the best choice of file systems for this partition if performance is the only concern?

○ a. FAT

○ b. NTFS

○ c. HPFS

○ d. CDFS

# Question 20

You need to configure the Replication service on your network to duplicate policies and profiles. Which systems can be used as recipients of replication data? [Check all correct answers]

❑ a. A Windows NT Server machine as a PDC or BDC

❑ b. Windows NT Server machines as member servers

❑ c. Windows NT Workstation machines

❑ d. Windows 95 clients

# Question 21

You want to improve the performance of your Windows NT Server system. Which of the following system changes may result in actual improved performance? [Check all correct answers]

❑ a. Deploy disk striping.

❑ b. Add a second disk controller and split the drives between the two controllers.

❑ c. Replace data drives with faster devices.

❑ d. Implement disk mirroring.

# Question 22

When you're moving files from an NTFS partition to a FAT partition, which of the following statements are true?

- ○ a.  LFNs are retained, and permissions are retained.
- ○ b.  LFNs are lost, and permissions are lost.
- ○ c.  LFNs are retained, and permissions are lost.
- ○ d.  LFNs are lost, and permissions are retained.

# Question 23

The accounting department prints hundreds of invoices each hour. The current high-speed laser printer is not fast enough to handle the load. Therefore, you decide to create a printer pool with four high-speed laser printers. Which of the following conditions must exist to create a printer pool? [Check all correct answers]

- ❏ a.  All print devices must be attached to the same printer port.
- ❏ b.  All print devices must be located in the same room.
- ❏ c.  All print devices must be managed by the same print server.
- ❏ d.  All print devices must be identical or at least use the same printer driver.

# Question 24

You're deploying Windows NT Server-hosted RAS. This dial-in server will be the connection point for over 50 remote clients, ranging from Windows 95 to OS/2 to Macintosh to Linux. Security is important to your organization. Which RAS setting provides the maximum level of security without preventing any authorized clients from gaining access?

- ○ a.  Require Microsoft Encrypted Authentication
- ○ b.  Use Only PPTP
- ○ c.  Require MS-CHAP
- ○ d.  Allow Any Authentication Including Clear Text

# Question 25

Which platform supported by Windows NT Server requires that a SCSI CD-ROM drive be present for installation?

○ a.  Intel

○ b.  Solaris

○ c.  80386

○ d.  NeXT

○ e.  RISC

# Question 26

While performing a regular system check, you notice that the Memory: Available Bytes counter displays a value of less than 1 on a consistent basis. What does this reading from Performance Monitor tell you about your system?

○ a.  A hard drive is about to fail.

○ b.  A second CPU is required.

○ c.  Excessive paging is occurring.

○ d.  The Registry is too large.

○ e.  The network interface is congested.

# Question 27

As a user who's a member of the Print Operators group, you perform daily backups of your personal data files. A power failure causes one of your files to become corrupted. When you attempt to recover the file from a backup, you're unable to do so. Why?

○ a.  You're not a member of the Account Operators group.

○ b.  You're not a member of the Backup Operators group.

○ c.  You failed to select the Enable Restoration checkbox when you performed the backup.

○ d.  Backups can only be restored to FAT partitions.

# Question 28

The primary hard drive on your PDC has failed. Fortunately, you implemented disk duplexing. The failed drive hosted both the boot and system partitions. What can you do to boot the system? [Check all correct answers]

❑ a.  Just reboot the system; Windows NT will handle booting from the duplexed drive automatically.

❑ b.  Remove the failed drive, install the duplexed drive in place of the failed drive, and set the duplexed drive's system partition to Active.

❑ c.  Create a Windows NT boot floppy and edit the BOOT.INI file to access the boot partition on the duplexed drive.

❑ d.  You must replace the failed drive, install Windows NT onto the new drive, and then copy the contents of the duplexed drive over the new drive.

# Question 29

Working from the PDC, which tool can you use to create a new share on a BDC housed in the next building?

○ a.  User Manager For Domains

○ b.  My Computer

○ c.  Server Manager

○ d.  Network Monitor

○ e.  Windows NT Diagnostics

○ f.  Network Neighborhood

# Question 30

You add a Windows NT Server system to an existing NetWare network. The NetWare network comprises several versions of NetWare; therefore, several IPX/SPX frame types are in use. When configuring Windows NT Server, you set it to autodetect the frame type. Which of the following frame types will your Windows NT Server system use to communicate with the NetWare network?

○ a. The 802.2 frame type

○ b. The 802.3 frame type

○ c. The 802.3 frame type with a SNAP header

○ d. The 802.5 frame type

○ e. The 802.5 frame type with a SNAP header

# Question 31

The manager of the accounting department must share a laser printer with all 26 accountants and secretaries in the department. What can you do to ensure the manager's documents print as soon as possible?

○ a. Set the logical printer used by the staff to have an access time from 5 P.M. to 8 A.M.

○ b. Create a second logical printer for the manager with a higher priority than the staff's logical printer.

○ c. Configure the logical printer to use separator pages.

○ d. Configure the logical printer to print directly without spooling.

# Question 32

Data files placed in a FAT partition on a Windows NT Server system can be accessed by network clients if which of the following are true? [Check all correct answers]

❑ a. The partition is shared.

❑ b. Users have file-level Read permissions.

❑ c. Users have the Log On Locally right.

❑ d. Users have Read access to the share.

# Question 33

Windows NT Workstation clients connecting to Windows NT Server RAS over a telephone line have the ability to perform which of the following activities? [Check all correct answers]

❑ a. Access printer shares.

❑ b. Use a roaming profile.

❑ c. Be logged onto the domain.

❑ d. Read data from network shares.

❑ e. Connect to the Internet over the LAN's proxy server.

# Question 34

Which of the types of disk configurations supported by Windows NT Server can contain the boot partition? [Check all correct answers]

❑ a. Stripe set

❑ b. Stripe set with parity

❑ c. Multipartition volume set

❑ d. Disk duplexing

❑ e. Disk mirroring

# Question 35

An existing BDC system is no longer needed to support the security database or to authenticate users because two new high-performance systems have been added to the network as BDCs. Which step must be taken to transform the BDC into a member server?

○ a. Demote the BDC to a member server though the Server Manager.

○ b. Remove the BDC service from the Services tab of the Network applet.

○ c. Reinstall Windows NT Server.

○ d. Reboot the BDC and at the logon prompt select "member server".

# Question 36

To implement disk duplexing, what's the minimum amount of hardware?

○ a. Two hard drives and two disk controllers

○ b. One hard drive and two disk controllers

○ c. Two hard drives and one disk controller

○ d. One hard drive and one disk controller

# Question 37

A network-attached printer is added to your network. It's a Hewlett-Packard laser jet, and you're using a JetDirect attachment. You launch the Add Printer Wizard but do not see the JetDirect port in the list. Why?

○ a. DLC has not been installed.

○ b. NetBIOS has been disabled.

○ c. TCP/IP Printing Services is not installed.

○ d. LPD has not been configured.

# Question 38

Your telemarketing group has been given access to a 25-station Windows NT Server-hosted domain. However, you have over 100 employees with a high rate of turnover. All the telemarketers need the same applications to perform their work, and no personal information is allowed on the system. What's the best way to configure the network?

○ a. Create individual roaming profiles.

○ b. Create a single roaming profile used by all user accounts.

○ c. Create a single user account with a roaming profile.

○ d. Create a single mandatory profile used by all user accounts.

# Question 39

You employ the NetWare migration tool to transform your NetWare-based network into a Windows NT Server network. You've already performed the following actions:

- Installed NWLink on Windows NT Server
- Installed Gateway Services for NetWare on Windows NT Server
- Created the NTGateway account group and a migration user account on the NetWare server
- Created an NTFS partition on Windows NT Server

In this situation, what can be migrated from NetWare to Windows NT Server using the migration tool? [Check all correct answers]

❏ a. NetWare files and directories

❏ b. NetWare volumes

❏ c. User and group accounts

❏ d. NetWare user passwords

# Question 40

Your Windows NT Server machine has the following logical drives: 400MB, 600MB, 1.2GB, and 3GB. What's the largest total size of a stripe set you can create with these drives?

○ a. 1,200MB

○ b. 1,600MB

○ c. 5.3GB

○ d. 1,800MB

○ e. 0MB

# Question 41

Your PDC is located in the central office. There are three BDCs, each located across a single B channel ISDN link to remote offices at the north, south, and west edges of the city. When the Replication service sends data to the BDCs, other traffic over the WAN links is interrupted for up to 15 minutes. You alter the ReplicationGovernor value through the Registry to improve performance over the links. However, your changes result in the replication activity no longer occurring. Why?

○ a. The ReplicationGovernor value was set too high.

○ b. The ReplicationGovernor value was set to 50.

○ c. The ReplicationGovernor value was set to 0.

○ d. The ReplicationGovernor value was set to 100.

# Question 42

A system administrator is taking a three-month leave of absence. What's the best way to secure her high-access account during her absence?

○ a. Delete it.

○ b. Disable it.

○ c. Rename it and change the password.

○ d. Remove it from all groups.

# Question 43

After making numerous changes to the Registry, you reboot your Windows NT Server system. However, the boot process stops after a blue screen appears displaying the version number. What's the easiest method for attempting to restore the system to normal operation?

○ a. Reinstall Windows NT Server.

○ b. Restore the system from a backup.

○ c. Use the Last Known Good Configuration (LKGC).

○ d. Use the ERD repair process.

# Question 44

On an older computer system that barely meets the minimum requirements, you attempt to install Windows NT Server. However, during the hardware-detection phase, the third SCSI hard drive is not recognized. What can you do to get Windows NT to recognize the hardware? [Check all correct answers]

❏ a. Abort the installation and start over.

❏ b. Remove the unrecognized device and replace it with a device listed on the HCL.

❏ c. Bypass automatic detection and install the storage device drivers manually.

❏ d. After installation, use the Add Drive command on the Hardware Profiles tab of the System applet.

❏ e. Complete the installation and then add the appropriate driver through the SCSI applet to access the device.

# Question 45

Several clients have been unable to consistently access resources offered by Windows NT Server systems on the network. You suspect too much traffic is occurring over the network. In order to convince the budget committee to spend money on faster network components, you need to show proof that the network is overtaxed. You launch Performance Monitor to view the % Network Utilization counter. However, this counter is not present. Why?

○ a. The NIC needs to be placed in promiscuous mode.

○ b. The Network Monitor agent is not installed.

○ c. **Diskperf -y** has not been executed.

○ d. The SNMP Service is not installed.

# Question 46

What does a consistent value of 4 for the System: Processor Queue length indicate?

○ a. Optimum network efficiency

○ b. High network load

○ c. Too little system RAM

○ d. Excessive paging

○ e. CPU lag

# Question 47

You change the permission level for a group's access to a resource from Read to Change. When will members of this group be able to use the enhanced access?

○ a.  Immediately

○ b.  After the next time they log in

○ c.  After the system reboots

○ d.  After you log out of the system

# Question 48

Where are the Internet resources saved through Internet Explorer stored for a user with a username of StormyG?

○ a.  %systemroot%\Profiles\Desktop\Favorites

○ b.  %systemroot%\Profiles\StormyG\Favorites

○ c.  %systemroot%\StormyG\IExplorer

○ d.  %systemroot%\Profiles\StormyG

○ e.  \Users\StormyG\Profile\Favorites

# Question 49

Which default groups of Windows NT Server grant their members the ability to log on locally? [Check all correct answers]

❏ a.  Administrators

❏ b.  Backup Operators

❏ c.  Server Operators

❏ d.  Account Operators

❏ e.  Print Operators

❏ f.  Users

❏ g.  Guests

❏ h.  Replicator

# Question 50

You've been assigned to perform a high-level network audit. Primarily, you need to collect the following information:

- The name of each computer
- The role of each computer
- The names of shared resources

Which of the following tools is best suited for obtaining this infor-mation?

○ a.  Windows Explorer

○ b.  Windows NT Diagnostics

○ c.  Disk Administrator

○ d.  Server Manager

○ e.  User Manager For Domains

○ f.  Network Monitor

# Question 51

Four managers have left for a week-long conference out of town. They'll not be accessing the office LAN while they're away. The second day they're gone, you notice several changes have been made to network shares and respec-tive permissions. You suspect a nonmanagerial employee is using one of the accounts of the out-of-town managers to perform these changes. What's the best single event type to audit to determine whether the manager accounts are being compromised?

○ a.  File and Object Access

○ b.  Use of User Rights

○ c.  Logon and Logoff

○ d.  Security Policy Changes

# Question 52

Which Windows NT Server network protocol is the most efficient yet still routable?

○ a. AppleTalk

○ b. TCP/IP

○ c. NWLink

○ d. NetBEUI

○ e. DLC

# Question 53

Which of the following files is not present on an ERD?

○ a. DEFAULT._

○ b. NTUSER.DA_

○ c. AUTOEXEC.NT

○ d. BOOT.INI

○ e. SETUP.LOG

# Question 54

You've added a UPS to your computer. However, each time you boot the Windows NT Server system, the UPS turns off the power. Which BOOT.INI switch can be added to prevent this?

○ a. **/DEBUG**

○ b. **/NOSERIALMICE**

○ c. **/SOS**

○ d. **/UPS**

# Question 55

A remote user is dialing into a Windows NT Server RAS server. However, the user is only able to access resources hosted by the RAS server, not resources elsewhere on the network. Why?

O a.  RAS clients are limited to resources on the RAS server.

O b.  NetBEUI is being used over the RAS link.

O c.  The modem is not NDIS compliant.

O d.  The Entire Network selection is not enabled.

# Windows NT Server 4 Answer Key #1

| | | | |
|---|---|---|---|
| 1. c | 15. c | 29. c | 43. c |
| 2. c | 16. d | 30. a | 44. b, c, e |
| 3. b | 17. e | 31. b | 45. b |
| 4. d | 18. b | 32. a, d | 46. e |
| 5. a | 19. a | 33. a, b, c, d, e | 47. b |
| 6. d | 20. a, b, c | 34. d, e | 48. b |
| 7. a | 21. a, b, c | 35. c | 49. a, b, c, d, e |
| 8. d | 22. c | 36. a | 50. d |
| 9. b | 23. c, d | 37. a | 51. c |
| 10. d | 24. d | 38. d | 52. c |
| 11. b | 25. e | 39. a, b, c | 53. d |
| 12. d | 26. c | 40. e | 54. b |
| 13. b | 27. b | 41. c | 55. d |
| 14. d | 28. b, c | 42. b | |

## Question 1

Answer c is correct. The system policies have not been duplicated to the BDCs, so users authenticated by a BDC do not have the system policies applied to them. System policies are not enabled through the User Manager For Domains. Therefore, answer a is incorrect. System policies can apply to users, groups, and computers. Therefore, answer b is incorrect. System policies do not need to be placed in every profile directory; they only need to be placed in a single location accessible from all systems (such as the NETLOGON share). Therefore, answer d is incorrect.

For more information, see Chapter 5 of *MCSE NT Server 4 Exam Cram*.

## Question 2

Answer c is correct. Installing File and Print Services for NetWare (FPNW) on the Windows NT Server machines will grant NetWare clients access to Windows NT-hosted resources. CSNW and GSNW grant Windows NT systems access to NetWare resources. Therefore, answers a and b are incorrect. There is no such product as NetWare Gateway Services for Microsoft. Therefore, answer d is incorrect.

For more information, see Chapter 7 of *MCSE NT Server 4 Exam Cram*.

## Question 3

Answer b is correct. You should force a domain synchronization, because the security changes made on the PDC have not been replicated to the BDC. This may require you to return to BLDG1 if you're unable to access the Server Manager from BLDG2. Changing your password on the BDC will not work, because the BDC cannot make changes to the security database. The request to change the password will be rejected when the BDC sends the message to the PDC. Therefore, answer a is incorrect. Rebooting the BDC will synchronize it with the PDC, but this will not update any other BDC and may cause resource or service disruption due to the system being offline. Therefore, answer c is incorrect. Changing your password again in BLDG1 is not required because in BLDG1, where the PDC is, the password is already changed. Therefore, answer d is incorrect.

For more information, see Chapter 5 of *MCSE NT Server 4 Exam Cram*.

## Question 4

Answer d is correct. You need to do nothing, because Windows NT Server automatically compensates for the failed drive. Rebooting Windows NT Server is not required. Therefore, answer a is incorrect. Breaking the set will cause all data to be lost. Therefore, answer b is incorrect. Restoring the data from backups to another volume is not required. Therefore, answer c is incorrect.

For more information, see Chapter 4 of *MCSE NT Server 4 Exam Cram.*

## Question 5

Answer a is correct. Choosing Execute Command File executes a command immediately before the operating system is shut down, and it's given 30 seconds to complete. Shut Down Command is not a valid command from the UPS applet. Therefore, answer b is incorrect. There is no option to remotely execute a file. Therefore, answer c is incorrect. There is never a case for shutting down a UPS remotely. Therefore, answer d is incorrect.

For more information, see Chapter 13 of *MCSE NT Server 4 Exam Cram.*

## Question 6

Answer d is correct. Realtime is priority level 24. Therefore, answers a, b, and c are incorrect.

For more information, see Chapter 5 of *MCSE NT Server 4 Exam Cram.*

## Question 7

Answer a is correct. Memory: Pages/Second measures the number of times the Virtual Memory Manager has to swap pages between the paging file and RAM. Excessive paging slows system performance. Memory: Transaction Faults/Second is the number of page faults resolved by recovering pages that were in transition (being written to disk). Therefore, answer b is incorrect. Physical Disk: Average Disk Queue Length is the average number of read/write requests queued during a time period, and is incorrect. Physical Disk: Average Disk Sec/Transfer is how long it took to transfer a file. Therefore, answers c and d are incorrect.

For more information, see Chapter 11 of *MCSE NT Server 4 Exam Cram.*

## Question 8

Answer d is correct. RAS does not support inbound SLIP, so clients must switch to PPP. RAS only supports outbound SLIP. Therefore, answer a is incorrect. There is no SLIP Services tool on the Resource Kit. Therefore, answer b is incorrect. RAS does not support SLIP no matter what the authentication settings are. Therefore, answer c is incorrect.

For more information, see Chapter 10 of *MCSE NT Server 4 Exam Cram.*

## Question 9

Answer b is correct. The correct ARC name for the Windows NT Server boot partition is multi(1)disk(0)rdisk(0)partition(2), being the second partition on the first drive on the second drive controller. The drive controllers are IDE, not SCSI without BIOS. Therefore, answer a is incorrect. The boot partition is not on the first drive controller. Therefore, answer c is incorrect. The boot partition is not the first partition. Therefore, answer d is incorrect. The boot partition is not the second SCSI drive. Therefore, answer e is incorrect.

For more information, see Chapter 12 of *MCSE NT Server 4 Exam Cram.*

## Question 10

Answer d is correct. Using the LKGC is the easiest method for restoring the system. Memorizing steps on a different system may work, but it's a lot of effort. Therefore, answer a is incorrect. Reinstalling is not the best option. Therefore, answer b is incorrect. The ERD repair process will not correct display problems. Therefore, answer c is incorrect. (Note that rebooting using the VGA mode is also an option, but it was left out of this question on purpose.)

For more information, see chapters 12 and 13 of *MCSE NT Server 4 Exam Cram.*

## Question 11

Answer b is correct. Non-BIOS enabled SCSI drive controllers require the Ntbootdd.sys driver. All the other files are fictitious. Therefore, answers a, c, and d are incorrect.

For more information, see chapters 12 and 13 of *MCSE NT Server 4 Exam Cram.*

## Question 12

Answer d is correct. This situation occurs when the print spooler is hung (that is, no longer functioning properly). To relieve this situation, the spooler must be stopped and restarted through the Services applet. An expired access time would not prevent print jobs from being deleted from the print queue. Therefore, answer a is incorrect. A lower priority logical printer would not prevent print jobs from being deleted from the print queue. Therefore, answer b is incorrect. A corrupt printer driver would not prevent print jobs from being deleted from the print queue. Therefore, answer c is incorrect.

For more information, see Chapter 8 of *MCSE NT Server 4 Exam Cram*.

## Question 13

Answer b is correct. RAS maintains a record of where resources are accessed. When a resource is accessed again, RAS automatically reestablishes the connection to that resource. There is no such thing as a RAS cache. Therefore, answer a is incorrect. Windows NT does not open the closest matching file. Therefore, answer c is incorrect. An error message is not displayed unless RAS is unable to reestablish the connection. Therefore, answer d is incorrect.

For more information, see Chapter 10 of *MCSE NT Server 4 Exam Cram*.

## Question 14

Answer d is correct. You should demote the new PDC through Server Manager. You cannot demote a PDC through the Network applet. Therefore, answer a is incorrect. Reinstalling Windows NT Server will not restore the system to its condition before the repair; instead, it will create a new server with a new SID. Therefore, answer b is incorrect. Just rebooting the new PDC will not demote it to a BDC. Therefore, answer c is incorrect.

For more information, see Chapter 5 of *MCSE NT Server 4 Exam Cram*.

## Question 15

Answer c is correct. The Microsoft recommended method for giving the new worker access is to rename and change the password for the old account. Allowing the new user to keep the same username and password used by the old user is inviting trouble. Therefore, answer a is incorrect. Creating a new account from scratch will not mimic the access of the old account. Therefore, answer b is incorrect. Just disabling the old account will not give the new user an account to use. Therefore, answer d is incorrect.

For more information, see Chapter 5 of *MCSE NT Server 4 Exam Cram*.

## Question 16

Answer d is correct. Creating roaming profiles is the only way to allow each user to maintain his or her own desktop environment. Making the Default User profile a mandatory profile by renaming the USER.DAT to USER.MAN will make every new user's profile a mandatory profile. These profiles will be duplicates of the Default User profile and they will not retain custom settings. Therefore, answer a is incorrect. Forcing all users to use a single profile will not retain individual settings; instead, as each user logs out, their settings will overwrite the existing settings, thus causing significant confusion. Therefore, answer b is incorrect. Just copying profiles to a network share without changing them to roaming profiles and editing the user accounts to pull profiles from the network share is an incomplete administrative action. Therefore, answer c is incorrect.

For more information, see Chapter 5 of *MCSE NT Server 4 Exam Cram*.

## Question 17

Answer e is correct. Inbound RAS connections can use TCP/IP, NWLink, and NetBEUI. Therefore, answers a, b, c, and d are incorrect.

For more information, see Chapter 10 of *MCSE NT Server 4 Exam Cram*.

## Question 18

Answer b is correct. Launching the installation routine from Windows 95 is one method for installing Windows NT Server in this situation. You'll need to use the **winnt /b** command so that all the data necessary for the installation, including the material from the three setup floppies, is copied to the hard drive. The installation process using the three setup floppies will not work with an unsupported CD-ROM drive. Therefore, answer a is incorrect. Formatting the hard drive will remove Windows 95, which is needed so that Windows NT Server can be installed on this system because the CD-ROM is not supported. Therefore, answer c is incorrect. Booting from the CD-ROM may start the installation (if the system even supports bootable CDs), but because the CD-ROM drive is not supported by Windows NT, the install process will fail. Therefore, answer d is incorrect.

For more information, see Chapter 2 of *MCSE NT Server 4 Exam Cram*.

## Question 19

Answer a is correct. FAT is the best choice because of its size. It has the least overhead and will be the most efficient file system for a partition of this size. NTFS will work, but it's not the most efficient file system for partitions this small. Therefore, answer b is incorrect. HPFS is not supported by Windows NT Server 4.0. Therefore, answer c is incorrect. CDFS is not a file system that can be used to format a partition. Therefore, answer d is incorrect.

For more information, see Chapter 3 of *MCSE NT Server 4 Exam Cram*.

## Question 20

Answers a, b, and c are correct. Windows NT Server machines, PDCs, BDCs, and member servers, as well as Windows NT Workstation machines can all be Replication service import systems. Windows 95 cannot participate in the Windows NT Replication service. Therefore, answer d is incorrect.

For more information, see Chapter 5 of *MCSE NT Server 4 Exam Cram*.

## Question 21

Answers a, b, and c are correct. Using disk striping, adding a second disk controller, and using faster drives all offer better performance. Disk mirroring is not any faster than a standalone drive, but it requires some additional system overhead. Therefore, answer d is incorrect.

For more information, see Chapter 4 of *MCSE NT Server 4 Exam Cram*.

## Question 22

Answer c is correct. Under Windows NT, when you move files from NTFS to FAT, LFNs are retained, and permissions are lost. Therefore, answers a, b, and d are incorrect.

For more information, see Chapter 3 of *MCSE NT Server 4 Exam Cram*.

## Question 23

Answers c and d are correct. A printer pool requires that all print devices in the pool be managed by the same print server, and that they all use the same printer driver. Two print devices cannot be attached to the same port. Therefore, answer a is incorrect. Printers do not need to be in the same room as long as they are managed from the same print server. Therefore, answer b is incorrect.

For more information, see Chapter 8 of *MCSE NT Server 4 Exam Cram*.

## Question 24

Answer d is correct. Because non-Microsoft clients need to connect, you must allow any authentication, including clear text. Because non-Microsoft clients do not support Microsoft Encrypted Authentication (MS-CHAP), it cannot be used. Therefore, answers a and c are incorrect. PPTP is a connection protocol used over the Internet, and it's not supported by some clients. Therefore, answer b is incorrect.

For more information, see Chapter 10 of *MCSE NT Server 4 Exam Cram*.

## Question 25

Answer e is correct. RISC systems require a SCSI CD-ROM drive. Intel systems can install from IDE CD-ROMs and SCSI CD-ROMs as well as over the network. Therefore, answer a is incorrect. Solaris, 80386, and NeXT systems are not supported by Windows NT. Therefore, answers b, c, and d are incorrect.

For more information, see Chapter 2 of *MCSE NT Server 4 Exam Cram*.

## Question 26

Answer c is correct. When the Memory: Available Bytes counter is consistently less than 1, your system is experiencing excessive paging. The Memory object does not offer information about hard drives, CPUs, the Registry, and the network interface. Therefore, answers a, b, d, and e are incorrect.

For more information, see Chapter 11 of *MCSE NT Server 4 Exam Cram*.

## Question 27

Answer b is correct. Backup Operators, Server Operators, and Administrators are the only groups that have the user right to Restore Files and Directories. This means users are able to back up files they see, but they're unable to restore them. The Account Operators group does not have the Restore user right. Therefore, answer a is incorrect. There is no Enable Restoration checkbox. Therefore, answer c is incorrect. Backups can be restored to FAT or NTFS when you have the Restore user right. Therefore, answer d is incorrect.

For more information, see Chapter 9 of *MCSE NT Server 4 Exam Cram*.

## Question 28

Answers b and c are correct. To boot the system after a drive failure, you can either remove the failed drive, install the duplexed drive in place of the failed drive and set the duplexed drive's system partition to Active, or create a Windows NT boot floppy and edit the BOOT.INI file to access the boot partition on the duplexed drive. Windows NT cannot handle the process of booting from the duplexed drive automatically. What's more, until booting occurs, the computer's BIOS controls the system, not Windows NT. Therefore, answer a is incorrect. Replacing the drive, installing Windows NT, and then copying the duplexed drive contents over the new drive will probably result in a DOA system. Therefore, answer d is incorrect.

For more information, see Chapter 4 of *MCSE NT Server 4 Exam Cram.*

## Question 29

Answer c is correct. Server Manager can be used to create new shares on remote systems. User Manager For Domains, My Computer, Network Monitor, Windows NT Diagnostics, and Network Neighborhood do not have the capability to create shares on remote systems. Therefore, answers a, b, d, e, and f are incorrect.

For more information, see Chapter 5 of *MCSE NT Server 4 Exam Cram.*

## Question 30

Answer a is correct. The autodetection of a frame type functions properly in an environment where only a single frame type is being used. In this situation, the frame type will default to 802.2. The other frame types can be detected, but only in a homogeneous environment. Therefore, answers b, c, d, and e are incorrect.

For more information, see Chapter 7 of *MCSE NT Server 4 Exam Cram.*

## Question 31

Answer b is correct. The best solution is to create a second logical printer for the manager with a higher priority than the staff's logical printer. Setting the access time to off hours will prevent the staff from obtaining printed documents during working hours. Therefore, answer a is incorrect. Using a separator page will not give the manager printing priority. Therefore, answer c is incorrect. Bypassing the spooler will not give the manager printing priority. Therefore, answer d is incorrect.

For more information, see Chapter 8 of *MCSE NT Server 4 Exam Cram.*

## Question 32

Answers a and d are correct. The partition must be shared and users must have Read access to the share. FAT does not have file-level permissions. Therefore, answer b is incorrect. The Log On Locally right is not required. Therefore, answer c is incorrect.

For more information, see Chapter 3 of *MCSE NT Server 4 Exam Cram*.

## Question 33

Answers a, b, c, d, and e are all correct. A RAS connection is exactly the same as a direct network connection, only it has slower throughput.

For more information, see Chapter 10 of *MCSE NT Server 4 Exam Cram*.

## Question 34

Answers d and e are correct. The boot partition can be involved in a disk duplex or disk mirror. The boot partition cannot be part of a volume set or a stripe set of any kind. Therefore, answers a, b, and c are incorrect.

For more information, see Chapter 4 of *MCSE NT Server 4 Exam Cram*.

## Question 35

Answer c is correct. The only way to transform a BDC (or PDC) into a member server is to reinstall Windows NT Server. The Server Manager cannot demote a BDC to a member server. Therefore, answer a is incorrect. There is no BDC service to be removed. Therefore, answer b is incorrect. There is no selection upon login to change a BDC to a member server. Therefore, answer d is incorrect.

For more information, see Chapter 5 of *MCSE NT Server 4 Exam Cram*.

## Question 36

Answer a is correct. Two hard drives and two disk controllers are required for disk duplexing. One drive and two controllers is no different than one drive and one controller, because the second controller will not be used. Therefore, answers b and d are incorrect. Two drives and one controller is the requirement for disk mirroring. Therefore, answer c is incorrect.

For more information, see Chapter 4 of *MCSE NT Server 4 Exam Cram*.

## Question 37

Answer a is correct. The HP network port will appear in the list of ports when the DLC protocol is installed. The lack of NetBIOS will not prevent the HP network port from being used. Therefore, answer b is incorrect. The TCP/IP Printing Services is not required. Therefore, answer c is incorrect. LPD is not required by Windows-supported printers. Therefore, answer d is incorrect.

For more information, see Chapter 8 of *MCSE NT Server 4 Exam Cram.*

## Question 38

Answer d is correct. The best way to maintain this environment is to create a single mandatory profile used by all user accounts. Allowing individual roaming profiles will not prevent personal information and settings from being placed and retained on the network. Therefore, answer a is incorrect. Using a single roaming profile for all user accounts, or having a single user account with a roaming profile, will produce the same result: Each time a user logs out, his or her changes to the environment will be saved, thus resulting in a profile that's a confusing mess. Therefore, answers b and c are incorrect.

For more information, see Chapter 5 of *MCSE NT Server 4 Exam Cram.*

## Question 39

Answers a, b, and c are the correct answers. The NetWare migration tool supports all the listed items, with the exception of passwords. User passwords must be re-created in the new Windows NT environment. Therefore, answer d is incorrect.

For more information, see Chapter 7 of *MCSE NT Server 4 Exam Cram.*

## Question 40

Answer e is correct. A stripe set is created from partitions on different physical drives, not logical drives. Therefore, this system would require the logical drives to be destroyed. However, even then, the question does not indicate whether the logical drives are all on the same physical drive. Therefore, answers a, b, c, and d are incorrect.

For more information, see Chapter 4 of *MCSE NT Server 4 Exam Cram.*

## Question 41

Answer c is correct. Setting the value to 0 would cause replication to never occur. The Registry key for ReplicationGovernor is 100% by default. Therefore, answers a and d are incorrect; they are not reasonable because the value can't be set higher than 100. Setting the value to 50 would impact the replication speed because ReplicationGovernor's value is a percentage of the available bandwidth. Replication would occur, but over a longer period of time. Therefore, answer b is incorrect.

For more information, see Chapter 5 of *MCSE NT Server 4 Exam Cram*.

## Question 42

Answer b is correct. Disabling the account is the only way to prevent someone else from using it while the system administrator is gone and still retain the account so that she can use it when she returns. Deleting the account will require that a new account be created. This will most likely result in a loss of access because the duplicate account is different due to its new SID. Therefore, answer a is incorrect. Renaming the account and changing the password retains the settings but leaves the account open for an unauthorized person to hack into. Therefore, answer c is incorrect. Removing the account from groups will partially remove its access, but this is a poor action, because it will need to be added again to these groups when the system administrator returns. Therefore, answer d is incorrect.

For more information, see Chapter 5 of *MCSE NT Server 4 Exam Cram*.

## Question 43

Answer c is correct. The easiest repair solution is to use the LKGC. Reinstalling Windows NT Server is a last-resort solution. Therefore, answer a is incorrect. Restoring the system from a backup is tedious and often requires the system to be bootable in order to access the restore utility. Therefore, answer b is incorrect. The ERD repair process may not correct the portion of the Registry damaged by your changes. Therefore, answer d is incorrect.

For more information, see chapters 12 and 13 of *MCSE NT Server 4 Exam Cram*.

## Question 44

Answers b, c, and e are correct. Replacing the device with an HCL device, bypassing automatic detection, and installing a driver after installation are all valid methods of resolving this situation. Restarting the installation will prob-ably not cause the system to recognize the device. Therefore, answer a is incorrect. There is no "Add Drive" command. Therefore, answer d is incorrect.

For more information, see chapters 2 and 13 of *MCSE NT Server 4 Exam Cram*.

## Question 45

Answer b is correct. The % Network Utilization counter is not present without the Network Monitor agent being installed. The NIC is not placed in promis-cuous mode to monitor network utilization by Performance Monitor. Therefore, answer a is incorrect. Diskperf is associated with disk counters, not network counters. Therefore, answer c is incorrect. The SNMP service is not associated with the % Network Utilization counter. Therefore, answer d is incorrect.

For more information, see Chapter 11 of *MCSE NT Server 4 Exam Cram*.

## Question 46

Answer e is correct. A consistent value of 2 or more for System: Processor Queue indicates a CPU bottleneck. Therefore, answers a, b, c, and d are incor-rect.

For more information, see Chapter 11 of *MCSE NT Server 4 Exam Cram*.

## Question 47

Answer b is correct. Access changes are not incorporated into a user's access token until the next time the user logs in. Access changes are not enjoyed immediately. Therefore, answer a is incorrect. The users don't need to wait until the system is rebooted. Therefore, answer c is incorrect. Users don't need to wait until you log out of the system—your logged-on status has no effect on access. Therefore, answer d is incorrect.

For more information, see Chapter 5 of *MCSE NT Server 4 Exam Cram*.

## Question 48

Answer b is correct. Favorites are stored in a user's profile (in this case, StormyG's) in %systemroot%\Profiles\StormyG\Favorites. Therefore, answers a, c, d, and e are incorrect.

For more information, see Chapter 5 of *MCSE NT Server 4 Exam Cram*.

## Question 49

Answers a, b, c, d, and e are correct. The Administrators, Backup Operators, Server Operators, Account Operators, and Print Operators groups have the Log On Locally right. The Users, Guests, and Replicator groups do not have this right. Therefore, answers f, g, and h are incorrect.

For more information, see Chapter 5 of *MCSE NT Server 4 Exam Cram*.

## Question 50

Answer d is correct. The Server Manager is used to obtain this information. The other listed applications may be able to show only part or one type of the information required. Therefore, answers a, b, c, e, and f are incorrect.

For more information, see Chapter 5 of *MCSE NT Server 4 Exam Cram*.

## Question 51

Answer c is correct. Logon and Logoff events will tell you whether an account is being used to log into the system. It will also record the time and station where the log on occurred. File and Object Access is used to monitor resource access, not logons. Therefore, answer a is incorrect. Use of User Rights and Security Policy Changes are not useful in this situation. Therefore, answers b and d are incorrect.

For more information, see Chapter 11 of *MCSE NT Server 4 Exam Cram*.

## Question 52

Answer c is correct. NWLink is the most efficient routable protocol of Windows NT. AppleTalk is not a protocol that can be used by Windows NT except to allow Macintosh client access. Therefore, answer a is incorrect. TCP/IP is not the most efficient routable protocol. Therefore, answer b is incorrect. NetBEUI is not routable. Therefore, answer d is incorrect. DLC is not a network protocol; it's used to communicate with IBM mainframes and network-attached printers. Therefore, answer e is incorrect.

For more information, see Chapter 6 of *MCSE NT Server 4 Exam Cram*.

## Question 53

Answer d is correct. An ERD does not contain the BOOT.INI file. The ERD contains the other listed files. Therefore, answers a, b, c, and e are incorrect.

For more information, see Chapter 13 of *MCSE NT Server 4 Exam Cram*.

## Question 54

Answer b is correct. The **/NOSERIALMICE** switch prevents Windows NT from polling the serial ports and inadvertently telling the UPS to cut the power. **/DEBUG** and **/SOS** do not aid with UPS devices. Therefore, answers a and c are incorrect. **/UPS** is a fictitious switch. Therefore, answer d is incorrect.

For more information, see Chapter 13 of *MCSE NT Server 4 Exam Cram*.

## Question 55

Answer d is correct. This situation indicates the protocol in use over the RAS link does not have the Entire Network selection enabled. RAS clients can be limited to RAS server resources, but they can also be granted access to the entire network. Therefore, answer a is incorrect. NetBEUI does not limit the reach of RAS clients due to a NetBEUI gateway. Therefore, answer b is incorrect. NDIS and modems are unassociated items. NDIS is a NIC standard. Plus, NDIS has nothing to do with the level of access for RAS clients. Therefore, answer c is incorrect.

For more information, see Chapter 10 of *MCSE NT Server 4 Exam Cram*.

# Windows NT Server 4 Practice Test #2

## Question 1

Windows NT Server supports fault-tolerant drive configurations. Which of the following RAID specifications represent drive configurations supported by Windows NT Server? [Check all correct answers]

- ❑ a. RAID 0
- ❑ b. RAID 1
- ❑ c. RAID 2
- ❑ d. RAID 4
- ❑ e. RAID 5

## Question 2

Which of the following technologies can be used to grant remote clients full network access when connecting to a Windows NT Server system running RAS over the Internet?

- ○ a. Serial Line Internet Protocol
- ○ b. Internet Information Server
- ○ c. Microsoft Encrypted Authentication
- ○ d. Point-to-Point Tunneling Protocol
- ○ e. Dynamic Host Configuration Protocol

# Question 3

You're using Performance Monitor to watch various counters. Which type of activity or reading level would indicate a problem or bottleneck in the Processor: % Processor Time counter?

- ○ a. Consistently under 30 percent
- ○ b. A random peak of 99 percent
- ○ c. Consistently over 90 percent
- ○ d. A constant variation between 10 percent and 60 percent

# Question 4

Two departments located on the same floor have decided to pool their technology resources. One network is NetWare based, and the other is Windows NT Server based. What needs to be deployed to allow clients to access resources on either network? [Check all correct answers]

- ❏ a. Gateway Services for NetWare
- ❏ b. TCP/IP Printing Services
- ❏ c. File and Print Services for NetWare
- ❏ d. Services for Macintosh
- ❏ e. Remote Access Service

# Question 5

Windows NT Server's Network Client Administrator can be used to build network startup disks for which of the following client types? [Check all correct answers]

- ❏ a. MS-DOS
- ❏ b. Windows 3.1
- ❏ c. Windows For Workgroups 3.11
- ❏ d. Microsoft Windows 95
- ❏ e. OS/2
- ❏ f. Windows NT Workstation 3.51

# Question 6

Your network hosts a single laser printer that's used by all network members. The managers have been complaining that they often have to wait 15 minutes or more to retrieve documents from the printer. Because most of the print jobs submitted by nonmanagers are not time dependant, how can you enable the managers' print jobs to complete sooner?

○ a. Set the logical printer to print directly to the printer.

○ b. Create a separate logical printer, assign rights to the managers, and set the printer priority to 1.

○ c. Create a separate logical printer, assign rights to the managers, and set the printer priority to 99.

○ d. Create a separate logical printer, assign rights to all nonmanagers, and set the access times for 5 P.M. to 8 A.M.

# Question 7

Your network has been attacked by a Trojan horse virus that deletes files. You've cleaned all the workstations but suspect the intruding software is still active on a server. What's the best audit event type to track to locate the intruding software?

○ a. Logon and Logoff

○ b. Use of User Rights

○ c. File and Object Access

○ d. Process Tracking

# Question 8

The source drive in a disk duplex has failed. Which of the following are valid actions that result in a restored bootable Windows NT Server system? [Check all correct answers]

❏ a. Replace the failed disk, re-create the duplex set, and restore the data from the secondary drive back to the primary.

❏ b. Place the secondary drive in the position of the primary and then reboot.

❏ c. Replace the failed disk. Windows NT Server will automatically restore the duplex set.

❏ d. Boot from a floppy with a modified BOOT.INI file.

❏ e. Nothing. Windows NT Server will automatically fail over to the secondary drive.

# Question 9

Several remote clients need to dial into your RAS server. Many support PPP, but several only have software offering SLIP connections. What can you do to enable all clients to connect to the RAS server?

○ a. Install the SLIP Service on Windows NT Server

○ b. Convert all clients to SLIP

○ c. Set authentication to accept clear text on Windows NT Server

○ d. Convert all clients to PPP

# Question 10

Disk striping with parity drive constructions can be formatted with which file system types under Windows NT Server? [Check all correct answers]

❏ a. FAT

❏ b. HPFS

❏ c. NFS

❏ d. NTFS

# Question 11

Which of the following actions will result in the greatest improvement in performance on a Windows NT Server system?

- ○ a.  Increasing L2 cache
- ○ b.  Increasing the size of the paging file
- ○ c.  Installing a second network interface card
- ○ d.  Implementing disk mirroring
- ○ e.  Installing faster hard drives

# Question 12

The Windows NT Migration Tool for NetWare can be used to perform which of the following functions? [Check all correct answers]

- ❑ a.  Duplicate user accounts and passwords from NetWare to Windows NT
- ❑ b.  Duplicate groups from NetWare to Windows NT
- ❑ c.  Duplicate user accounts but not passwords from Windows NT to NetWare
- ❑ d.  Maintain file and directory security from NetWare to Windows NT
- ❑ e.  Duplicate file and directory information from Windows NT to NetWare
- ❑ f.  Duplicate user accounts with a standardized password from NetWare to Windows NT

# Question 13

You send a document to a printer. When you retrieve the pages from the printer, you notice they're filled with nonsense instead of your desired document. Why?

- ○ a.  The print spooler is hung.
- ○ b.  DLC is not installed.
- ○ c.  There's not enough drive space for spooling.
- ○ d.  The wrong printer driver is installed.

## Question 14

A Windows NT Server system is configured with two 1GB SCSI hard drives. Both drives are attached to the same SCSI drive controller with an operating onboard BIOS. Each disk contains a single primary partition. The Windows NT system files reside on Disk 2, and the boot files reside on Disk 1. Which of the following ARC names correctly identifies the boot partition that appears in the BOOT.INI file?

O  a.  multi(0)disk(0)rdisk(0)partition(1)

O  b.  multi(0)disk(1)rdisk(0)partition(1)

O  c.  multi(0)disk(0)rdisk(1)partition(1) ‹

O  d.  multi(1)disk(0)rdisk(0)partition(0)

O  e.  multi(0)disk(0)rdisk(1)partition(0)

## Question 15

You have a computer that has four nonpartitioned drives of the following sizes: 900MB, 1.6GB, 2.4GB, and 3GB. You want to implement disk striping with parity. What's the largest amount of usable space you can obtain on such a drive configuration after you install Windows NT Server onto this computer?

O  a.  2.7GB

O  b.  3GB

O  c.  3.2GB

O  d.  4.8GB

O  e.  7GB

## Question 16

Which of the following files would be found on the system partition of an Intel system? [Check all correct answers]

❏  a.  BOOT.INI

❏  b.  NTLDR

❏  c.  NTOSKRNL.EXE

❏  d.  NTBOOTDD.SYS

❏  e.  OSLOADER.EXE

❏  f.  BOOTSECT.DOS

# Question 17

Which of the following counters can be monitored to help determine whether your Windows NT Server system is in need of more physical RAM?

○ a.  Processor: % Processor Time

○ b.  Memory: Pages/Thread

○ c.  Memory: Pages/Second

○ d.  LogicalDisk: Avg. Disk Bytes/Transfer

# Question 18

Using NTBACKUP, you need to perform a backup of all the important data on your network servers, including the Registry. You plan on performing the operation from a BDC. You'll be pulling data from the PDC, two other BDCs, and six member servers. How can you perform or initiate this operation to ensure a successful backup operation?

○ a.  Manually initiate the backup process.

○ b.  Schedule the backup to run after hours using the Scheduler service.

○ c.  Create an ERD before starting the backup.

○ d.  Use a third-party backup tool.

# Question 19

An NWLink network employs a star topology to connect all servers and clients through a single central hub. One Windows NT Server machine, which is a member server, is unable to communicate with the network. No other clients or servers are experiencing any difficulty. Which of the following is the most likely cause of this problem?

○ a.  The hub is offline.

○ b.  The PDC has a bad connection to the network.

○ c.  An incorrect frame type is in use.

○ d.  Only a single NIC is present in the problematic system.

# Question 20

As a member of the Domain Users group, you have Read access to the SalesDocs share. The files and folders accessed through this share are set with the NTFS permission of Change for the Everyone group. Which level of access do you have for these files?

○ a. No Access

○ b. Read

○ c. Change

○ d. Full Control

# Question 21

After modifying various aspects of Windows NT Server through the Registry, you reboot the system. Once the blue screen displaying the version and build appears, all drive access stops. After several minutes, you realize the system is hung. You cycle the power, only to get the same thing. What's your best option for restoring the system so it will boot?

○ a. Create a boot floppy.

○ b. Use the ERD repair process.

○ c. Use the Last Known Good Configuration.

○ d. Reinstall Windows NT Server and restore from backup.

# Question 22

Which of the following are true statements about Windows NT Server's Gateway Services for NetWare? [Check all correct answers]

❑ a. GSNW includes the functionality of Client Services for NetWare.

❑ b. GSNW requires all other NetWare clients be removed.

❑ c. GSNW allows each client to access NetWare using a unique NetWare account.

❑ d. GSNW will install NWLink if it's not already present on the system.

# Question 23

The system and boot partitions of a Windows NT Server machine can partici-pate in all supported fault-tolerant drive configurations.

○ a.  True

○ b.  False

# Question 24

Windows NT Server offers a true upgrade installation path from which of the following operating systems? [Check all correct answers]

❑ a.  MS-DOS

❑ b.  Windows For Workgroups 3.11

❑ c.  Windows 95

❑ d.  Windows NT Workstation 3.51

# Question 25

A network has a single BDC remaining online after its PDC fails. Which of the following statements are true? [Check all correct answers]

❑ a.  Users can log into the domain.

❑ b.  Users can change their passwords.

❑ c.  The BDC is automatically promoted to a PDC.

❑ d.  A member server needs to be promoted to a PDC.

❑ e.  Logon scripts, system policies, and profiles are still available.

# Question 26

You do not have the three Windows NT setup disks, but you do have access to the CD-ROM via DOS drivers. What's the best action for initiating an installa-tion of Windows NT Server?

○ a.  Execute **winnt** from the i386 directory on the CD.

○ b.  Execute **winnt32 /b** from the i386 directory on the CD.

○ c.  Execute **winnt /ox** from the i386 directory on the CD.

○ d.  Execute **winnt /b** from the i486 directory on the CD.

# Question 27

The drive controller supporting the SCSI drive hosting the Windows NT Server boot partition fails. You replace it with a spare that does not have onboard BIOS, just like the original. Which change needs to be made to the system to allow the system to boot?

○ a. Alter the BOOT.INI file to use SCSI() instead of MULTI().

○ b. Alter the BOOT.INI file to use the second drive controller instead of the first.

○ c. Alter the BOOT.INI file to use RDISK() instead of DISK().

○ d. None of the above.

# Question 28

You intend to use DHCP on your Windows NT Server-hosted network to manage TCP/IP client configurations. Which of the following settings can be defined for clients by DHCP? [Check all correct answers]

❑ a. Default IP gateway address

❑ b. DNS server address

❑ c. WINS server address

❑ d. IP address

❑ e. NetBIOS name

❑ f. MAC address

❑ g. NetBIOS name resolution type

❑ h. Remote boot services for BOOTP clients

# Question 29

Your Windows NT Server network uses TCP/IP as its networking protocol exclusively. Performing traffic analysis using Network Monitor has revealed that over 10 percent of the traffic on the network is due to broadcast traffic (a level over five times normal). Which of the following actions is the best solution for reducing broadcast traffic?

○ a. Reduce FQDN resolution requests by installing DNS.

○ b. Migrate from TCP/IP to NetBEUI.

○ c. Deploy a WINS server.

○ d. Install more BDCs.

# Question 30

The print server's boot partition only has 15MB of free space. Users have complained that they're unable to send more than 12 pages of a document to the printer at one time. Most of the print jobs consist of 50 to 200 pages. What's the best course of action to resolve this issue?

○ a. Instruct users to print only 12 pages at a time.

○ b. Set the logical printer to print directly to the printer.

○ c. Move the spooler to a drive with more free space.

○ d. Increase the priority of the spooler.

# Question 31

A UPS is attached to your Windows NT Server machine. The UPS is rated to provide 15 minutes of power during an outage and then signal the system to shut itself down. You configure the UPS applet to the appropriate settings. After making sure the UPS is fully charged, you test the setup by unplugging the UPS from the wall. When the battery finally runs out, you realize the computer did not perform a graceful shutdown. What could have caused this? [Check all correct answers]

❏ a. The wrong cable was used to connect the UPS to the computer.

❏ b. The wrong COM port was identified in the UPS applet.

❏ c. A command file was not defined through the UPS applet.

❏ d. The wrong voltage was defined for Remote UPS Shutdown in the UPS applet.

❏ e. The battery recharge time was improperly defined through the UPS applet.

# Question 32

Which restriction is placed on the paging file when STOP error recovery options are selected?

○ a. The paging file must be 12MB larger than the amount of physical RAM.

○ b. There must be 12MB free on the system partition.

○ c. There must be 2MB free on the boot partition.

○ d. There must be at least 2MB free on any partition.

# Question 33

A network administrator has left your organization. A replacement is hired. Which method does Microsoft recommend for granting the new employee the same access levels as the previous worker?

○ a. Create a new user account from scratch that matches the group memberships of the old network administrator's account.

○ b. Create a copy of the old network administrator's account for the new employee and disable the old account.

○ c. Rename the old account and change the password for the new employee.

○ d. Create a copy of the old network administrator's account for the new employee and delete the old account.

# Question 34

Your network has been growing very quickly. It contains several member servers hosting applications, but no BDCs. You decide that transforming three systems into BDCs to assist the PDC will improve network performance and balance the load of authentication. Which of the following methods is the best course of action for transforming a member server into a BDC?

○ a. Use the Promote To BDC command from the Computer menu of the Server Manager on a PDC to promote the member servers.

○ b. Install the BDC Service from the Service tab of the Network applet on each member server.

○ c. Reinstall Windows NT Server on the systems to make them BDCs.

○ d. On the Windows NT Setup tab of the Add/Remove Software applet, add the DC Components selection on each member server.

# Question 35

Which characteristics do Windows NT FAT and MS-DOS FAT have in common? [Check all correct answers]

❑ a. Volume size of 2GB

❑ b. No limit of files in root directory

❑ c. File-level security

❑ d. LFN support

❑ e. Over 512 files in nonroot directories

# Question 36

Your computer currently hosts Windows 98. You want to replace this operating system with Windows NT Server. However, your original distribution CD is damaged. Fortunately, you made a complete copy of it on a network share before the damage occurred. If you want the boot partition of the new system to be formatted with NTFS, what's the best method you can use to install Windows NT Server? [Check all correct answers]

❑  a.  Use the three setup floppies to initiate the installation.

❑  b.  Execute a **WINNT32** command from Windows 98.

❑  c.  Execute a **WINNT** command from Windows 98.

❑  d.  Boot with a client disk created through Network Client Administrator from another operational Windows NT Server machine, and then execute a **WINNT32** command.

❑  e.  Boot with a client disk created through Network Client Administrator from another operational Windows NT Server machine, and then execute a **WINNT** command.

# Question 37

Firewalls are devices that block unwanted access to a network. Which Windows NT Server RAS security features can act like a firewall for all types of RAS clients? [Check all correct answers]

❑  a.  Callback

❑  b.  PPTP

❑  c.  Encrypted authentication

❑  d.  User-based dial-in access

❑  e.  The Entire Network/This Computer Only setting

# Question 38

Moving the paging file to a physical drive other than the one(s) hosting the boot and system partitions offers which benefit?

○ a. It reduces wear and tear on the primary physical drive.

○ b. It improves performance by separating the burden of system activity from memory activity.

○ c. It improves fault tolerance because the failure of the paging file drive will not affect the system.

○ d. It guarantees that the paging file can expand to 150MB, as recommended by Microsoft.

# Question 39

The Network Client Administrator utility from Windows NT Server can be used to perform which of the following functions? [Check all correct answers]

❑ a. Create installation disk sets

❑ b. View client local boot information

❑ c. Create Windows NT Server startup disks

❑ d. Make network installation startup disks

❑ e. Copy client-based network administration tools

# Question 40

You've been assigned the task of creating 130 new user accounts for the new group of research assistants. Which of the following is the most efficient manner in which these accounts can be created?

○ a. Manually create each one, making sure to properly duplicate all settings.

○ b. Create a single complete user account and make copies of it for all other accounts.

○ c. Use the Template option in User Manager to create a user form to base all accounts on.

○ d. Use the **NET USERS** command to create a batch file to create all the accounts.

# Question 41

While booting, you see an error message stating that at least one driver or service has failed to load during startup. Where can you go to view more information about this error?

○ a.  Windows NT Diagnostics

○ b.  Dr. Watson

○ c.  Event Viewer

○ d.  DEVICE.LOG

○ e.  Server Manager

# Question 42

Which of the following statements is true?

○ a.  Global user accounts can be members of local groups only.

○ b.  Global groups can contain local groups.

○ c.  Local user accounts can be members of global groups only.

○ d.  Local groups can contain local users and global groups.

# Question 43

While booting a system hosting Windows NT Server, the following error is displayed:

```
Couldn't open boot sector file
multi(0)disk(0)rdisk(0)partition(1):\Bootsect.dos
```

What does this error imply?

○ a.  Booting to Windows NT Server is not possible.

○ b.  The BOOT.INI file is missing.

○ c.  NTDETECT.COM is missing a supporting file.

○ d.  Booting to non-Windows NT operating systems is not possible.

## Question 44

Which of the following statements are true? [Check all correct answers]

☐ a. Windows NT enables all possible binding orders by default.

☐ b. Binding NetBEUI before TCP/IP is always the best option.

☐ c. Adding a protocol after initial installation requires you to manually set all bindings.

☐ d. Binding should be prioritized on the workstation to maximize network performance.

☐ e. Removing bindings where functionality is not needed can improve security and performance.

## Question 45

Which of the following clients and/or systems require printer drivers to be installed locally when a Windows NT Server system is the print server? [Check all correct answers]

☐ a. Windows For Workgroups 3.11

☐ b. Windows 95

☐ c. Windows NT Workstation 3.51

☐ d. OS/2 Warp clients

☐ e. NetWare servers

☐ f. Windows NT Advanced Server 3.1

## Question 46

When a print job fails to produce output on a printer, what's the first thing you should check?

○ a. Physical connections

○ b. The status of the spooler service

○ c. The print priority of your logical printer

○ d. Your print permission levels

○ e. The Event Viewer

# Question 47

Which of the following are requirements for a computer to be configured as a BDC on an existing network? [Check all correct answers]

- ❑ a.  A local CD-ROM drive
- ❑ b.  A network interface card
- ❑ c.  A pointing device
- ❑ d.  120MB of free drive space
- ❑ e.  16MB of RAM

# Question 48

How can you restrict a user's access to Control Panel applets, prevent wall-paper changes, and require network logon to gain local system access from a Windows NT Server PDC?

- ○ a.  Deploy mandatory profiles.
- ○ b.  Define a hardware profile for each client.
- ○ c.  Specify the settings for each user account through User Manager.
- ○ d.  Deploy system policies.

# Question 49

In which directory on a Windows NT Server BDC will user roaming profiles be found?

- ○ a.  USERS\\*<username>* (a custom shared directory)
- ○ b.  *%winnt_root%*\\*<username>*
- ○ c.  *%winnt_root%*\Profiles\\*<username>*
- ○ d.  *%winnt_root%*\Ntusers\\*<username>*

# Question 50

Through which Windows NT Server utility can you obtain a list of network resources currently being accessed on a system-by-system basis?

○ a.  Network Monitor

○ b.  Server Manager

○ c.  Windows NT Diagnostics

○ d.  Windows NT Explorer

# Question 51

The replication import server's default destination directory can be viewed through which of the following?

○ a.  *%winnt_root%*\Repl\Import\

○ b.  Repl\Import\

○ c.  *%winnt_root%*\System32\Repl

○ d.  NETLOGON

# Question 52

Which of the following is a requirement of Services for Macintosh?

○ a.  TCP/IP

○ b.  An NTFS volume

○ c.  NetBIOS

○ d.  DLC

○ e.  8.3 share names

# Question 53

Which of the following RAS-related logs can only be enabled through the Registry? [Check all correct answers]

☐ a. MODEMLOG.TXT

☐ b. DRWTSN32.LOG

☐ c. DEVICE.LOG

☐ d. PPP.LOG

☐ e. DEBUG.LOG

# Question 54

The OSLOADER.EXE file used by RISC systems replaces which files employed by Intel systems? [Check all correct answers]

☐ a. BOOTSECT.DOS

☐ b. NTDETECT.COM

☐ c. HAL.DLL

☐ d. NTLDR

☐ e. BOOT.INI

# Question 55

RAS supports outbound connections using either PPP or SLIP. Which of the following statements are true about these connection protocols? [Check all correct answers]

☐ a. SLIP does not support DHCP.

☐ b. PPP only supports TCP/IP.

☐ c. SLIP is used exclusively to access Unix servers.

☐ d. PPP is the most widely used WAN protocol.

☐ e. SLIP supports encrypted passwords.

☐ f. SLIP can be used to aggregate multiple links into a single, larger communication pipeline.

# Windows NT
# Server 4
# Answer Key #2

| | | | |
|---|---|---|---|
| 1. a, b, e | 15. c | 29. c | 43. d |
| 2. d | 16. a, b, c, d, f | 30. c | 44. a, d, e |
| 3. c | 17. c | 31. a, b, d | 45. a, d, e |
| 4. a, c | 18. d | 32. c | 46. a |
| 5. a, c, e | 19. c | 33. c | 47. b, e |
| 6. c | 20. b | 34. c | 48. d |
| 7. c | 21. c | 35. a, e | 49. a |
| 8. b, d | 22. a, b, d | 36. c, e | 50. b |
| 9. d | 23. b | 37. d, e | 51. d |
| 10. a, d | 24. d | 38. b | 52. b |
| 11. e | 25. a, e | 39. a, d, e | 53. c, d |
| 12. b, d, f | 26. a | 40. d | 54. a, b, d |
| 13. d | 27. d | 41. c | 55. a, d |
| 14. c | 28. a, b, c, d, g, h | 42. d | |

# Question 1

Answers a, b, and e are correct. Windows NT Server supports RAID 0 (stripe sets without parity), RAID 1 (disk mirroring and disk duplexing), and RAID 5 (stripe sets with parity). RAID 2 and RAID 4 are not supported by Windows NT Server. Therefore, answers c and d are incorrect.

For more information, see Chapter 4 of *MCSE NT Server 4 Exam Cram.*

# Question 2

Answer d is correct. PPTP offers a full, reliable, and secure network connection over the Internet for remote clients. SLIP will not offer access over the Internet, and it cannot be used to dial into a Windows NT Server. Therefore, answer a is incorrect. IIS offers only WWW, FTP, and Gopher services, not access to the entire network, and without additional security. Therefore, answer b is incorrect. Microsoft Encrypted Authentication is a high-level security setting, but it does not directly relate to establishing a connection over the Internet, and it doesn't imply access to the network. Therefore, answer c is incorrect. DHCP is a client configuration protocol—it does not offer remote network connections. Therefore, answer e is incorrect.

For more information, see Chapter 10 of *MCSE NT Server 4 Exam Cram.*

# Question 3

Answer c is correct. Only a consistent reading of over 90 percent would indicate a bottleneck. Operations under 30 percent, random peaks, and variations are normal system activities that do not indicate problems. Therefore, answers a, b, and d are incorrect.

For more information, see Chapter 11 of *MCSE NT Server 4 Exam Cram.*

# Question 4

Answers a and c are correct. GSNW and FPNW should be installed to grant clients access to resources on either network. TCP/IP Printing Services is only required when interacting with Unix or other LPD/LPR-type printers. Therefore, answer b is incorrect. Services for Macintosh is only needed for Macintosh clients. Therefore, answer d is incorrect. RAS is only required to grant remote, dial-up clients network access. Therefore, answer e is incorrect.

For more information, see Chapter 7 of *MCSE NT Server 4 Exam Cram.*

# Question 5

Answers a, c, and e are correct. Network Client Administrator can be used to build network startup disks for MS-DOS, Windows For Workgroups 3.11, and OS/2. Network Client Administrator does not build disks for Windows 3.1, Windows 95, or Windows NT Workstation 3.51. Therefore, answers b, d, and f are incorrect.

For more information, see Chapter 2 of *MCSE NT Server 4 Exam Cram*.

# Question 6

Answer c is correct. The best solution is to create a separate logical printer, assign rights to the managers, and set the printer priority to 99. Sending print jobs directly to the printer will not print the managers' print jobs first; instead, it will just prevent all print jobs from being spooled. Therefore, answer a is incorrect. Setting the priority to 1 will not give managers priority, because that's the lowest setting. Therefore, answer b is incorrect. Setting a logical printer for off-hour access will cause all print jobs submitted during the day to be printed at night. This is probably not the best solution, because the printer can run out of paper and experience print jams while no one is around to resolve the problems. Therefore, answer d is incorrect.

For more information, see Chapter 8 of *MCSE NT Server 4 Exam Cram*.

# Question 7

Answer c is correct. The best audit event is File and Object Access, because each action by the Trojan horse will be recorded and you'll at least be able to determine which system it's operating from. Logon and Logoff would be used to track compromised user accounts, not software. Use of User Rights would be used to track a compromised user account's activities, not software activities. Process Tracking is used to monitor VM usage and conflict errors, not software's interaction with files. Therefore, answers a, b, and d are incorrect.

For more information, see Chapter 7 of *MCSE NT Server 4 in the Enterprise Exam Cram*.

## Question 8

Answers b and d are correct. The valid actions are "Place the secondary drive in the position of the primary and then reboot" and "Boot from a floppy with a modified BOOT.INI file." It's not possible to re-create the duplex set without booting into Windows NT. In addition, even if it were possible, this would cause the loss of the data on the secondary drive. Also, copying the data from the secondary drive back to the primary drive is not possible if the partitions use NTFS, because Windows NT is not bootable and no DOS utilities support this action. Therefore, answer a is incorrect. Windows NT won't automatically restore the mirror set by replacing the failed drive, and it won't fail over to the secondary drive—plus Windows NT cannot even boot in this situation, so it couldn't perform these actions even if they were supported. Therefore, answers c and e are incorrect.

For more information, see Chapter 4 of *MCSE NT Server 4 Exam Cram*.

## Question 9

Answer d is correct. The only way to enable all clients to dial into a Windows NT Server RAS server is to convert them to PPP. There is no SLIP Service—RAS only supports SLIP for dial-out access to non-Windows NT systems. Therefore, answer a is incorrect. RAS does not support inbound SLIP connections; SLIP clients cannot establish a connection. Therefore, answer b is incorrect. Setting authentication to clear text will not allow RAS to accept inbound SLIP connections. Therefore, answer c is incorrect.

For more information, see Chapter 10 of *MCSE NT Server 4 Exam Cram*.

## Question 10

Answers a and d are correct. FAT and NTFS can be used on all Windows NT Server-supported drive constructions. Windows NT Server does not support HPFS or NFS. Therefore, answers b and c are incorrect.

For more information, see Chapter 4 of *MCSE NT Server 4 Exam Cram*.

## Question 11

Answer e is correct. Installing faster hard drives offers the most performance improvement because it improves the slowest component of the system. Adding L2 cache offers only a minor performance improvement. Therefore, answer a is incorrect. Increasing the paging file size either will not affect or will adversely affect performance. Therefore, answer b is incorrect. A second NIC will not change performance, at least internally. Therefore, answer c is incorrect. Disk mirroring is actually slower than other drive configurations. Therefore, answer d is incorrect.

For more information, see Chapter 11 of *MCSE NT Server 4 Exam Cram*.

## Question 12

Answers b, d, and f are correct. The Windows NT Migration Tool for NetWare can be used to duplicate groups, maintain file and directory security, and duplicate user accounts with a standardized password from NetWare to Windows NT. The tool cannot duplicate passwords. Therefore, answer a is incorrect. The tool migrates from NetWare to Windows NT, not from Windows NT to NetWare. Therefore, answers c and e are incorrect.

For more information, see Chapter 7 of *MCSE NT Server 4 Exam Cram*.

## Question 13

Answer d is correct. If an incorrect printer driver has been installed, documents may print illegibly. A hung print spooler would not print anything. Therefore, answer a is incorrect. DLC is not required for locally attached printers. What's more, even if the printer were a network-attached printer, nothing would be printed without DLC. Therefore, answer b is incorrect. If there's insufficient drive space for spooling, nothing would be printed. Therefore, answer c is incorrect.

For more information, see Chapter 8 of *MCSE NT Server 4 Exam Cram*.

## Question 14

Answer c is correct. The multi(0)disk(0)rdisk(1)partition(1) ARC name is correct because it indicates the first partition on the second drive on the one and only SCSI drive controller with an operating onboard BIOS. RDISK(0) indicates the first drive, which does not host the boot partition. Therefore, answer a is incorrect. DISK(1) should not be used because this is not a SCSI drive controller without onboard BIOS. Therefore, answer b is incorrect. MULTI(1) indicates a second drive controller. Therefore, answer d is incorrect. PARTITION(0) is an invalid construction. Therefore, answer e is incorrect.

For more information, see Chapter 12 of *MCSE NT Server 4 Exam Cram*.

# Question 15

Answer c is correct. Because one drive must be used to host Windows NT Server, the best choice is the 900MB drive. The remaining three drives can contribute a 1.6GB partition to the stripe set with parity, thus making a disk configuration with 3.2GB of usage space because one-third of the configuration will be used to store parity information (1/n, where n is the number of partitions in the configuration). 2.7GB is the amount of usable space if all four drives contribute 900MB to a stripe set with parity, but this is not the largest possible. A four-drive set is possible if 700MB, 1.5GB, or 2.1GB or less from drive 2, 3, or 4, respectively, is used to host Windows NT Server. Therefore, answer a is incorrect. 3GB is possible if 1.5GB from drives 2, 3, and 4 are used, but this is not the largest possible. Therefore, answer b is incorrect. 4.8GB is the size of the entire disk configuration of drives 2, 3, and 4, not the usable space from the configuration. Therefore, answer d is incorrect. 7GB is the size of a volume set with drives 2, 3, and 4. Therefore, answer e is incorrect.

For more information, see Chapter 4 of *MCSE NT Server 4 Exam Cram.*

# Question 16

Answers a, b, c, d, and f are correct. All these files appear on Intel systems. BOOT.INI and NTLDR appear on all Intel system partitions. NTOSKRNL.EXE appears on Intel boot partitions. BOOTSECT.DOS appears on Intel system partitions on multiboot systems with non-Windows NT operating systems. NTBOOTDD.SYS appears on Intel system partitions when a SCSI drive controller without onboard BIOS is employed. OSLOADER.EXE is the only listed file that appears on RISC systems. Therefore, answer e is incorrect.

For more information, see Chapter 12 of *MCSE NT Server 4 Exam Cram.*

# Question 17

Answer c is correct. The Memory: Pages/Second counter should be watched to decide whether you need more RAM. If you want to find out the percentage of elapsed time a processor is busy, you would look at % Processor Time. Therefore, answer a is incorrect. There is no Pages/Thread counter. Therefore, answer b is incorrect. The LogicalDisk: Avg. Disk Bytes/Transfer counter indicates the amount of bytes transferred to and from a disk, but it does not relate to memory. Therefore, answer d is incorrect.

For more information, see Chapter 11 of *MCSE NT Server 4 Exam Cram.*

## Question 18

Answer d is correct. The Registry cannot be remotely backed up using NTBACKUP. A third-party tool needs to be used to accomplish this task. None of the other options will enable remote Registry backup. Therefore, answers a, b, and c are incorrect.

For more information, see Chapter 9 of *MCSE NT Server 4 Exam Cram*.

## Question 19

Answer c is correct. An incorrect frame type is the most likely cause of this problem. If the hub were offline, other systems would have problems. Therefore, answer a is incorrect. If the PDC had a bad connection, other systems would have problems. Therefore, answer b is incorrect. A second NIC in the member server will not resolve the issue if the wrong frame type is being used. Therefore, answer d is incorrect.

For more information, see chapters 6 and 7 of *MCSE NT Server 4 Exam Cram*.

## Question 20

Answer b is correct. The least permissive of the share and NTFS permissions results in Read access to these files. As an authenticated user, you're a member of the Everyone group. Neither No Access nor Full Control is defined for the Domain Users group or the Everyone group for the SalesDocs share. Change is the access level of just the Everyone group, but when used in conjunction with the SalesDocs share, the least permissive of the combined share permissions versus the NTFS permissions wins. Therefore, answers a, c, and d are incorrect.

For more information, see chapters 3 and 5 of *MCSE NT Server 4 Exam Cram*.

## Question 21

Answer c is correct. The LKGC is the best option; it should remove the recent Registry changes and allow the system to boot normally. A boot disk will not restore the Registry but will bypass the system partition. Therefore, answer a is incorrect. The ERD repair process may restore the system, but the ERD does not contain a complete copy of the Registry—plus, it may not be a recent ERD. Therefore, answer b is incorrect. Reinstalling is a last-resort option, because it will change the SID and will only restore the system to the point of the most recent backup. Therefore, answer d is incorrect.

For more information, see Chapter 13 of *MCSE NT Server 4 Exam Cram*.

## Question 22

Answers a, b, and d are correct. All three of these statements are true. GSNW grants each client access to NetWare through the same NetWare account. Therefore, answer c is incorrect.

For more information, see Chapter 7 of *MCSE NT Server 4 Exam Cram*.

## Question 23

Answer b is correct. This is a false statement. The system and boot partitions can be the primary drive in a disk duplex or disk mirror configuration, but no other fault-tolerant drive configuration is supported by Windows NT Server boot and system partitions.

For more information, see Chapter 4 of *MCSE NT Server 4 Exam Cram*.

## Question 24

Answer d is correct. Windows NT Server only offers a true upgrade installation path from Windows NT. MS-DOS cannot be upgraded in any sense. Therefore, answer a is incorrect. Some information is retained from WFW and Windows 95 if installation is made into their main Windows directories, but this is not considered a true upgrade. Therefore, answers b and c are incorrect.

For more information, see Chapter 2 of *MCSE NT Server 4 Exam Cram*.

## Question 25

Answers a and e are correct. Users can log into the domain. Also, if replication is properly configured, logon scripts, system policies, and profiles are still available. Users cannot change their passwords because BDCs cannot alter the security database. Therefore, answer b is incorrect. A BDC is not automatically promoted to a PDC—this operation must be performed manually. Therefore, answer c is incorrect. A member server cannot be promoted to a PDC—it must be reinstalled for the domain controller components to be added to it. Therefore, answer d is incorrect.

For more information, see Chapter 5 of *MCSE NT Server 4 Exam Cram*.

## Question 26

Answer a is correct. The only valid option from this list is to execute **winnt** from the i386 directory on the CD. **Winnt32** cannot be used from DOS. Therefore, answer b is incorrect. /OX creates the boot floppies but does not start the installation—another step is required, so the better option is answer a. Therefore, answer c is incorrect. The directory is named i386, not i486. Therefore, answer d is incorrect.

For more information, see Chapter 2 of *MCSE NT Server 4 Exam Cram*.

## Question 27

Answer d is correct. This system does not require any changes because the original and the replacement drive controllers are similar in function (that is, SCSI without BIOS). Changing from MULTI to SCSI is only required when the original controller has an operational BIOS and the replacement does not. Therefore, answer a is incorrect. Indicating a second controller would only be required if two controllers were added to the system and the system partition was hosted on the second one. Therefore, answer b is incorrect. RDISK is only used with MULTI; DISK is used with SCSI. Therefore, answer c is incorrect.

For more information, see Chapter 12 of *MCSE NT Server 4 Exam Cram*.

## Question 28

Answers a, b, c, d, g, and h are correct. DHCP can provide a default gateway address, a DNS server address, a WINS server address, an IP address, and a NetBIOS name resolution type. It also supports remote boot services for BOOTP clients. DHCP cannot provide a NetBIOS name or MAC address to clients. The NetBIOS name is defined locally on the client, and the MAC address is determined by the NIC's manufacturer. Therefore, answers e and f are incorrect.

For more information, see Chapter 6 of *MCSE NT Server 4 Exam Cram*.

## Question 29

Answer c is correct. Deploying a WINS server will reduce NetBIOS b-node traffic because clients will use h-node traffic to communicate with the WINS server for name resolution first before resorting back to b-node. B-node traffic is most likely the source of most of the broadcast traffic on a TCP/IP network. DNS will not reduce b-node traffic. Therefore, answer a is incorrect. NetBEUI is more likely to increase the broadcast traffic than to reduce it. Therefore, answer b is incorrect. Additional BDCs will not reduce b-node traffic. Therefore, answer d is incorrect.

For more information, see Chapter 6 of *MCSE NT Server 4 Exam Cram*.

## Question 30

Answer c is correct. The best action is to move the spooler folder to a drive with more free space. Instructing users to print only 12 pages at a time does not resolve the issue. Therefore, answer a is incorrect. Printing directly to the printer bypasses the spooler and will cause print server and client delays. The client may not be able to perform any other activity while the print job is sent to the printer one page at a time. Therefore, answer b is incorrect. The priority of the spooler has no effect on how many pages at a time a user can send, especially when the problem is free space. Therefore, answer d is incorrect.

For more information, see Chapter 8 of *MCSE NT Server 4 Exam Cram*.

## Question 31

Answers a, b, and d are correct. Possible explanations for this situation are the wrong cable, wrong port, and wrong voltage are used. A command file is not necessary to perform a graceful shutdown; it simply offers the ability to execute a program just before shutdown. Therefore, answer c is incorrect. The recharge time value has no effect on the ability to perform a graceful shutdown. The only time the recharge time valve may affect the situation is when the UPS has not fully recharged between outages. Therefore, answer e is incorrect.

For more information, see Chapter 13 of *MCSE NT Server 4 Exam Cram*.

## Question 32

Answer c is correct. The restriction is a 2MB paging file on the boot partition when STOP error recovery options are selected. 12MB larger than physical RAM is the default size of the paging file. Therefore, answer a is incorrect. 12MB on the system partition is not a requirement for any aspect of Windows NT. Therefore, answer b is incorrect. At least 2MB on any partition is not quite correct—it must be on the boot partition. Therefore, answer d is incorrect.

For more information, see Chapter 13 of *MCSE NT Server 4 Exam Cram*.

## Question 33

Answer c is correct. Microsoft's recommended course of action is to rename the old account and change the password for the new employee. The other options are not recommended by Microsoft. Therefore, answers a, b, and d are incorrect. Creating a new user from scratch will not ensure the same level of access. Copying the old account and then disabling it will retain the old account for security audits, but because Microsoft does not have a security audit tool, there is no need to retain old accounts. Copying the old account and then deleting it is a useful option if you want to create a new account with a new SID and remove the old account from the system.

For more information, see Chapter 5 of *MCSE NT Server 4 Exam Cram*.

## Question 34

Answer c is correct. The only valid method for transforming a member server to a BDC is to reinstall Windows NT Server. The domain controller components are not present on a member server. There is no Promote to BDC command that will promote members servers. Therefore, answer a is incorrect. There is no BDC Service. Therefore, answer b is incorrect. There is no DC Components selection available through the Add/Remove Software applet. Therefore, answer d is incorrect.

For more information, see Chapter 2 of *MCSE NT Server 4 Exam Cram*.

## Question 35

Answers a and e are correct. Windows NT FAT and MS-DOS FAT both support 2GB volumes and over 512 files in nonroot directories. Windows NT FAT actually supports a maximum of 4GB, but the selection does not mention maximum. Neither Windows NT FAT nor MS-DOS FAT support unlimited root directory entries and file-level security. Therefore, answers b and c are incorrect. Windows NT FAT supports LFNs, but MS-DOS FAT does not. Therefore, answer d is incorrect.

For more information, see Chapter 3 of *MCSE NT Server 4 Exam Cram*.

# Question 36

Answers c and e are correct. The only two valid options from this list are "Execute a **WINNT** command from Windows 98" and "Boot with a client disk created through Network Client Administrator from another operational Windows NT Server machine and then execute a **WINNT** command." The three setup floppies method of installation cannot access the distribution files from a network share. Therefore, answer a is incorrect. **WINNT32** can only be executed from a Windows NT system, not Windows 98 or MS-DOS. Therefore, answers b and d are incorrect.

For more information, see Chapter 2 of *MCSE NT Server 4 Exam Cram*.

# Question 37

Answers d and e are correct. The features of user-based dial-in access and the Entire Network/This Computer Only setting are RAS security features, which act like firewalls to all types of RAS clients. User-based dial-in access is somewhat like a firewall, only granting communication access to specific users or computers. The Entire Network/This Computer Only setting is like a firewall in that it can limit access to a network. Callback is similar to ARP's reverse lookup for verifying a client's IP address, but because callback is not supported over PPTP connections, it isn't available for all types of RAS clients. Therefore, answer a is incorrect. PPTP provides secure communications over the Internet, but it's not a firewall-like activity. Therefore, answer b is incorrect. Encrypted authentication ensures proper identification, but it's not a firewall-like activity. Therefore, answer c is incorrect.

For more information, see Chapter 10 of *MCSE NT Server 4 Exam Cram*.

# Question 38

Answer b is correct. The benefit is improved performance due to separating the burden of system activity from memory activity. The level of wear and tear on a drive due to normal paging file activity is negligible over the lifetime of a physical drive. Therefore, answer a is incorrect. Fault tolerance is not improved, because the failure of the paging file host drive will cause a system failure. Therefore, answer c is incorrect. The paging file is, by default, 12MB larger than physical RAM; Microsoft and non-Microsoft resources recommend a paging file of about two times that of physical RAM. There's never a mention of 150MB as a specific size for the paging file. 150MB is associated with the amount of free space required to install Windows NT Server. Therefore, answer d is incorrect.

For more information, see Chapter 11 of *MCSE NT Server 4 Exam Cram*.

## Question 39

Answers a, d, and e are correct. The Network Client Administrator can be used to create installation disk sets, make network installation startup disks, and copy client-based network administration tools. Viewing local boot client information is an invalid action—the real function is to view *remote* boot client information. Therefore, answer b is incorrect. The three setup floppies must be built with either **WINNT** or **WINNT32**. Therefore, answer c is incorrect.

For more information, see Chapter 2 of *MCSE NT Server 4 Exam Cram*.

## Question 40

Answer d is correct. The **NET USERS** command is the most efficient means by which to create 130 similar user accounts. Manually creating 130 user accounts is not the most efficient method and will probably result in several configuration errors. Therefore, answer a is incorrect. Making copies of a correct account is a good method for creating 130 user accounts, but it isn't the most efficient method. Therefore, answer b is incorrect. There is no Template option in User Manager. Therefore, answer c is incorrect.

For more information, see Chapter 5 of *MCSE NT Server 4 Exam Cram*.

## Question 41

Answer c is correct. The Event Viewer is the only place you can view further information about system-level errors. Windows NT Diagnostics, Dr. Watson, and Server Manager do not offer history lists of errors for review. Therefore, answers a, b, and e are incorrect. DEVICE.LOG records communications over a serial port to a communications device; it does not record system boot errors. Therefore, answer d is incorrect.

For more information, see Chapter 13 of *MCSE NT Server 4 Exam Cram*.

## Question 42

Answer d is correct. "Local groups can contain local users and global groups" is the true statement in this list. Global user accounts can be members of either local or global groups. Therefore, answer a is incorrect. Global groups can only contain users. Therefore, answer b is incorrect. Local user accounts can be members of either local or global groups. Therefore, answer c is incorrect.

For more information, see Chapter 5 of *MCSE NT Server 4 Exam Cram*.

# Question 43

Answer d is correct. This error means the BOOTSECT.DOS file is missing or corrupt, thus preventing non-Windows NT operating systems from being booted. Windows NT Server does not use the BOOTSECT.DOS file to boot. Therefore, answer a is incorrect. If BOOT.INI were missing, the file would not have been able to select a non-Windows NT operating system to attempt to boot to cause this error. Therefore, answer b is incorrect. NTDETECT.COM is only used when booting to Windows NT, not to a non-Windows NT operating system. Therefore, answer c is incorrect. (Note: The question stated that the system hosted Windows NT Server, not that Windows NT Server was the operating system being booted to.)

For more information, see Chapter 13 of *MCSE NT Server 4 Exam Cram*.

# Question 44

Answers a, d, and e are correct. These are all true statements. Binding NetBEUI before TCP/IP is not always the best option, especially when broadcast traffic needs to be kept to a minimum. Therefore, answer b is incorrect. When a new network component is installed, even after the initial installation of the operating system, Windows NT will enable all bindings by default—you don't have to manually enable bindings to use the new component. Therefore, answer c is incorrect.

For more information, see Chapter 6 of *MCSE NT Server 4 Exam Cram*.

# Question 45

Answers a, d, and e are correct. WFW, OS/2, and NetWare systems all require local installation of printer drivers for Windows NT Server print server-hosted printers. Windows 95, Windows NT Workstation 3.51, and Windows NT Advanced Server 3.1 can pull print drivers from the print server each time a print job is submitted. Therefore, answers b, c, and f are incorrect.

For more information, see Chapter 8 of *MCSE NT Server 4 Exam Cram*.

# Question 46

Answer a is correct. Physical connections should be checked first, because they're the most common points of failure for printers. The spooler service is a valid trouble-shooting checkpoint, but it isn't the first thing to look into. Therefore, answer b is incorrect. The priority of your logical printer should not affect your ability to print documents—it just means your print jobs are printed before or after others. This is probably one of the last items you should check when troubleshooting printers.

Therefore, answer c is incorrect. Your print permission levels are good to check, but they aren't the first thing to check. Therefore, answer d is incorrect.

For more information, see Chapter 8 of *MCSE NT Server 4 Exam Cram*.

## Question 47

Answers b and e are correct. Windows NT Server requires 16MB of RAM, but to become a BDC, the server must have network access, so a NIC is also required. A local CD-ROM drive is not required because network access to the distribution files is possible. Therefore, answer a is incorrect. A pointing device makes the installation easier, but it can be managed through the keyboard. Therefore, answer c is incorrect. Windows NT Server requires 150MB of free space, not 120MB, which is the requirement of Windows NT Workstation. Therefore, answer d is incorrect.

For more information, see Chapter 2 of *MCSE NT Server 4 Exam Cram*.

## Question 48

Answer d is correct. System policies are used to restrict a user's access to Control Panel applets, prevent wallpaper changes, and require network logon to gain local system access. Mandatory profiles do not restrict Control Panel applet access or require network logon. (However, mandatory profiles do prevent permanent changes to the desktop wallpaper.) Therefore, answer a is incorrect. Hardware profiles do not perform any of these functions; instead, hardware profiles are used to add or remove device drivers based on available peripherals or connections. Therefore, answer b is incorrect. The User Manager does not offer these controls on a user basis; the System Policy Editor must be used to create system policies. Therefore, answer c is incorrect.

For more information, see Chapter 5 of *MCSE NT Server 4 Exam Cram*.

## Question 49

Answer a is correct. Roaming profiles are placed in any network share accessible from any client. Therefore, the USERS\<*username*> (a custom shared directory) is the most likely selection. The *%winnt_root%*\Profiles\<*username*> directory is where local profiles, not roaming profiles, are stored. Therefore, answer c is incorrect. The *%winnt_root%*\\<*username*> and *%winnt_root%*\ Ntusers\<*username*> directory choices are both designed to steer your attention to the local profile storage area and away from the only correct answer—a custom share. Therefore, answers b and d are incorrect.

For more information, see Chapter 5 of *MCSE NT Server 4 Exam Cram*.

## Question 50

Answer b is correct. Server Manager can be used to obtain a list of network resources currently being accessed on a system-by-system basis. Network Monitor, Windows NT Diagnostics, and Windows NT Explorer do not offer a list of network resource access. Therefore, answers a, c, and d are incorrect.

For more information, see Chapter 5 of *MCSE NT Server 4 Exam Cram.*

## Question 51

Answer d is correct. NETLOGON is the share of the *%winnt_root%\* System32\Repl\Import folder that's the default destination of the replication import server. The other three answers are invalid locations of the default destination. Therefore, answers a, b, and c are incorrect.

For more information, see Chapter 5 of *MCSE NT Server 4 Exam Cram.*

## Question 52

Answer b is correct. Services for Macintosh requires an NTFS partition. Services for Macintosh does not require TCP/IP, NetBIOS, DLC or 8.3 share names. Therefore, answers a, c, d, and e are incorrect.

For more information, see chapters 3 and 6 of *MCSE NT Server 4 Exam Cram.*

## Question 53

Answers c and d are correct. DEVICE.LOG and PPP.LOG are the two RAS-related logs in this list that can be enabled only through the Registry. MODEMLOG.TXT can be enabled through the Modem applet. Therefore, answer a is incorrect. DRWTSN32.LOG is not related to RAS and is enabled though the Dr. Watson utility. Therefore, answer b is incorrect. DEBUG.LOG is not related to RAS and is enabled through command-line functions. Therefore, answer e is incorrect.

For more information, see Chapter 10 of *MCSE NT Server 4 Exam Cram.*

## Question 54

Answers a, b, and d are correct. BOOTSECT.DOS, NTDETECT.COM, and NTLDR are all replaced on RISC systems by OSLOADER.EXE. HAL.DLL is present on RISC systems but not on Intel systems. Therefore, answer c is incorrect. BOOT.INI is not contained in the OSLOADER.EXE file; instead, it's stored in an area of nonvolatile memory on a RISC system. Therefore, answer e is incorrect.

For more information, see Chapter 12 of *MCSE NT Server 4 Exam Cram*.

## Question 55

Answers a and d are correct. "SLIP does not support DHCP" and "PPP is the most widely used WAN protocol" are the only two true statements in this list. SLIP only supports TCP/IP; PPP supports NetBEUI, NWLink, and TCP/IP. Therefore, answer b is incorrect. SLIP and PPP can be used to access Unix servers. Therefore, answer c is incorrect. PPP supports encrypted passwords, SLIP does not. Therefore, answer e is incorrect. PPP can be used to aggregate multiple links (Multilink PPP or MPPP); SLIP cannot. Therefore, answer f is incorrect.

For more information, see Chapter 10 of *MCSE NT Server 4 Exam Cram*.

# Windows NT Server 4 In The Enterprise Practice Test #1

**9**

## Question 1

A user belongs to both the Engineering and the Sales global groups. Group profiles exist for both groups. The user does not have a specific user policy. How will the user's system profile be determined?

- ○ a. The Default User profile will be applied first, and then the group profiles will be applied in the order specified in the Group Priority dialog box.

- ○ b. The user will receive the Default User profile.

- ○ c. The group profiles will be applied in the order specified in the Group Priority dialog box, and the Default User profile will be ignored.

- ○ d. The group profiles will be applied in the order specified in the Group Priority dialog box, and then the Default User profile will be applied.

## Question 2

In order to troubleshoot startup problems, you can have Windows NT list driver names while they're being loaded by Ntldr. What must be done for this to happen?

- ○ a. Boot to Windows NT using a fault-tolerant boot disk.

- ○ b. Edit the Boot.ini file to include the **/sos** switch.

- ○ c. Boot to Windows NT using the Emergency Repair Disk.

- ○ d. Edit the Boot.ini file to include the **/drivers** switch.

# Question 3

International Computer Corp has four domains: Americas, Asia, Europe, and Australia. Users in the Asia, Europe, and Australia domains need access to a Windows NT Server in the Americas domain that stores corporate directory information. What trust relationships must be in place?

○ a. Configure Asia, Europe, and Australia to trust the Americas domain.

○ b. Configure Asia, Europe, and Australia to be trusted by the Americas domain.

○ c. Configure three two-way trusts between Americas and Asia, Europe, and Australia.

○ d. No trust relationships are required.

# Question 4

You need to reboot a server that stores a database that's shared on the network. You want to know how many users will be affected if the shared database goes offline. Where can you check to see how many users are connected to the share?

○ a. Server Manager|Properties|In Use

○ b. Server Manager|Properties

○ c. Server Manager|Properties|Replication

○ d. Server Manager|Properties|Shares

○ e. Server Manager|Properties|Alerts

# Question 5

Windows NT provides various options for hard drive configurations. Which of the following fault-tolerant configurations are available in Windows NT? [Check all correct answers]

❑ a. Stripe sets

❑ b. Stripe sets with parity

❑ c. Disk mirroring

❑ d. Volume sets

❑ e. Mirrored stripe sets

# Question 6

You want NetWare clients to be able to print to the new high-speed laser printer attached to a Windows NT Server. What must be installed on the Windows NT Server for this to work? [Check all correct answers]

❑ a.  File and Print Services for NetWare

❑ b.  Gateway Services for NetWare

❑ c.  NWLink protocol

❑ d.  Migration Tool for NetWare

# Question 7

You have Windows NT Server installed on a computer as a member server in the Corporate domain. You decide to make this computer a Backup Domain Controller (BDC) for this domain. What's the easiest way to accomplish this task?

○ a.  Change the role of the server from Server Manager on the Primary Domain Controller.

○ b.  Reinstall Windows NT Server and select Backup Domain Controller for the server role.

○ c.  Rename the computer and create a new computer account on the Primary Domain Controller specifying the Backup Domain Controller.

○ d.  Change the computer's role from the Network Properties dialog box on the computer.

# Question 8

Your company wants to implement a fault-tolerance standard for all Windows NT Servers on the network.

Required result:

- The servers should be able to recover from a single disk failure.

Optional desired results:

- You must provide fault tolerance for the system partitions.
- You want to provide protection from a drive controller failure.

Proposed solution:

- Implement disk mirroring.

Which results does the proposed solution satisfy?

○ a. The proposed solution produces the required result and both the optional desired results.

○ b. The proposed solution produces the required result and only one of the optional desired results.

○ c. The proposed solution produces the required result but does not produce either of the optional desired results.

○ d. The proposed solution does not produce the required result.

# Question 9

You're troubleshooting network performance and suspect that synchronization traffic may be a problem. You want to increase the time between synchronizations. Which of the following actions would accomplish this task?

○ a. Increase the value of the **Pulse** parameter in the Registry.

○ b. Increase the value of the **PulseConcurrency** parameter in the Registry.

○ c. Decrease the value of the **Pulse** parameter in the Registry.

○ d. Decrease the value of the **PulseConcurrency** parameter in the Registry.

# Question 10

You want the sales representatives for your company to be able to dial into your Windows NT network from remote customer sites in order to obtain up-to-date pricing information. They use Windows NT Workstation on their portable computers. The information that they'll be accessing is extremely sensitive.

Required result:

- The sales representatives should be able to use RAS to dial in from any customer location. All transmitted data, including logon information, should be encrypted.

Optional desired results:

- Telephone numbers the sales representatives are calling from should be able to be authenticated before access is granted to the network.

- The sales representatives should only be allowed access to the network during business hours.

Proposed solution:

- Grant dial-up access to the sales representatives. Configure the workstations and the RAS server to use Microsoft Encrypted Authentication. Set callback security to the Set By Caller option. On the RAS server's Properties dialog box, check the Required Data Encryption box.

Which results does the proposed solution satisfy?

- ○ a.  The proposed solution produces the required result and both the optional desired results.

- ○ b.  The proposed solution produces the required result and only one of the optional desired results.

- ○ c.  The proposed solution produces the required result but does not produce either of the optional desired results.

- ○ d.  The proposed solution does not produce the required result.

# Question 11

Which of the following tasks can be completed as part of the emergency repair process? [Check all correct answers]

❑ a. Inspect the boot sector.

❑ b. Repair missing or corrupt Windows NT system files.

❑ c. Inspect the startup environment.

❑ d. Inspect Registry files.

# Question 12

In a multiple master domain model, how should trusts be configured? [Check all correct answers]

❑ a. Each master domain should have a two-way trust with each other master domain.

❑ b. Each master domain should trust each resource domain.

❑ c. Each resource domain should trust each master domain.

❑ d. Each resource domain should have a two-way trust with each other resource domain.

# Question 13

Windows NT typically comes with three setup floppies that can be used to troubleshoot startup problems. How can you re-create these floppies if you lose the originals?

○ a. From a Windows 95 computer, run Winnt.exe from the I386 folder of the Windows NT CD with the **/b** switch.

○ b. From a Windows 95 computer, run Winnt.exe from the I386 folder of the Windows NT CD with the **/ox** switch.

○ c. From a Windows NT computer, run Winnt.exe from the I386 folder of the Windows NT CD with the **/b** switch.

○ d. From a Windows NT computer, run Winnt.exe from the I386 folder of the Windows NT CD with the **/ox** switch.

# Question 14

What's the purpose of an LMHOSTS file?

- ○ a. To map fully qualified domain names to IP addresses
- ○ b. To map NetBIOS names to IP addresses
- ○ c. To provide the IP address of the Primary Domain Controller for logon authentication
- ○ d. To provide a list of Backup Domain Controllers to the Primary Domain Controller for replication

# Question 15

You're the administrator of a school computer lab that uses all Windows NT Workstation computers as part of a Windows NT domain. Students using the computers do not necessarily log onto the same computer each day. What's the best way to ensure that each student receives his or her user profile regardless of which computer he or she logs onto?

- ○ a. Have each student log onto each computer and configure the settings the same on all of them.
- ○ b. Store each student's profile in his or her home folder and properly specify the profile path in User Manager For Domains.
- ○ c. Configure a mandatory profile for each computer for all students.
- ○ d. Store each student's profile in the Netlogon share on all domain controllers.

# Question 16

Your company has 30,000 users located in four different locations. Administrators at each location want control of local resources, but they do not want to manage user accounts. Which domain model would be most appropriate in this scenario?

- ○ a. Master domain model
- ○ b. Multiple master domain model
- ○ c. Single domain
- ○ d. Complete trust model

## Question 17

You install a new network driver on your Windows NT computer and are no longer able to log on. What's the easiest way to resolve this problem?

○ a. Reinstall Windows NT and restore from tape backup.

○ b. Restart the computer and select the Last Known Good Configuration option.

○ c. Use the emergency repair process.

○ d. Boot from a fault-tolerant boot disk.

## Question 18

What's the primary function of a Dynamic Host Configuration Protocol server?

○ a. To provide IP configuration to DHCP-enabled clients

○ b. To provide IP addresses for fully qualified domain names

○ c. To provide client computers with the IP address of a WINS server

○ d. To provide IP addresses for NetBIOS computer names

## Question 19

You suspect that your disk subsystem may be a bottleneck on your Windows NT Server. You open Performance Monitor and add counters for the Physical Disk object. You notice that all values for these counters are zero, even during high periods of activity. What needs to be done?

○ a. Run chkdsk to verify the integrity of the hard drives.

○ b. Install an updated driver for the disk controller.

○ c. Turn on the disk counters by running diskperf with the **−y** switch.

○ d. Turn on the disk counters by running diskperf with the **−n** switch.

# Question 20

Suppose the following situation exists:

Your growing company is experiencing higher demand for storage resources on the server. There are four drives in your server computer. Two are mirrored and contain the system and boot files. The other two are mirrored and contain data files. Your company's current solution implements disk mirroring for ease of recovery owing to any failed drive, but company management feels that 100 percent disk overhead is excessive.

Required result:

- Provide for recovery of any single drive failure.

Optional desired results:

- Support maximum performance.

- Implement a fault-tolerance strategy that uses disk space effectively.

Proposed solution:

- Combine all drives into a single stripe set.

Which results does the proposed solution satisfy?

- ○ a.  The proposed solution produces the required result and both the optional desired results.

- ○ b.  The proposed solution produces the required result and only one of the optional desired results.

- ○ c.  The proposed solution produces the required result but does not produce either of the optional desired results.

- ○ d.  The proposed solution does not produce the required result.

# Question 21

Users complain that one server on your network responds very slowly. You suspect that there's insufficient memory on the server. Which utility can you use to check the current memory usage?

○ a. Task Manager

○ b. Server Manager

○ c. Windows NT Diagnostics

○ d. Network Monitor

# Question 22

You want to install Windows NT Server on a new computer as a Backup Domain Controller for your domain. However, you want Windows NT Server installed by an offsite consultant before attaching it to your domain. What's the best way to achieve this?

○ a. Have the consultant install Windows NT Server as a Primary Domain Controller for your domain and then demote it to a BDC after attaching the computer to the network.

○ b. Have the consultant install Windows NT Server as a Backup Domain Controller for your domain.

○ c. Have the consultant install Windows NT Server as a standalone server and then promote it to a BDC after attaching the computer to the network.

○ d. This will not work. The system must be attached to the network during the installation.

# Question 23

Suppose the following situation exists:

Your company has two primary locations. The company headquarters is located in Chicago, with a sales office in Los Angeles. The two offices are configured as a single domain connected by an ISDN line. All domain controllers, WINS servers, and DNS servers are located in Chicago.

Required result:

- Reduce the bandwidth used by logon validation over the ISDN line.

Optional desired results:

- Increase performance of fully qualified domain name resolution for users in Los Angeles.
- Decrease the time required to log on for users in Los Angeles.

Proposed solution:

- Place a BDC in Los Angeles with WINS installed.

Which results does the proposed solution satisfy?

- ○ a. The proposed solution produces the required result and both the optional desired results.
- ○ b. The proposed solution produces the required result and only one of the optional desired results.
- ○ c. The proposed solution produces the required result but does not produce either of the optional desired results.
- ○ d. The proposed solution does not produce the required result.

# Question 24

You've just shared a folder containing your company's accounting database on your Windows NT Server for the first time. What is the default share permission for the Everyone group?

- ○ a. Full Control
- ○ b. Change
- ○ c. Read
- ○ d. No Access

# Question 25

Which of the following built-in global groups have the ability to back up files and folders by default? [Check all correct answers]

❏ a. Domain Admins

❏ b. Domain Users

❏ c. Domain Guests

❏ d. Server Operators

❏ e. Backup Operators

# Question 26

You have a Windows NT Server with IIS installed, and you want to host three Web sites on this server. Each site will have its own registered domain name and IP address. Which of the following actions must you perform to accommodate this situation?

○ a. Set up DHCP Relay Agent.

○ b. Install DNS and add an entry for each site in the DNS database.

○ c. Assign each IP address to the network interface card of the server and associate each IP address with the appropriate Web directory.

○ d. Create a HOSTS file with an entry for each domain name with corresponding IP addresses.

# Question 27

You have two domains: Corp is a master domain, and Sales is a resource domain. Both Corp and Sales have a PDC, BDC, member servers, and several Windows NT Workstation computers. You want to create a group called CorpBackup to back up the PDC, BDC, member servers, and all Windows NT Workstation computers in both domains.

Required result:

- Members of the CorpBackup group must be able to back up both domain controllers.

Optional desired results:

- Members of the CorpBackup group must be able to back up all member servers.

- Members of the CorpBackup group must be able to back up all workstations.

Proposed solution:

- Create a global group called CorpBackup in the Corp domain and add this new global group to the local Backup Operators group on all domain controllers, member servers, and workstations in both domains.

Which results does the proposed solution satisfy?

- ○ a.  The proposed solution produces the required result and both the optional desired results.

- ○ b.  The proposed solution produces the required result and only one of the optional desired results.

- ○ c.  The proposed solution produces the required result but does not produce either of the optional desired results.

- ○ d.  The proposed solution does not produce the required result.

# Question 28

You're transferring user accounts from a NetWare server to a Windows NT domain controller using the Migration Tool for NetWare. You want this process to replace existing Windows NT user accounts that have the same name. How would you accomplish this?

○ a.  Do nothing. Existing accounts are replaced by default.

○ b.  Select the Replace Existing Accounts checkbox.

○ c.  This cannot be done.

○ d.  Use a user mapping file.

# Question 29

You have three domains: Sales, Admin, and SrvrShare. Users in the Sales domain need to access a database in the SrvrShare domain. What type of trust must be established to make such access possible?

○ a.  A two-way trust must be established between Sales and SrvrShare.

○ b.  The Sales domain must trust the SrvrShare domain.

○ c.  The SrvrShare domain must trust the Admin domain.

○ d.  The SrvrShare domain must trust the Sales domain.

# Question 30

Which parameters can be adjusted to regulate domain synchronization traffic in the HKEY_LOCAL_MACHINE\SystemCurrentControlSet\Services\Netlogon \Parameters key of the Registry? [Check all correct answers]

❑ a.  **PulseConcurrency**

❑ b.  **Pulse**

❑ c.  **ReplicationGovernor**

❑ d.  **ReplicationTimeout**

# Question 31

Your company has one location with 500 employees. There are four departments spread over two floors in the same building. Centralized user and resource administration is necessary. Which domain model is best for this situation?

- ○ a. Complete trust
- ○ b. Single domain
- ○ c. Master domain
- ○ d. Multiple master domain

# Question 32

What's the recommended method of giving permissions to users for resources in a domain environment?

- ○ a. Place users in local groups and give permissions to local groups.
- ○ b. Give permissions for resources directly to individual users.
- ○ c. Place users in global groups, place global groups in local groups, and assign permissions to local groups.
- ○ d. Place users in local groups, place local groups in global groups, and assign permissions to global groups.

# Question 33

You have a Windows NT Server on your network that contains only one physical drive with a single NTFS partition. There's a database on this server that contains critical information. You want to implement fault tolerance. How can this be accomplished?

- ○ a. Add two more hard drives and create a stripe set with parity.
- ○ b. Create a mirror with a network drive located on another server.
- ○ c. Add another hard drive and implement disk mirroring.
- ○ d. Implement directory replication.

# Question 34

You're purchasing a new server that's to have Windows NT Server preinstalled. You want the new server to be a member server in your Corp domain. How should Windows NT be installed?

○ a. Install the computer as a member server in the Corp workgroup and change it to the Corp domain once the computer is connected to the network.

○ b. Install the computer as a member server in the Corp domain.

○ c. Install the computer as a PDC in the Corp domain and demote it to a member server once the computer is connected to the network.

○ d. Windows NT cannot be installed on the computer as a member server without being connected to the network during installation.

# Question 35

You implemented a stripe set with parity from three hard drives on your file server to protect your data from a single drive failure. One of the drives in the set fails. How should you restore the array?

○ a. Replace the failed drive and do nothing else. This stripe set will regenerate automatically.

○ b. Replace the failed drive, delete the partitions that were part of the original stripe set, and then create a new stripe set with parity and restore from a tape backup.

○ c. Remove the failed drive and convert the remaining two drives to a mirror set.

○ d. Replace the failed drive. Use Disk Administrator to create a new partition on the drive equal in size to the one that failed, select the stripe set and the new partition, and then select Regenerate from the Fault Tolerance menu.

# Question 36

What is your effective permission to a shared folder if you're logged on locally, your share permission is No Access, and your NTFS permission is Read?

○ a. Change

○ b. Full Control

○ c. Read

○ d. No Access

# Question 37

Your company uses a multiple master domain model with master domains in Chicago and Dallas. Jim's computer is part of the Sales resource domain. Jim logs on from his computer to the Dallas domain. Which shared folders will Jim be able to view?

○ a.   Jim will be able to view only shared folders in the Sales domain for which the Sales\Domain Users group has at least Read permission.

○ b.   Jim will be able to view only shared folders in the Sales domain for which the Dallas\Domain Users group has at least Read permission.

○ c.   Jim will be able to view all shared folders in all three domains to which the Dallas\Domain Users group has at least Read permission.

○ d.   Jim will be able to view only shared folders in the Dallas and Chicago domains for which the Sales\Domain Users group has at least Read permission.

# Question 38

Which application is used to view the contents of a memory dump file after a STOP error occurs?

○ a.   DUMPEXAM.EXE

○ b.   Kernel Debugger

○ c.   Notepad

○ d.   Event Viewer

# Question 39

You're installing Windows NT Server on a new computer whose sole responsibility will be to authenticate users in an existing domain. Which role should you choose for this computer?

○ a.   Primary Domain Controller for the domain

○ b.   Backup Domain Controller for the domain

○ c.   Member server for the domain

○ d.   Member server in a workgroup

# Question 40

The first drive in your mirror set fails. How can you boot to the second drive?

○ a. Boot from the Emergency Repair Disk.

○ b. Start a new installation and select the Repair option.

○ c. Boot from a fault-tolerant boot disk.

○ d. Do nothing. Windows NT will boot to the second drive automatically.

# Question 41

You have three domains: Texas, Nevada, and Arizona. Currently, you have the following trusts configured: Texas trusts Nevada, and Nevada trusts Arizona. What's the minimum that needs to be done for a user in the Arizona domain to access resources in the Texas domain?

○ a. Nothing. Texas trusts Arizona by virtue of trusting Nevada, because Nevada trusts Arizona.

○ b. Configure a trust relationship so that Texas trusts Arizona.

○ c. Configure a complete trust for all domains.

○ d. Configure a trust relationship so that Arizona trusts Texas.

# Question 42

You've implemented a stripe set with four physical drives. The second drive of the set fails. How do you restore the array?

○ a. Replace the failed drive, re-create the array, and restore from tape.

○ b. Replace the failed drive and choose Re-create from the Fault Tolerance menu in Disk Administrator.

○ c. Replace the failed drive and choose Regenerate from the Fault Tolerance menu in Disk Administrator.

○ d. Replace the failed drive and allow the array to regenerate automatically.

# Question 43

Your network has two primary groups of users who share data with other members of their group. Each group needs access to information from the other group from time to time. You've noticed that network performance seems to be getting worse as more users are added, and you believe that segmenting the network will provide some relief.

Required result:

- Segment the network so that each group is on a different segment.

Optional desired results:

- Users in each group should still have occasional access to computers maintained by the other group.

- Reduce the amount of broadcast traffic each computer receives.

Proposed solution:

- Install a router on the network so that all users from one group are on one segment, and all users of the other group are on a different segment. Install NetBEUI on all computers as the only protocol.

Which results does the proposed solution satisfy?

- ○ a. The proposed solution produces the required result and both the optional desired results.

- ○ b. The proposed solution produces the required result and only one of the optional desired results.

- ○ c. The proposed solution produces the required result but does not produce either of the optional desired results.

- ○ d. The proposed solution does not produce the required result.

# Question 44

Which of the following items concerning how Windows NT should respond to STOP errors can be configured in the Startup/Shutdown tab of the System Properties page? [Check all correct answers]

- ❏ a. Write an error event to the System log.

- ❏ b. Send an Administrative alert.

- ❏ c. Write a dump file.

- ❏ d. Run Chkdsk on next boot.

- ❏ e. Automatically reboot.

# Question 45

Which of the following networking protocols are built into Windows NT? [Check all correct answers]

❑ a. AppleTalk

❑ b. Data Link Control (DLC)

❑ c. TCP/IP

❑ d. NetBEUI

❑ e. NWLink IPX/SPX

# Question 46

Which networking components are needed for a Windows NT Server system to provide access to NetWare resources? [Check all correct answers]

❑ a. Gateway Service for NetWare

❑ b. File and Print Services for NetWare

❑ c. NWLink Protocol

❑ d. Migration Tool for NetWare

# Question 47

You want to use Network Monitor to capture all the frames sent from a network computer named Steve. What's the best way to set up the capture filter?

○ a. **INCLUDE Steve —> ANY**

○ b. **INCLUDE Steve <— ANY**

○ c. **INCLUDE Steve <—> ANY**

○ d. **INCLUDE ANY <— Steve**

# Question 48

Several print jobs have been submitted and are not printing. The print jobs cannot be deleted manually either. How can you resolve this problem with the minimal amount of effort?

○ a.  Restart the server.

○ b.  Cycle the power on the printer.

○ c.  Stop and restart the spooler service.

○ d.  Give users administrative rights to the printer and have them delete and resubmit their print jobs.

# Question 49

Which performance counters would you monitor if you suspect that the disk subsystem is a bottleneck for your server? [Check all correct answers]

❑ a.  Current Disk Queue Length

❑ b.  Pages/sec

❑ c.  % Disk Time

❑ d.  Interrupts/sec

# Question 50

When should you monitor a system to create a performance baseline?

○ a.  Data should be taken during times of high activity.

○ b.  Data should be taken at regular intervals throughout the day for several days.

○ c.  Data should be taken during times of low activity.

○ d.  Data should be taken at one time during the day for several days.

# Question 51

You have a shared printer that's used by the sales team and its managers. What can you do to ensure that documents printed by the managers have priority over those printed by the sales team?

○ a. Have the managers send a message when they're printing to tell the sales team not to print.

○ b. Create two logical printers—one for each group. Set the priority of the logical printer for the managers to 1 and for the sales team to 99.

○ c. Create two logical printers—one for each group. Set the priority of the logical printer for the managers to 99 and for the sales team to 1.

○ d. Give the managers administrative privileges to the printer and give the sales team Print permission only.

# Question 52

What information can be provided to a client machine from a DHCP server? [Check all correct answers]

❑ a. IP address

❑ b. Frame type

❑ c. WINS server IP address

❑ d. Subnet mask

# Question 53

Which of the following statements is false?

○ a. When installing Windows NT as a Backup Domain Controller, you must have connectivity to the Primary Domain Controller.

○ b. When installing Windows NT as a Primary Domain Controller, you're actually creating a new domain.

○ c. When installing Windows NT as a Primary Domain Controller, you cannot have another Primary Domain Controller on the network.

○ d. When installing Windows NT as a member server, you can join either a domain or a workgroup.

## Question 54

Which tool would you use to view all processes currently running on a Windows NT computer?

○ a.  Network Monitor

○ b.  Performance Monitor

○ c.  Task Manager

○ d.  Server Manager

## Question 55

When is a good time to update your Emergency Repair Disk? [Check all correct answers]

❑ a.  During the installation of Windows NT

❑ b.  Anytime the hard drive configuration is changed

❑ c.  After making significant changes to your accounting database

❑ d.  After completing a virus scan

# Windows NT Server 4 In The Enterprise Answer Key #1

**10**

1. c
2. b
3. b
4. d
5. b, c
6. a, c
7. b
8. b
9. a
10. b
11. a, b, c, d
12. a, c
13. b
14. b

15. b
16. b
17. b
18. a
19. c
20. d
21. a
22. d
23. b
24. a
25. a
26. c
27. a
28. c

29. d
30. a, b, c
31. b
32. c
33. c
34. a
35. d
36. c
37. c
38. a
39. b
40. c
41. b
42. a

43. b
44. a, b, c, e
45. a, b, c, d, e
46. a, c
47. a
48. c
49. a, c
50. b
51. c
52. a, c, d
53. c
54. c
55. a, b

## Question 1

Answer c is correct. If group profiles exist for a user, these profiles are applied in the order specified in the Group Priority dialog box, and the Default User profile is ignored. The Default User profile is only applied when both individual user and group profiles do not exist for the user. Therefore, answers a, b, and d are incorrect.

For more information, see Chapter 5 of *MCSE NT Server 4 in the Enterprise Exam Cram.*

## Question 2

Answer b is correct. The **/sos** switch in the Boot.ini file will cause Ntldr to display driver names while they're being loaded. Booting from a fault-tolerant boot disk is used to troubleshoot startup problems related to missing or corrupt system files. Therefore, answer a is incorrect. The Emergency Repair Disk is not a bootable disk. Therefore, answer c is incorrect. The **/drivers** switch for the Boot.ini file does not exist. Therefore, answer d is incorrect.

For more information, see Chapter 15 of *MCSE NT Server 4 in the Enterprise Exam Cram.*

## Question 3

Answer b is correct. In trust relationships, users are in one domain and resources are in another. Relate this to a parent and child. The parent has the car, and the child wants it. The parent must trust the child in order for the child to use the car. The parent is *trusting*, and the child is *trusted*. The user, therefore, is the child, and the resource, held by the parent, is the car. The trust arrow points from the resource to the user. Answer b is correct because the parent, or Americas, trusts its Asia, Europe, and Australia domain children. Answer a is incorrect because it does no good for the child to trust the parent to get a resource—it must be the other way around. The two-way trusts mentioned in answer c will work, but creating the additional trusts just creates more maintenance work and might give users in the Americas domain unnecessary access to resources in the other three domains. Therefore, answer c is not the best answer. Answer d is incorrect because without trusts, users in one domain cannot access resources in another domain.

For more information, see Chapter 3 of *MCSE NT Server 4 in the Enterprise Exam Cram.*

## Question 4

Answer d is correct. The Shares button shows you a list of all shares; when you select any particular share, it displays a list of connected users, time, and whether the share is in use. In Use shows the computer's open shared resources but not the number of users. Therefore, answer a is incorrect. Answer b opens the Properties dialog box but leaves you one mouse click short. Therefore, answer b is incorrect. Replication manages directory replication, not shares. Therefore, answer c is incorrect. Alerts permits registration to receive administrative alerts but says nothing about shares. Therefore, answer e is also incorrect.

For more information, see Chapter 5 of *MCSE NT Server 4 in the Enterprise Exam Cram.*

## Question 5

Answers b and c are correct. The only fault-tolerant configurations available in Windows NT are disk mirroring (RAID 1) and striping with parity (RAID 5). Stripe sets (RAID 0) and volume sets are also available but are not fault-tolerant solutions. Therefore, answers a and d are incorrect. Windows NT does not support mirroring stripe sets. Therefore, answer e is incorrect.

For more information, see Chapter 6 of *MCSE NT Server 4 in the Enterprise Exam Cram.*

## Question 6

Answers a and c are correct. The NWLink protocol must be installed to allow NetWare clients to communicate with the Windows NT Server. File and Print Services for NetWare allows NetWare clients to access shared folders and printers on a Windows NT Server. Gateway Services for NetWare allows a Windows NT Server to connect to NetWare servers. Therefore, answer b is incorrect. The Migration Tool for NetWare is a utility that aids in the migration of users, groups, and files from a NetWare server to a Windows NT Server. Therefore, answer d is incorrect.

For more information, see chapters 12 and 13 of *MCSE NT Server 4 in the Enterprise Exam Cram.*

## Question 7

Answer b is correct. The only way to change the role of a Windows NT Server from member server to domain controller (and vice versa) is by reinstalling Windows NT Server and selecting the appropriate role during installation. Therefore, answers a, c, and d are incorrect.

For more information, see Chapter 5 of *MCSE NT Server 4 in the Enterprise Exam Cram.*

## Question 8

Answer b is correct. Disk mirroring does have the ability to recover from a single drive failure, as does disk striping with parity. A Windows NT mirror set can also contain the system and boot partitions, whereas a stripe set cannot. Disk mirroring does not, however, protect from a controller failure. Disk duplexing would be a better solution to meet all required and desired results.

For more information, see Chapter 6 of *MCSE NT Server 4 in the Enterprise Exam Cram.*

## Question 9

Answer a is correct. The **Pulse** parameter dictates the frequency with which synchronization occurs. Increasing this value will increase the time between synchronizations. The **PulseConcurrency** parameter defines the maximum number of BDCs that can be synchronized simultaneously. Therefore, answers b and d are incorrect. Decreasing the **Pulse** parameter has the opposite result of what is required by the question. Therefore, answer c is incorrect.

For more information, see Chapter 5 of *MCSE NT Server 4 in the Enterprise Exam Cram.*

## Question 10

Answer b is correct. The required result is met by specifying that Microsoft Encrypted Authentication must be used, checking the Required Data Encryption box, and granting dial-up permission to the sales representatives. The first desired result is met by using callback security. The second desired result is not met by the proposed solution. The times that the sales representative can connect to the network can be limited through the Logon Hours dialog box in User Manager For Domains.

For more information, see Chapter 14 of *MCSE NT Server 4 in the Enterprise Exam Cram.*

## Question 11

Answers a, b, c, and d are correct. The emergency repair process presents you with the following options: Inspect Registry Files, Inspect Startup Environment, Verify Windows NT System Files, Inspect Boot Sector.

For more information, see Chapter 15 of *MCSE NT Server 4 in the Enterprise Exam Cram.*

## Question 12

Answers a and c are correct. In the multiple master domain model, each master domain must trust each other master domain with a two-way trust relationship. The resource domains must trust the master domains in order for users to access the resources. Remember that all user accounts are stored in the master domains. There is no need for the user domain to trust the resource domain. Therefore, answers b and d are incorrect.

For more information, see Chapter 2 of *MCSE NT Server 4 in the Enterprise Exam Cram.*

## Question 13

Answer b is correct. To create setup floppies from the Windows NT installation CD, you can run Winnt.exe (on a Windows 95/DOS computer) or Winnt32.exe (on a Windows NT computer) with the /ox switch. The /b switch is to perform a "floppyless" installation. The disks can also be created during installation by running Winnt.exe or Winnt32.exe with no switches. Therefore, answers a and c are incorrect. You cannot run Winnt.exe on a Windows NT computer. Therefore, answer d is incorrect.

For more information, see Chapter 15 of *MCSE NT Server 4 in the Enterprise Exam Cram.*

## Question 14

Answer b is correct. An LMHOSTS file is a static mapping of NetBIOS names (or friendly names) to IP addresses. The WINS service performs the same function but provides dynamic mapping. Fully qualified domain names can be mapped to IP addresses by using a HOSTS file or the DNS service. Therefore, answer a is incorrect. LMHOSTS files have nothing to do with domain controllers. Therefore, answers c and d are incorrect.

For more information, see Chapter 9 of *MCSE NT Server 4 in the Enterprise Exam Cram.*

# Question 15

Answer b is correct. Although answers a and c might work, answer b is the *best* answer. User profiles can be stored on any accessible share in the domain or any trusting domain. This path must be specified for the user in User Manager For Domains. This method will make a single profile for a user that's available to that user regardless of which computer he or she logs onto. Therefore, any changes made to the profile from one computer will be present when the user logs onto another computer.

For more information, see Chapter 5 of *MCSE NT Server 4 in the Enterprise Exam Cram.*

# Question 16

Answer b is correct. The multiple master domain model is appropriate for this situation. There are too many users for the master domain model. Therefore, answer a is incorrect. A single domain does not provide decentralization of resource management and cannot support that many users. Therefore, answer c is incorrect. Complete trust does not provide for centralization of user account management. Therefore, answer d is incorrect.

For more information, see Chapter 2 of *MCSE NT Server 4 in the Enterprise Exam Cram.*

# Question 17

Answer b is correct. Answer a will work, but it's far more work than is required. The Last Known Good Configuration is not updated until there is a successful logon. Therefore, if you're unable to logon, you can use the Last Known Good Configuration to get back to the configuration used at the last successful logon. The emergency repair process will not work in this situation. Therefore, answer c is incorrect. Booting from a fault-tolerant disk will not fix the problem. Therefore, answer d is incorrect.

For more information, see Chapter 15 of *MCSE NT Server 4 in the Enterprise Exam Cram.*

# Question 18

Answer a is correct. A DHCP server is primarily responsible for providing and maintaining IP address information to client computers. DNS servers resolve fully qualified domain names to IP addresses. Therefore, answer b is incorrect. Although a DHCP server can provide the IP address of a WINS server to client computers, that's not its primary function. Therefore, answer c is incorrect. WINS servers resolve NetBIOS names to IP addresses. Therefore, answer d is incorrect.

For more information, see Chapter 9 of *MCSE NT Server 4 in the Enterprise Exam Cram.*

## Question 19

Answer c is correct. By default, physical and logical disk counters are disabled. To enable these counters, you must run **diskperf -y**. Running chkdsk and updating the controller driver will have no effect on this situation. Therefore, answers a and b are incorrect. The **-n** switch disables the disk counters. Therefore, answer d is incorrect.

For more information, see Chapter 11 of *MCSE NT Server 4 in the Enterprise Exam Cram.*

## Question 20

Answer d is correct. Although a stripe set supplies higher performance than mirroring, and takes advantage of all available disk space, it does not meet the required result of being able to recover from a single drive failure. In addition, a stripe set cannot contain the Windows NT system and boot partitions. Because the required result is not met, answers a, b, and c are incorrect.

For more information, see Chapter 6 of *MCSE NT Server 4 in the Enterprise Exam Cram.*

## Question 21

Answer a is correct. Task Manager will show current memory usage as well as a short history in graphical form. Task Manager also shows currently running applications, processes, and CPU usage. You could also use Performance Monitor counters for the Memory object to track memory usage. Server Manager, Windows NT Diagnostics, and Network Monitor cannot provide information on memory usage. Therefore, answer b, c, and d are incorrect.

For more information, see Chapter 11 of *MCSE NT Server 4 in the Enterprise Exam Cram.*

## Question 22

Answer d is correct. Backup Domain Controllers are assigned the same domain security identifier as the Primary Domain Controller. Therefore, when you're installing a BDC, the computer must be physically attached to the network where the PDC resides. Answer a is incorrect because the domain SID will be different for the new computer. You cannot install Windows NT Server to be a Backup Domain Controller for a network unless it is attached to the network. Therefore, answer b is incorrect. Answer c is incorrect because it's not possible to promote a standalone server to a domain controller.

For more information, see Chapter 5 of *MCSE NT Server 4 in the Enterprise Exam Cram*.

## Question 23

Answer b is correct. Placing a BDC at the remote site will reduce logon traffic across the WAN link as well as decrease the time for the remote users to log on. Installing WINS on the remote BDC will aid in the performance of NetBIOS name resolution but will not affect name resolution performance of fully qualified domain names. The remote users will still have to get FQDN resolution across the WAN link.

For more information, see Chapter 9 of *MCSE NT Server 4 in the Enterprise Exam Cram*.

## Question 24

Answer a is correct. The default share permissions for a new share is Full Control for Everyone. Therefore, answers b, c, and d are incorrect.

For more information, see Chapter 4 of *MCSE NT Server 4 in the Enterprise Exam Cram*.

## Question 25

Answer a is correct. By default, the only built-in global group that has the right to back up files and folders is the Domain Admins group. This is due to the fact that the Domain Admins group is automatically added to the Administrators local group, which has this right. The Domain Users, Domain Guests, and Server Operators Groups do not have the right to back up files and folders by default. Therefore, answers b, c, and d are incorrect. Although the Backup Operators group also has this right, the Backup Operators group is a local group, not a global group. Therefore, answer e is incorrect.

For more information, see Chapter 4 of *MCSE NT Server 4 in the Enterprise Exam Cram*.

## Question 26

Answer c is correct. All you need to do to host multiple Web sites on IIS when connected to the Internet is to assign the IP addresses of each site to the server and associate those IP addresses with the respective Web directories. The DHCP Relay Agent is not related to this situation. Therefore, answer a is incorrect. You don't need to install DNS, because DNS name resolution for registered domain names will be handled by InterNIC. A HOSTS file is not needed for the same reason. Therefore, answers b and d are also incorrect.

For more information, see Chapter 9 of *MCSE NT Server 4 in the Enterprise Exam Cram.*

## Question 27

Answer a is correct. In the master domain model, the master domain is trusted by the resource domain. Therefore, global groups created in the master domain can be added to local groups and assigned permissions to resources in the re-source domains. By adding the CorpBackup global group of the trusted domain to all local Backup Operators groups, you have effectively given that group the right to back up all computers in both domains.

For more information, see Chapter 4 of *MCSE NT Server 4 in the Enterprise Exam Cram.*

## Question 28

Answer c is correct. By default, accounts with duplicate names are not trans-ferred at all. There is no Replace Existing Accounts checkbox. Therefore, answer b is incorrect. A user-mapping file maps account names in NetWare to differ-ent account names in Windows NT. Therefore, answer d is incorrect. There is no way for the Migration Tool for NetWare to simply replace existing Win-dows NT user accounts. Therefore, answer a is incorrect.

For more information, see Chapter 12 of *MCSE NT Server 4 in the Enterprise Exam Cram.*

## Question 29

Answer d is correct. For a group in one domain to access resources in another domain, the domain with the resource must trust the domain with the group. A two-way trust is not necessary. Therefore, answer a is incorrect. The trust relationship in answer b is reversed. Therefore, answer b is incorrect. A trust between Sales and Admin is not necessary. Therefore, answer c is incorrect.

For more information, see Chapter 3 of *MCSE NT Server 4 in the Enterprise Exam Cram*.

## Question 30

Answers a, b, and c are correct. Domain synchronization can be regulated by adjusting the Netlogon parameters in the Registry. The **Pulse** parameter determines the frequency of synchronization. **PulseConcurrency** defines the maximum number of BDCs that are synchronized at one time. The **ReplicationGovernor** parameter defines the packet size used in synchronization. There is no such parameter as **ReplicationTimeout**. Therefore, answer d is incorrect.

For more information, see Chapter 5 of *MCSE NT Server 4 in the Enterprise Exam Cram*.

## Question 31

Answer b is correct. A single domain can easily support the number of users given, and it provides for centralized user and resource administration. Although other domain models could work, they would produce more administrative overhead than needed. Therefore, answers a, c, and d are incorrect.

For more information, see Chapter 2 of *MCSE NT Server 4 in the Enterprise Exam Cram*.

## Question 32

Answer c is correct. The recommended method of assigning permissions is to place users into global groups, global groups into local groups, and assign permissions to the local groups. You can assign permissions for a resource directly to local groups and users; however, this is not the recommended method. Therefore, answers a and b are incorrect. Answer d is incorrect because you cannot put local groups into global groups.

For more information, see Chapter 4 of *MCSE NT Server 4 in the Enterprise Exam Cram*.

## Question 33

Answer c is correct. Implementing disk mirroring is the only way to achieve fault tolerance in this scenario without the addition of a hardware RAID controller. Answer a is incorrect because the Windows NT boot and system partitions cannot be part of a stripe set. Answer b is also incorrect because you can only create a mirror set with a drive on the same system. Directory replication is designed to replicate user profiles, logon scripts, and system policies to multiple domain controllers. Therefore, answer d is incorrect.

For more information, see Chapter 6 of *MCSE NT Server 4 in the Enterprise Exam Cram.*

## Question 34

Answer a is correct. A computer can be installed as a member server while disconnected from the network; however, it must be able to contact the PDC of the domain to be installed as part of the domain. Therefore, answer b is incorrect. Answer c is incorrect because you cannot demote a PDC to a member server. Answer d is a false statement and is therefore incorrect.

For more information, see Chapter 5 of *MCSE NT Server 4 in the Enterprise Exam Cram.*

## Question 35

Answer d is correct. This is the recommended approach for restoring a disk array. Stripe sets do not regenerate automatically. Therefore, answer a is incorrect. Answer b would work, but it would defeat the purpose of having a stripe set with parity and would cause more work than necessary. Answer c is incorrect because it's not possible to take partitions that are part of a stripe set and covert them to a mirror set. To create a mirror with the remaining two drives, the existing partitions would first have to be removed, causing you to lose your data.

For more information, see Chapter 6 of *MCSE NT Server 4 in the Enterprise Exam Cram.*

## Question 36

Answer c is correct. Read access is the effective cumulative permission. The cumulative permission does not result in Change or Full Control Access. Therefore, answers a and b are incorrect. Answer d would be correct if you were accessing the resource from the network, but share permissions are irrelevant when you're logged on locally.

For more information, see Chapter 4 of *MCSE NT Server 4 in the Enterprise Exam Cram.*

## Question 37

Answer c is correct. In a multiple master domain model, each master domain trusts the other master domains, and each resource domain trusts each master domain. Therefore, a user logging onto a master domain will have access to any resource in the resource domain and both master domains for which that user has permissions. None of the other answers correctly identify the resources to which Jim will have access. Therefore, answers a, b, and d are incorrect.

For more information, see Chapter 3 of *MCSE NT Server 4 in the Enterprise Exam Cram.*

## Question 38

Answer a is correct. The DUMPEXAM.EXE utility is used to view the contents of a memory dump. Kernel Debugger records the activity of Windows NT during a boot and when a stop error occurs. Therefore, answer b is incorrect. Notepad does not provide system information. Therefore, answer c is incorrect. Event Viewer is used to view a list of STOP errors and what time they occurred. Therefore, answer d is incorrect.

For more information, see Chapter 15 of *MCSE NT Server 4 in the Enterprise Exam Cram.*

## Question 39

Answer b is correct. To authenticate users, the computer must be installed as a domain controller. If the computer is installed as a PDC, a new domain will be created. Therefore, answer a is incorrect. Member servers do not authenticate users for a domain. Therefore, answers c and d are incorrect.

For more information, see Chapter 5 of *MCSE NT Server 4 in the Enterprise Exam Cram.*

## Question 40

Answer c is correct. A fault-tolerant boot disk is a disk formatted with Windows NT that contains the following files: Ntldr, Ntdetect.com, Boot.ini, Ntbootdd.sys, and Bootsect.dos (the latter two only if needed). The Boot.ini file must be modified to correctly point to the second drive on the controller if the first drive is the failed drive. Booting from the ERD will not work in this situation. Therefore, answer a is incorrect. It is not necessary to perform a repair installation. Therefore, answer b is incorrect. Windows NT will not boot to the second drive automatically. Therefore, answer d is incorrect.

For more information, see Chapter 6 of *MCSE NT Server 4 in the Enterprise Exam Cram.*

## Question 41

Answer b is correct. The domain with the resource must trust the domain with the user wanting access to that resource. Answer a is incorrect because trusts are not transitive. Answer c would work, but it's not correct because it would be more trouble than answer b. Establishing a relationship in which Arizona trusts Texas is not necessary. Therefore, answer d is incorrect.

For more information, see Chapter 3 of *MCSE NT Server 4 in the Enterprise Exam Cram.*

## Question 42

Answer a is correct. A stripe set does not provide any fault tolerance. Therefore, if a drive fails, the only way to recover it is to re-create the array and restore from backup. There is no Re-create option from the Fault Tolerance menu. Therefore, answer b is incorrect. You cannot automatically regenerate a stripe set. Therefore, answers c and d are incorrect.

For more information, see Chapter 6 of *MCSE NT Server 4 in the Enterprise Exam Cram.*

## Question 43

Answer b is correct. The required solution is met by installing the router. The amount of broadcast traffic each computer must process is also reduced by adding the router, because broadcasts are not passed through routers. The other optional result of providing access between groups is not met because the NetBEUI protocol is being used exclusively. The NetBEUI protocol is not routable.

For more information, see Chapter 8 of *MCSE NT Server 4 in the Enterprise Exam Cram.*

## Question 44

Answers a, b, c, and e are correct. From the Startup/Shutdown tab of the System Properties page, you can configure Windows NT to do the following when a STOP error occurs: write an error event to the System log, send an Administrative alert, write a dump file, and automatically reboot. Running Chkdsk on the next boot can't be configured from the Startup/Shutdown tab of the System Properties page. Therefore, answer d is incorrect.

For more information, see Chapter 15 of *MCSE NT Server 4 in the Enterprise Exam Cram.*

## Question 45

Answers a, b, c, d, and e are correct. AppleTalk, DLC, TCP/IP, NetBEUI, and NWLink IPX/SPX are all protocols that are included with Windows NT.

For more information, see Chapter 8 of *MCSE NT Server 4 in the Enterprise Exam Cram.*

## Question 46

Answers a and c are correct. Gateway Service for NetWare and the NWLink Protocol are necessary for a Windows NT Server to provide access to NetWare resources for Microsoft clients. File and Print Services for NetWare provides NetWare clients access to Windows NT resources. Therefore, answer b is incorrect. Microsoft's Migration Tool for NetWare transfers user and group information from a NetWare server to a Windows NT Server. Therefore, answer d is incorrect.

For more information, see Chapter 12 of *MCSE NT Server 4 in the Enterprise Exam Cram.*

## Question 47

Answer a is correct. To capture all frames being sent from Steve, the capture filter should have the line **INCLUDE Steve → ANY.** The arrow pointing the other way would capture all frames being sent to Steve. Therefore, answer b is incorrect. Answer c captures all frames sent either to or from Steve. Therefore, answer c is incorrect. Answer d would not capture any frames sent from Steve. Therefore, answer d is incorrect.

For more information, see Chapter 10 of *MCSE NT Server 4 in the Enterprise Exam Cram.*

## Question 48

Answer c is correct. The problem is most likely caused by a stalled print spooler. Stopping and restarting the spooler service should fix the problem. The problem can also be fixed by restarting the computer, because all services will be stopped and restarted, but this is more effort. Therefore, answer a is incorrect. Shutting down and restarting the printer would not solve the problem. Therefore, answer b is incorrect. You should never give users administrative rights. Therefore, answer d is incorrect.

For more information, see Chapter 13 of *MCSE NT Server 4 in the Enterprise Exam Cram.*

## Question 49

Answers a and c are correct. In order to monitor disk performance, you first must ensure that the disk counters are enabled. Disk counters can be enabled by executing diskperf with the −y switch. The Pages/sec counter should be monitored if memory is the suspected bottleneck. Therefore, answer b is incorrect. Interrupts/sec can be monitored if you suspect that a hardware device is malfunctioning. Therefore, answer d is incorrect.

For more information, see Chapter 11 of *MCSE NT Server 4 in the Enterprise Exam Cram.*

## Question 50

Answer b is correct. Performance baselines can be used comparatively to see whether a given counter is operating within its normal range. Baseline data should be gathered throughout the entire day at specific intervals over several days in order to get a good idea of "normal" operation. Monitoring data during times of high activity would not provide a correct baseline of normal operation. Therefore, answer a is incorrect. Likewise, only monitoring data at times of low activity would not provide a correct baseline. Therefore, answer c is incorrect. Only monitoring at a specific time would not provide a correct baseline either. Therefore, answer d is incorrect.

For more information, see Chapter 11 of *MCSE NT Server 4 in the Enterprise Exam Cram.*

## Question 51

Answer c is correct. You have the ability to create more than one logical printer for a single print device. These logical printers can have different settings. A priority of 99 will take precedence over a priority of 1. Answer a will work, of course, but this should not be necessary in the age of computers. Answer b will give a higher priority to the sales team, which is the opposite of what is requested by the question. Therefore, answer b is incorrect. Answer d does not affect the priority of print jobs. Therefore, answer d is incorrect.

For more information, see Chapter 13 of *MCSE NT Server 4 in the Enterprise Exam Cram.*

## Question 52

Answers a, c, and d are correct. DHCP provides TCP/IP configuration information to DHCP-enabled clients. This information can include the IP address, the subnet mask, the default gateway, the WINS server addresses, and the DNS server address. Frame type is a configuration parameter for NWLink and is not provided by a DHCP server. Therefore, answer b is incorrect.

For more information, see Chapter 8 of *MCSE NT Server 4 in the Enterprise Exam Cram.*

## Question 53

Answer c is correct. You can install a new Primary Domain Controller on the same network as an existing Primary Domain Controller, provided that you're creating a separate domain. All of the other statements are true. Therefore, answers a, b, and d are incorrect.

For more information, see Chapter 5 of *MCSE NT Server 4 in the Enterprise Exam Cram.*

## Question 54

Answer c is correct. Task Manager will give you a current view of open application processes that are running, including resources used by each, current memory usage, and current processor usage. Network Monitor is used to capture and analyze traffic on your network. Therefore, answer a is incorrect. Performance Monitor will allow you to monitor various counters for different objects, such as processor and memory. Therefore, answer b is incorrect. Server Manager allows operations such as domain controller promotion, domain synchronization, and adding computer accounts. Therefore, answer d is incorrect.

For more information, see Chapter 11 of *MCSE NT Server 4 in the Enterprise Exam Cram.*

## Question 55

Answers a and b are correct. You should update the ERD when you install Windows NT and when you make changes to your hard drive configuration. Choices c and d do not necessitate updating the ERD, because they do not make changes to the information contained on this disk. Therefore, answers c and d is incorrect. If you create your ERD using RDISK.EXE with the /S switch, Windows NT will save all current Registry settings to disk.

For more information, see Chapter 15 of *MCSE NT Server 4 in the Enterprise Exam Cram.*

# Windows NT Server 4 In The Enterprise Practice Test #2

## Question 1

A user belongs to both the Engineering and Sales global groups. Group policies exist for both groups. The user also has a specific user policy profile. How will the user's system policy be determined?

○ a. The Default User profile will be applied first, the group profiles will be applied in the order specified the Group Priority dialog box, and then the specific user profile will be applied.

○ b. The user will receive the Default User profile and the others will be ignored.

○ c. The user will receive the specific user profile and the others will be ignored.

○ d. The group profiles will be applied in the order specified in the Group Priority dialog box, and both the specific user profile and the Default User profile will be ignored.

## Question 2

If the Boot.ini file is not pointing to the correct path for the Windows NT boot partition, which of the following messages is most likely to occur?

○ a. BOOT: Couldn't find NTLDR. Please insert another disk.

○ b. Windows could not start because the following file is missing or corrupt: \ *%systemroot%*\system32\ntoskrnl.exe

○ c. NTDETECT failed

○ d. I/O Error accessing boot sector file: multi(0)disk(0)rdisk(0)partition(1):\bootsect.dos

## Question 3

Your company has two domains: Corp and Accounting. Users in the Accounting domain need access to the personnel files stored in the Corp domain. Which trust relationship must be in place?

○ a. Accounting must trust Corp.

○ b. Corp must trust Accounting.

○ c. Both domains must trust each other.

○ d. No trust relationship is required.

## Question 4

From where in Windows NT would you promote your Backup Domain Controller to a Primary Domain Controller?

○ a. Regedt32.exe

○ b. Network Properties page

○ c. Windows NT Diagnostics

○ d. Server Manager

○ e. User Manager For Domains

# Question 5

Windows NT provides various options for hard drive configurations. Which of the following hard drive configurations are available in Windows NT Server? [Check all correct answers]

❑ a. Stripe sets

❑ b. Stripe sets with parity

❑ c. Disk mirroring

❑ d. Volume sets

❑ e. Mirrored stripe sets

# Question 6

You want to use Microsoft's Migration Tool for NetWare to transfer files from a NetWare server to a computer running Windows NT Server. Which of the following must be installed on the Windows NT Server? [Check all correct answers]

❑ a. Gateway Services for NetWare

❑ b. File and Print Services for NetWare

❑ c. NWLink protocol

❑ d. Client Services for NetWare

# Question 7

What's the function of using diskperf.exe with the **-y** switch?

○ a. It writes signatures to the hard drives so that they're available in Disk Administrator.

○ b. It enables logical and physical disk counters for monitoring.

○ c. It allows you to convert a FAT partition to NTFS.

○ d. It enables auditing of disk resources.

# Question 8

Your company is currently using disk mirroring and wants to implement a fault tolerance standard for all Windows NT Servers on the network.

Required result:

- The servers should be able to recover from a single disk failure.

Optional desired results:

- You want to achieve better usage of your hard drives.
- You want to provide protection from a drive controller failure.

Proposed solution:

- Implement stripe sets with parity.

Which result does the proposed solution satisfy?

- ○ a. The proposed solution produces the required result and both the optional desired results.
- ○ b. The proposed solution produces the required result and only one of the optional desired results.
- ○ c. The proposed solution produces the required result but does not produce either of the optional desired results.
- ○ d. The proposed solution does not produce the required result.

# Question 9

You're troubleshooting network performance and suspect that synchronization traffic may be a problem due to the large number of BDCs on your network. How can you decrease synchronization traffic without changing the frequency of synchronization?

- ○ a. Decrease the value of the **PulseConcurrency** parameter in the Registry.
- ○ b. Increase the value of the **PulseConcurrency** parameter in the Registry.
- ○ c. Decrease the value of the **Pulse** parameter in the Registry.
- ○ d. Increase the value of the **Pulse** parameter in the Registry.

# Question 10

You want the sales representatives for your company to be able to dial into your Windows NT network from remote customer sites to obtain up-to-date pricing information. They use Windows NT Workstation on their portable computers. The information that they'll be accessing is extremely sensitive.

Required result:

- The sales representatives must use RAS to dial in from any customer location. All transmitted data, including logon information, must be encrypted.

Optional desired results:

- Telephone numbers the sales representatives are calling from must be authenticated before access is granted to the network.

- The sales representatives should only be allowed access to the network during business hours.

Proposed solution:

- Grant dial-up access to the sales representatives. Configure the workstations and the RAS server to use Microsoft Encrypted Authentication. Set callback security to the Set By Caller option. On the RAS server's Properties dialog box, check the Required Data Encryption box.

Which result does the proposed solution satisfy?

- ○ a. The proposed solution produces the required result and both the optional desired results.

- ○ b. The proposed solution produces the required result and only one of the optional desired results.

- ○ c. The proposed solution produces the required result but does not produce either of the optional desired results.

- ○ d. The proposed solution does not produce the required result.

# Question 11

Which of the following utilities can be used to back up the Registry? [Check all correct answers]

- ❑ a. Windows NT Backup
- ❑ b. Disk Administrator
- ❑ c. Regedit
- ❑ d. Regedt32
- ❑ e. Rdisk

# Question 12

Which of the following can be used for fully qualified domain name resolution? [Check all correct answers]

- ❑ a. DNS server
- ❑ b. WINS server
- ❑ c. HOSTS file
- ❑ d. LMHOSTS file

# Question 13

How can you perform a floppyless installation of Windows NT?

- ○ a. From a Windows 95 computer, run Winnt.exe from the I386 folder of the Windows NT CD-ROM with the **/ox** switch.
- ○ b. From a Windows 95 computer, run Winnt.exe from the I386 folder of the Windows NT CD-ROM with the **/b** switch.
- ○ c. From a Windows NT computer, run Winnt.exe from the I386 folder of the Windows NT CD-ROM with the **/b** switch.
- ○ d. From a Windows NT computer, run Winnt.exe from the I386 folder of the Windows NT CD-ROM with the **/ox** switch.

# Question 14

What's the purpose of an LMHOSTS file?

○ a.  To map fully qualified domain names to IP addresses.

○ b.  To map NetBIOS names to IP addresses.

○ c.  To provide the IP address of the Primary Domain Controller for logon authentication.

○ d.  To provide a list of Backup Domain Controllers to the Primary Domain Controller for replication.

# Question 15

You've just created a new profile for a user. What must be done to allow the user access to the new profile and make it a mandatory profile?

○ a.  Copy the profile into the user's home folder and change the file extension from .POL to .MAN.

○ b.  Copy the profile to a shared location, specify the share path in User Manager For Domains, and change the file extension from .POL to .MAN.

○ c.  Copy the profile to a shared location, specify the share path in User Manager For Domains, and change the attributes of the file to Read Only.

○ d.  Copy the profile to the Netlogon share and change the attributes of the file to Read Only.

# Question 16

What trust relationships must be in place in the master domain model?

○ a.  Each resource domain must trust every other resource domain and trust the master domain.

○ b.  Each resource domain must trust the master domain.

○ c.  The master domain must trust each resource domain.

○ d.  The master domain must have a two-way trust with each resource domain.

## Question 17

When is the Last Known Good Configuration updated?

○ a.  After the server service has started

○ b.  After a successful logon

○ c.  After Ntdetect.com begins

○ d.  After all services have started

## Question 18

Which of the following Windows NT protocols is not routable?

○ a.  NetBEUI

○ b.  NWLink

○ c.  TCP/IP

○ d.  AppleTalk

## Question 19

Which Windows NT utility allows you to view current information on open applications, running processes, and performance data?

○ a.  Network Monitor

○ b.  Performance Monitor

○ c.  Task Manager

○ d.  Windows NT Diagnostics

# Question 20

You want to implement a fault tolerance standard for your company. Currently, all servers are equipped with two hard drives that are mirrored. You're only concerned with providing fault tolerance for partitions containing data.

Required result:

- Provide for recovery of any single drive failure.

Optional desired results:

- Support higher performance.

- Implement a fault tolerance strategy that uses disk space effectively.

Proposed solution:

- Add more hard drives and use disk striping with parity. Separate all data from the system and boot partitions.

Which result does the proposed solution satisfy?

- ○ a. The proposed solution produces the required result and both the optional desired results.

- ○ b. The proposed solution produces the required result and only one of the optional desired results.

- ○ c. The proposed solution produces the required result but does not produce either of the optional desired results.

- ○ d. The proposed solution does not produce the required result.

# Question 21

Which view should be used in Performance Monitor when you're producing a performance baseline?

- ○ a. Alert view
- ○ b. Chart view
- ○ c. Log view
- ○ d. Report view

# Question 22

You're creating a new domain and have two new servers. One will become the Primary Domain Controller and the other will be the Backup Domain Controller. How should you install these servers to finish as quickly as possible?

- ○ a. You can install both simultaneously as long as they're connected to the network.
- ○ b. You should install both as BDCs and then promote one to the PDC when complete.
- ○ c. Install one as the PDC and the other as a standalone at the same time. When complete, promote the standalone to a BDC.
- ○ d. The installation of the PDC must be completed before the BDC can be installed.

# Question 23

Your company has two primary locations. The company headquarters is located in Chicago, with a sales office in Los Angeles. The two offices are configured as a single domain connected by an ISDN line. All domain controllers, WINS servers, and DNS servers are located in Chicago.

Required result:

- Reduce the bandwidth used by logon validation over the ISDN line.

Optional desired results:

- Increase performance of fully qualified domain name resolution for users in Los Angeles.
- Decrease the time required to log on for users in Los Angeles.

Proposed solution:

- Configure each office as a separate domain and install a DNS server at each location.

Which result does the proposed solution satisfy?

- ○ a. The proposed solution produces the required result and both the optional desired results.
- ○ b. The proposed solution produces the required result and only one of the optional desired results.
- ○ c. The proposed solution produces the required result but does not produce either of the optional desired results.
- ○ d. The proposed solution does not produce the required result.

# Question 24

You've just created a new NTFS partition. What's the default security permission for the Everyone group?

○ a. Full Control

○ b. Change

○ c. Read

○ d. No Access

# Question 25

Which of the following are standard NTFS file permissions? [Check all correct answers]

❑ a. Read

❑ b. Change

❑ c. Add

❑ d. List

❑ e. No Access

# Question 26

You have a Windows NT Server system with IIS installed, and you want to host three Web sites on this server for your local intranet. Each site will have its own domain name and IP address. Which of the following tasks must you perform to accommodate this situation? [Check all correct answers]

❑ a. Set up the DHCP Relay Agent.

❑ b. Install DNS and add an entry for each site in the DNS database. Configure DNS to use WINS for NetBIOS name resolution.

❑ c. Assign each IP address to the network interface card of the server and associate each IP address with the appropriate Web directory.

❑ d. Install a WINS server and add entries to the WINS database for each site.

# Question 27

Your company has two domains: Corp and Sales. Corp is the master domain and Sales is a resource domain. Corp and Sales each have a PDC, a BDC, member servers, and several Windows NT Workstations. You want to create a group called CorpBackup to be able to back up the PDCs, BDCs, member servers, and Windows NT Workstations in both domains.

Required result:

- Members of the CorpBackup group must be able to back up both domain controllers.

Optional desired results:

- Members of the CorpBackup group must be able to back up all member servers.

- Members of the CorpBackup group must be able to back up all workstations.

Proposed solution:

- Create a Global group called CorpBackup in the Corp domain and add this new global group to the global Domain Admins group on the Primary Domain Controller of each domain.

Which result does the proposed solution satisfy?

- ○ a. The proposed solution produces the required result and both the optional desired results.

- ○ b. The proposed solution produces the required result and only one of the optional desired results.

- ○ c. The proposed solution produces the required result but does not produce either of the optional desired results.

- ○ d. The proposed solution does not produce the required result.

## Question 28

You're transferring user accounts from a NetWare server to a Windows NT domain controller using the Migration Tool for NetWare. By default, how are duplicate account names handled?

○ a. The NetWare account will replace the Windows NT account.

○ b. The NetWare account will automatically be renamed and then transferred.

○ c. The Windows NT account will be renamed, and the NetWare account transferred will be unchanged.

○ d. The NetWare account will not be transferred.

## Question 29

Your company has two separate domains: Far and Away. The Far domain trusts the Away domain. If you belong to the Far domain and log onto the Away domain, what resources will you have access to?

○ a. All folders in the Away domain that the Far\Domain Users group has access to.

○ b. All folders in the Far domain that the Far\Domain Users group has access to.

○ c. All folders in either domain that the Far\Domain Users group has access to.

○ d. All folders in the either domain that the Away\Domain Guests group has access to.

## Question 30

Which of the following actions could lead to reduced network traffic due to BDC synchronization? [Check all correct answers]

❑ a. Increasing the **PulseConcurrency** value.

❑ b. Decreasing the **PulseConcurrency** value.

❑ c. Increasing the **Pulse** value.

❑ d. Decreasing the **Pulse** value.

# Question 31

Which of the following programs would you use to view the contents of a memory dump file resulting from a STOP error?

○ a.  DUMPCHK.EXE

○ b.  DUMPEXAM.EXE

○ c.  Windows NT Diagnostics

○ d.  Event Viewer

# Question 32

What's the recommended method of giving permissions to users for resources in a domain environment?

○ a.  Add users to global groups and give permissions to global groups.

○ b.  Give permissions for resources directly to individual users.

○ c.  Add users to global groups, place global groups into local groups, and assign permissions to local groups.

○ d.  Add users to local groups, place local groups into global groups, and assign permissions to global groups.

# Question 33

You have one print device and two groups of users—Sales and Marketing—in your office. Sales prints customer invoices all day that are usually only one to two pages and are usually needed immediately. Marketing prints product price lists that can be up to 100 pages long and are not usually needed until the following day. What's the best way to ensure that the large documents printed by Marketing do not cause delays in Sales being able to get their documents quickly?

○ a.  Create two logical printers. Set the priority of the printer for Sales to 99 and that of Marketing to 1.

○ b.  Create two logical printers. Set the priority of the printer for Sales to 1 and that of Marketing to 99.

○ c.  Create two logical printers. Set the Marketing group's printer to only be available after hours.

○ d.  Buy a new printer so that each group has its own device.

# Question 34

You're purchasing a new server that's to have Windows NT Server preinstalled. You want the new server to be a Backup Domain Controller in your Corp domain. How should Windows NT be installed?

○ a. Install the computer as a member server and promote it to a Backup Domain Controller once it's attached to the network.

○ b. Install the computer as a PDC in the Corp domain and demote it to a BDC once the computer is connected to the network.

○ c. Have only the first phase of the installation completed and resume installation once the computer is attached to the network.

○ d. Install the computer as a Backup Domain Controller in the Corp workgroup and change it to the Corp domain once it's attached to the network.

# Question 35

You've implemented a mirror set on your file server to protect your data from a single-drive failure. One of the drives in the set fails. How should you re-store the mirror set?

○ a. Replace the failed drive. Using Disk Administrator, choose Regener-ate from the Fault Tolerance menu.

○ b. Replace the failed drive. Using Disk Administrator, choose Re-create from the Partition menu.

○ c. Replace the failed drive and do nothing else. This mirror set will regenerate automatically.

○ d. Using Disk Administrator, choose Break Mirror from the Fault Tolerance menu. Replace the failed drive and then re-create the mirror set.

# Question 36

You're accessing the folder from the network, your share permission is Change, and your NTFS permission is Read. What are your effective permissions to a shared folder?

○ a. Change

○ b. Full Control

○ c. Read

○ d. No Access

# Question 37

Which type of information cannot be provided by a DCHP server?

○ a. WINS server address

○ b. Default gateway

○ c. MAC address

○ d. Subnet mask

# Question 38

You have shared a folder, and you've given a user Full Control share permission to this folder. The user reports that he's unable to copy a file to the share but can view the contents of the folder. Which of the following is not a reason why this would occur?

○ a. The user is unable to make a connection to the server.

○ b. The user belongs to a group that has No Access share permission.

○ c. The user only has an NTFS permission of Read.

○ d. The user does not have any specific NTFS permissions for the folder but belongs to a group that has the List permission.

# Question 39

You're installing Windows NT Server on a new computer that will be running SQL Server and storing the accounting database for users in the domain. You expect this application to place a heavy load on the server. Which role should you choose for this computer?

○ a. Primary Domain Controller for the domain

○ b. Backup Domain Controller for the domain

○ c. Member server in the domain

○ d. Member server in a workgroup

# Question 40

You boot your system after installing an updated video driver. After you log on, you notice that the screen has a lot of distortion and is extremely hard to navigate. You're able to shut the system down. How should this problem be fixed?

- ○ a. Use the Last Known Good Configuration option during the boot process.
- ○ b. Use the emergency repair process.
- ○ c. Boot the system using the VGA option.
- ○ d. Reinstall Window NT.

# Question 41

You have three domains: X, Y, and Z. The following trust relationships are currently in place: X trusts Y and Z; Y trusts Z. Which of the following statements is false?

- ○ a. Users in the X domain will have access to resources in the Y domain.
- ○ b. Users in the Y domain will have access to resources in the X domain.
- ○ c. Users in the Z domain will have access to resources in the X domain.
- ○ d. Users in the Z domain will have access to resources in the Y domain.

# Question 42

A user complains that she does not have access to the corporate database that's stored on a FAT partition. To appease the user, you grant her the Read permission to the folder where the database is stored, but she still has no access. What must be done for the user to access the database?

- ○ a. The user must log off and back on.
- ○ b. The user must map a drive to the share.
- ○ c. You must reboot the server where the database is stored.
- ○ d. You must reboot the user's system.

# Question 43

Your company has three branch offices, located in Sacramento, New Orleans, and Springfield. Each office has approximately 1,200 users. Each office is connected to the corporate headquarters in Austin by ISDN. Your job is to determine the domain model to be used.

Required results:

- Users in the branch offices must have access to the corporate directory store in Austin.

- Authentication traffic must be minimized across the WAN links.

- Centralized account management must be in place.

Optional desired results:

- Each branch office should have control of local resources.

- NetBIOS name resolution should be minimized across the WAN links.

Proposed solution:

- Use a single-domain model. Place at least one BDC in each location.

Which result does the proposed solution satisfy?

- ○ a. The proposed solution produces the required results and both the optional desired results.

- ○ b. The proposed solution produces the required results and only one of the optional desired results.

- ○ c. The proposed solution produces the required results but does not produce either of the optional desired results.

- ○ d. The proposed solution does not produce the required result.

# Question 44

Which of the following items can be controlled using the user account policy? [Check all correct answers]

- ❑ a. Password age

- ❑ b. Password length

- ❑ c. Password uniqueness

- ❑ d. User cannot change password

- ❑ e. User must log on in order to change password

# Question 45

Which of the following protocols are used for routing? [Check all correct answers]

❑ a. AppleTalk

❑ b. RIP

❑ c. DLC

❑ d. DHCP Relay Agent

❑ e. NWLink IPX/SPX

# Question 46

Which networking components are needed for a Windows NT Server system to provide NetWare clients access to Windows NT resources? [Check all correct answers]

❑ a. Gateway Service for NetWare

❑ b. File and Print Services for NetWare

❑ c. NWLink protocol

❑ d. Migration Tool for NetWare

# Question 47

Which Microsoft product includes a fully functional version of Network Monitor?

○ a. Systems Management Server

○ b. SQL Server

○ c. Windows NT Server

○ d. Proxy Server

# Question 48

In Performance Monitor, you notice that the Pages/sec counter is consistently high. What's the best solution to this problem?

○ a. Add another processor to the system.

○ b. Add a faster disk controller to the system.

○ c. Add more RAM to the system.

○ d. Use a network interface card that can support high bandwidth.

# Question 49

You add a new Windows NT Workstation to the network and configure it to join the domain. In addition to the domain name, which of the following items are needed to perform this action? [Check all correct answers]

❑ a. The username and password for an account with administrative rights

❑ b. A domain user account

❑ c. A domain computer account

❑ d. Administrative rights to the workstation

# Question 50

Your company network uses a single domain model. You want Joe to be able to back up all Windows NT Server computers and Windows NT Workstation computers in the domain. Joe is currently a member of the Domain Users global group only. What's the easiest way to give Joe backup rights on the domain computers?

○ a. Add Joe's account to the Backup Operators global group.

○ b. Add Joe's account to the Domain Admins global group.

○ c. Add Joe's account to the Backup Operators local group on all Windows NT computers in the domain.

○ d. Add Joe's account to the Administrators local group on all Windows NT computers in the domain.

# Question 51

Your Windows NT Server machine has three hard drives. The first hard drive has a single partition that contains the Windows NT system files, which uses 100 percent of the drive. Which fault-tolerant configurations are available in this situation? [Check all correct answers]

❏ a.  Disk mirroring

❏ b.  Disk duplexing

❏ c.  Stripe set

❏ d.  Stripe set with parity

# Question 52

Which types of information cannot be provided to a client machine from a DHCP server? [Check all correct answers]

❏ a.  IP address

❏ b.  Frame type

❏ c.  WINS server IP address

❏ d.  Subnet mask

❏ e.  Location of LMHOSTS file

# Question 53

When added to the Boot.ini file, which of the following switches will display driver names as they're loaded by NTLDR?

○ a.  **/BaseVideo**

○ b.  **/NoSerialMice**

○ c.  **/sos**

○ d.  **/Drivers**

# Question 54

Which tool would you use to view the current CPU usage on a Windows NT computer?

○ a.  Network Monitor

○ b.  Performance Monitor

○ c.  Task Manager

○ d.  Server Manager

# Question 55

Your company has 6,000 employees in a single domain. How many Backup Domain Controllers need to be installed on the network?

○ a.  None

○ b.  3

○ c.  5

○ d.  10

# Windows NT Server 4 In The Enterprise Answer Key #2

| | | | |
|---|---|---|---|
| 1. c | 15. b | 29. d | 43. c |
| 2. b | 16. b | 30. b, c | 44. a, b, c, e |
| 3. b | 17. b | 31. b | 45. b, d |
| 4. d | 18. a | 32. c | 46. b, c |
| 5. a, b, c, d | 19. c | 33. c | 47. a |
| 6. a, c | 20. a | 34. c | 48. c |
| 7. b | 21. c | 35. d | 49. a, c |
| 8. b | 22. d | 36. c | 50. b |
| 9. a | 23. a | 37. c | 51. a, b |
| 10. b | 24. a | 38. a | 52. b, e |
| 11. a, b, c, d, e | 25. a, b, e | 39. c | 53. c |
| 12. a, c | 26. b, c, d | 40. c | 54. c |
| 13. b | 27. a | 41. a | 55. b |
| 14. b | 28. d | 42. a | |

# Question 1

Answer c is correct. If a specific user profile exists for a user, the user will receive that profile—any group profiles will be ignored along with the Default User profile. If no individual user profile exists, group policies are applied in the order specified in the Group Priority dialog box, and the Default User profile is ignored. The Default User profile is only applied when both individual user and group policies do not exist for the user. Therefore, answers a, b, and d are incorrect.

For more information, see Chapter 5 of *MCSE NT Server 4 in the Enterprise Exam Cram.*

# Question 2

Answer b is correct. If the ARC path within the Boot.ini file is not pointing to the Windows NT boot partition, you'll receive an error indicating the Ntoskrnl.exe file is missing or corrupt. Answer a occurs when Ntldr is missing or a Windows NT-formatted floppy is accidentally left in the A: drive. "NTDETECT failed" typically occurs when the Ntdetect.com file is missing. Answer d occurs if the Bootsect.dos file is missing. Therefore, answers a, c, and d are incorrect.

For more information, see Chapter 15 of *MCSE NT Server 4 in the Enterprise Exam Cram.*

# Question 3

Answer b is correct. In trust relationships, users are in one domain and resources are in another. The domain that contains the resource (in this case, Corp) must trust the domain containing the user needing access to the resource (in this case, Accounting). Answer a reverses the necessary trust. Therefore, answer a is incorrect. A two-way trust between the two domains would also provide users in Accounting access to resources in Corp, but it's more than is needed in this situation. Therefore, answer c is incorrect. A trust relationship is required. Therefore, answer d is incorrect.

For more information, see Chapter 3 of *MCSE NT Server 4 in the Enterprise Exam Cram.*

# Question 4

Answer d is correct. Server Manager is used to promote a BDC to a PDC. Regedt32.exe is used to edit the Registry. Therefore, answer a is incorrect. You can change only the domain name (on a PDC) or domain membership (on a standalone) from the Network Properties page. Therefore, answer b is incorrect. Windows NT Diagnostics is used to display resource allocation information. Therefore, answer c is incorrect. User Manager For Domains is used to manage user information and create trust relationships. Therefore, answer e is incorrect.

For more information, see Chapter 5 of *MCSE NT Server 4 in the Enterprise Exam Cram.*

## Question 5

Answers a, b, c, and d are correct. Through Windows NT Server Disk Administrator, in addition to primary and extended partitions and logical drives, you can create mirror sets, stripe sets, stripe sets with parity, and volume sets. The only fault-tolerant configurations available in Windows NT Server are disk mirroring (RAID 1) and striping with parity (RAID 5). Windows NT Server does not support mirroring stripe sets. Therefore, answer e is incorrect.

For more information, see Chapter 6 of *MCSE NT Server 4 in the Enterprise Exam Cram.*

## Question 6

Answers a and c are correct. For a NetWare migration to work, you need the NWLink protocol for connectivity and Gateway Services for NetWare to provide access the NetWare resources. File and Print Services for NetWare provides NetWare clients access to Windows NT resources. Therefore, answer b is incorrect. Client Service for NetWare is only found in Windows NT Workstation but is included as part of Gateway Services for NetWare. Therefore, answer d is incorrect.

For more information, see Chapter 12 of *MCSE NT Server 4 in the Enterprise Exam Cram.*

## Question 7

Answer b is correct. The diskperf utility is used to enable and disable disk counters for monitoring in Performance Monitor. Using the -y switch enables disk counters. The -n switch disables the counters. None of the other answers provide the correct result of applying the -y switch. Therefore, answers a, c, and d are incorrect.

For more information, see Chapter 11 of *MCSE NT Server 4 in the Enterprise Exam Cram.*

## Question 8

Answer b is correct. A stripe set with parity does have the ability to recover from a single drive failure; therefore, the required result is met. This solution also makes better use of drive space than disk mirroring. With a stripe set with parity, $1/n$ of the total space is lost to storage of parity information ($n$ is the number of drives in the array). A stripe set with parity does not provide controller fault tolerance, but disk duplexing does.

For more information, see Chapter 6 of *MCSE NT Server 4 in the Enterprise Exam Cram*.

## Question 9

Answer a is correct. The **PulseConcurrency** parameter defines the maximum number of BDCs that can be synchronized simultaneously. Decreasing this value decreases the number of BDCs that take place in synchronization concurrently. Increasing the **PulseConcurrency** parameter will have the opposite effect. Therefore, answer b is incorrect. The Pulse parameter dictates the frequency with which synchronization occurs. Therefore, answers c and d are incorrect.

For more information, see Chapter 5 of *MCSE NT Server 4 in the Enterprise Exam Cram*.

## Question 10

Answer b is correct. The required result is met by requiring that Microsoft Encrypted Authentication be used, checking the Required Data Encryption box, and granting dial-up permission to the sales representatives. The first optional desired result is met by using callback security. The second optional desired result is not met by the proposed solution. The times that the sales representative can connect to the network can be limited through the Logon Hours dialog box in User Manager For Domains.

For more information, see Chapter 14 of *MCSE NT Server 4 in the Enterprise Exam Cram*.

## Question 11

Answers a, b, c, d, and e are correct. All these utilities can be used to back up the Registry. From Disk Administrator, you can only back up the SYSTEM key. To back up the Registry using Windows NT Backup, you must back up at least one file. To back up the Registry using Rdisk, you must use the /s switch.

For more information, see Chapter 15 of *MCSE NT Server 4 in the Enterprise Exam Cram.*

## Question 12

Answers a and c are correct. Fully qualified domain names can be resolved to IP addresses using either a DNS server or a HOSTS file. WINS servers and LMHOSTS files are used to resolve NetBIOS computer names. Therefore, answers b and d are incorrect.

For more information, see Chapter 9 of *MCSE NT Server 4 in the Enterprise Exam Cram.*

## Question 13

Answer b is correct. To perform a floppyless installation, you can run Winnt.exe (on a Windows 95/DOS computer) or Winnt32.exe (on a Windows NT computer) with the /b switch. Therefore, answer c is incorrect. The /ox switch allows you to create a set of setup floppies. Therefore, answers a and d are incorrect.

For more information, see Chapter 2 of *MCSE NT Server 4 Exam Cram.*

## Question 14

Answer b is correct. An LMHOSTS file is a static mapping of NetBIOS (or friendly) names to IP addresses. The WINS service performs the same function but provides dynamic mapping. None of the other answers are correct representations of the function of the LMHOSTS file. Therefore, answers a, c, and d are incorrect.

For more information, see Chapter 9 of *MCSE NT Server 4 in the Enterprise Exam Cram.*

## Question 15

Answer b is correct. Renaming the Ntconfig.pol file to Ntconfig.man makes the profile mandatory. To make the file accessible, you must copy it to a share location and then specify the full UNC pathname in the User Environment Profile page in User Manager For Domains. None of the other answers will make the profile mandatory. Therefore, answers a, c, and d are incorrect.

For more information, see Chapter 5 of *MCSE NT Server 4 in the Enterprise Exam Cram.*

## Question 16

Answer b is correct. In the master domain model, the master domain contains all the user accounts for the organization. Each resource domain must trust the master domain so that users can access the resources in the resource domains. None of the other answers will create the needed trust for this type of domain model. Therefore, answers a, c, and d are incorrect.

For more information, see chapters 2 and 3 of *MCSE NT Server 4 in the Enterprise Exam Cram.*

## Question 17

Answer b is correct. The Last Known Good Configuration is a backup of all Registry settings that existed at the last successful logon. As soon as a user logs onto the system, this information is updated. This is the only time that the LKGC is created. Therefore, answers a, c, and d are incorrect.

For more information, see Chapter 15 of *MCSE NT Server 4 in the Enterprise Exam Cram.*

## Question 18

Answer a is correct. NetBEUI, although fast and efficient, is not routable. This makes it a poor choice in the enterprise environment. All the other listed protocols are routable. Therefore, answers b, c, and d are incorrect.

For more information, see Chapter 8 of *MCSE NT Server 4 in the Enterprise Exam Cram.*

## Question 19

Answer c is correct. Task Manager gives you a current view of your server. From Task Manager, you can end applications and processes as well as launch new processes. Network Monitor is used to capture and analyze network traffic. Therefore, answer a is incorrect. Performance Monitor is used to monitor performance and activity of processes and resources. Therefore, answer b is incorrect. Windows NT Diagnostics provides resource configuration information. Therefore, answer d is incorrect.

For more information, see Chapter 11 of *MCSE NT Server 4 in the Enterprise Exam Cram.*

## Question 20

Answer a is correct. Using a stripe set with parity for your data partitions will provide protection from a single-drive failure, thus achieving the required result. The system and boot partitions, however, cannot be part of a stripe set with parity. Both optional desired results are met as well. Stripe sets with parity provide better disk usage and high performance than mirror sets.

For more information, see Chapter 6 of *MCSE NT Server 4 in the Enterprise Exam Cram.*

## Question 21

Answer c is correct. Log view should be used when you're creating a performance baseline in Performance Monitor. Alert view allows you to set and view alerts. Therefore, answer a is incorrect. Chart view allows viewing of realtime performance data. Therefore, answer b is incorrect. Report view creates custom performance reports. Therefore, answer d is incorrect.

For more information, see Chapter 11 of *MCSE NT Server 4 in the Enterprise Exam Cram.*

## Question 22

Answer d is correct. To establish a new domain, the Primary Domain Controller must be completely installed. Backup Domain Controllers cannot be installed without network connectivity to an existing PDC. Therefore, answers a and b are incorrect. A standalone server cannot be promoted to a domain controller. Therefore, answer c is incorrect.

For more information, see Chapter 5 of *MCSE NT Server 4 in the Enterprise Exam Cram.*

## Question 23

Answer a is correct. Although this may not be an ideal solution, it does meet all the required and optional results because it creates the need for administration of users and permissions at the Los Angeles office.

For more information, see Chapter 9 of *MCSE NT Server 4 in the Enterprise Exam Cram.*

## Question 24

Answer a is correct. The default security permissions for a new NTFS partition is Full Control for Everyone. Therefore, answers b, c, and d are incorrect.

For more information, see Chapter 4 of *MCSE NT Server 4 in the Enterprise Exam Cram.*

## Question 25

Answers a, b, and e are correct. The four standard NTFS file permissions are Read, Change, Full Control, and No Access. The seven standard NTFS folder permissions are List, Read, Add, Add And Read, Change, Full Control, and Full Access. Therefore, answers c and d are incorrect.

For more information, see Chapter 4 of *MCSE NT Server 4 in the Enterprise Exam Cram.*

## Question 26

Answers b, c, and d are correct. All that's needed to host multiple Web sites on IIS when you're connected to the Internet is to assign the IP address of each site to the server and associate each IP address with its respective Web directory. On an internal network, however, you also need some type of name resolution capability. DNS should be used to resolve fully qualified domain names, and WINS should be used to resolve NetBIOS names. The DHCP Relay Agent is not needed in this situation. Therefore, answer a is incorrect.

For more information, see Chapter 9 of *MCSE NT Server 4 in the Enterprise Exam Cram.*

## Question 27

Answer a is correct. In the master domain model, the master domain is trusted by the resource domain. Therefore, global groups created in the master domain can be added to local groups and assigned permissions to resources in the resource domain. By adding the CorpBackup global group of the trusted domain to the Domain Admins group of each domain, you effectively give that group the right to back up all computers in both domains. Remember, by default, the Domain Admins global group is added to the Administrators local group and all Windows NT computers in the domain.

For more information, see Chapter 4 of *MCSE NT Server 4 in the Enterprise Exam Cram.*

## Question 28

Answer d is correct. By default, accounts with duplicate names are not transferred at all. Therefore, answers a, b, and c are incorrect.

For more information, see Chapter 12 of *MCSE NT Server 4 in the Enterprise Exam Cram.*

## Question 29

Answer d is correct. In this situation, your user account does not exist in the Away domain. Therefore, when you log onto the Away domain, you're treated as a member of the Domain Guests group and have the same permissions as the Domain Guests group. Therefore, answers a, b, and c are incorrect.

For more information, see Chapter 3 of *MCSE NT Server 4 in the Enterprise Exam Cram.*

## Question 30

Answers b and c are correct. Domain synchronization can be regulated by decreasing the **PulseConcurrency** parameter and increasing the **Pulse** parameter in the Registry. The **Pulse** parameter determines the frequency of synchronization. Increasing this value increases the time between synchronizations, thus reducing network traffic. **PulseConcurrency** defines the maximum number of BDCs synchronized at one time. Decreasing this value will also reduce network traffic. The other answers will not produce the desired effect. Therefore, answers a and d are incorrect.

For more information, see Chapter 5 of *MCSE NT Server 4 in the Enterprise Exam Cram.*

## Question 31

Answer b is correct. DUMPEXAM.EXE is used to view the contents of a dump file. DUMPCHK.EXE is used to verify the creation of dump files. Therefore, answer a is incorrect. Windows NT Diagnostics provides resource configuration information. Therefore, answer c is incorrect. Event Viewer shows the time and date that a STOP error occurred. Therefore, answer d is incorrect.

For more information, see Chapter 15 of *MCSE NT Server 4 in the Enterprise Exam Cram.*

## Question 32

Answer c is correct. The recommended method of assigning permissions is to add users into global groups, add global groups into local groups, and then assign permissions to the local groups. You can assign permissions for a resource directly to global groups and users; however, this is not the recommended method. Therefore, answers a and b are incorrect. You cannot put local groups into global groups. Therefore, answer d is incorrect.

For more information, see Chapter 4 of *MCSE NT Server 4 in the Enterprise Exam Cram*.

## Question 33

Answer c is correct. You can make certain printers available only during certain hours. This is beneficial in this case, where two different groups need access to the same print device but have different needs. Answer d would work as well, but it's not necessary. Setting the priority of the Sales group higher allows their documents to print sooner but does not stop the large documents from Marketing being printed during work hours. Therefore answers a and b are incorrect.

For more information, see Chapter 13 of *MCSE NT Server 4 in the Enterprise Exam Cram*.

## Question 34

Answer c is correct. The first phase of installation can be completed before having to be attach the computer to the network. To complete the installation of a BDC, however, connectivity to the PDC must be established. You cannot promote a member server to BDC status. Therefore, answer a is incorrect. If the computer is installed as a PDC, a new domain will be created. Therefore, answer b is incorrect. You cannot install a BDC as a member of a workgroup. Therefore, answer d is incorrect.

For more information, see Chapter 5 of *MCSE NT Server 4 in the Enterprise Exam Cram*.

## Question 35

Answer d is correct. To restore a mirror set, the original mirror must be broken. The mirror set can then be created using the new drive. None of the other options provide the correct sequence of events to reestablish the mirror set. Therefore, answers a, b, and c are incorrect.

For more information, see Chapter 6 of *MCSE NT Server 4 in the Enterprise Exam Cram.*

## Question 36

Answer c is correct. When combining share and NTFS permissions, the most restrictive permission becomes the effective permission. In this case, the NTFS permission of Read is more restrictive and therefore determines the effective permission. None of the other answers list the correct permission. Therefore, answers a, b, and d are incorrect.

For more information, see Chapter 4 of *MCSE NT Server 4 in the Enterprise Exam Cram.*

## Question 37

Answer c is correct. The MAC address is a unique address assigned to a network interface card by the card manufacturer. This information cannot be supplied by a DHCP server. The WINS server address, default gateway, and subnet mask are all things that can be provided. Therefore, answers a, b, and d are incorrect.

For more information, see Chapter 9 of *MCSE NT Server 4 in the Enterprise Exam Cram.*

## Question 38

Answer a is correct. The user can obviously make a connection to the server if he can view the contents of the folder. Even if the user has Full Control share and NTFS permissions but belongs to a group assigned No Access, No Access will be the resultant effective permission. Therefore, answer b is incorrect. It's possible to have NTFS folder permissions that are more restrictive than the share permissions on the same folder. Therefore, answers c and d are incorrect.

For more information, see chapters 4 and 15 of *MCSE NT Server 4 in the Enterprise Exam Cram.*

## Question 39

Answer c is correct. In this scenario, the best option would be to choose Stand-Alone Server during installation and then join the domain so that domain security can be used for access to the database. It's typically not recommended that you configure heavily used application servers as domain controllers. Therefore, answers a and b are incorrect. Windows NT Server machines cannot be members of a workgroup. Therefore, answer d is incorrect.

For more information, see Chapter 5 of *MCSE NT Server 4 in the Enterprise Exam Cram.*

## Question 40

Answer c is correct. Problems due to incorrect display settings can be cured by choosing the VGA option and correcting the display properties once you're logged on. Using the Last Known Good Configuration option would do no good in this scenario due to your ability to log on successfully. Therefore, answer a is incorrect. The emergency repair process is not appropriate for this situation. Therefore, answer b is incorrect. Reinstalling Window NT would probably correct the situation, but it's not necessary in this case. Therefore, answer d is incorrect.

For more information, see Chapter 15 of *MCSE NT Server 4 in the Enterprise Exam Cram.*

## Question 41

Answer a is correct. The domain with the resource must trust the domain with the user wanting access to that resource. In this scenario, X is not trusted by Y and Z. Therefore, users in X do not have access to resources in the other two domains. All other statements are true. Therefore, answers b, c, and d are incorrect.

For more information, see Chapter 3 of *MCSE NT Server 4 in the Enterprise Exam Cram.*

## Question 42

Answer a is correct. An access token is created for a user upon logon. The only time it changes is when the user logs off and back on. Changing permissions without the user logging off will have no effect. The user does not have to map a drive to the share. Therefore, answer b is incorrect. Rebooting the database server will not solve this problem and may actually cause additional problems if other users are accessing the database server. Therefore, answer c is incorrect. Although rebooting the system will force the user to log back on, it's not a necessary step. Therefore, answer d is incorrect.

For more information, see Chapter 4 of *MCSE NT Server 4 in the Enterprise Exam Cram.*

## Question 43

Answer c is correct. A single domain model provides central user account management and allows all users access to all resources. By placing a BDC at each location, authentication traffic is minimized. Therefore, the required result is met. The single-domain model does not allow for local management of resources at the branch location. No solution is offered to minimize WAN name resolution.

For more information, see Chapter 2 of *MCSE NT Server 4 in the Enterprise Exam Cram.*

## Question 44

Answers a, b, c, and e are correct. In the Account Policy dialog box, you can manage password restrictions, account lockout properties, whether users are disconnected when logon hours expire, and whether users must log on before changing their passwords. The option "User cannot change password" is set in the User Properties dialog box. Therefore, answer d is incorrect.

For more information, see Chapter 7 of *MCSE NT Server 4 in the Enterprise Exam Cram.*

## Question 45

Answers b and d are correct. For a Windows NT computer to provide routing functions, it must have more than one NIC installed on different network segments. The Multi Protocol Router (MPR) is a service that provides routing functions to Windows NT. This service comprises RIP (Routing Information Protocol) for TCP/IP, RIP for IPX, and BOOTP Relay Agent for DHCP (or DHCP Relay Agent). AppleTalk, DLC, and NWLink are not required in this situation. Therefore, answers a, c and e are incorrect.

For more information, see Chapter 8 of *MCSE NT Server 4 in the Enterprise Exam Cram.*

## Question 46

Answers b and c are correct. File and Print Services for NetWare and the NWLink protocol are necessary for NetWare clients access to Windows NT resources. Gateway Service for NetWare allows a Windows NT Server system to provide access to NetWare resources for Microsoft clients. Therefore, answer a is incorrect. Microsoft's Migration Tool for NetWare transfers user and group information from a NetWare server to a Windows NT Server system. Therefore, answer d is incorrect.

For more information, see Chapter 12 of *MCSE NT Server 4 in the Enterprise Exam Cram.*

## Question 47

Answer a is correct. SMS ships with a version of Network Monitor that has more functionality than the version shipped with Windows NT Server. SQL Server is a database server and does not include Network Monitor. Therefore, answer b is incorrect. The version of Network Monitor that ships with Windows NT Server is not fully functional. Therefore, answer c is incorrect. Proxy Server is used as a central point of access to Internet services for your network. Therefore, answer d is incorrect.

For more information, see Chapter 10 of *MCSE NT Server 4 in the Enterprise Exam Cram.*

## Question 48

Answer c is correct. Typically, a high value for Pages/sec indicates that the system is low on memory. Adding more RAM to the system can solve this problem. None of the other options will improve this situation as much as adding more RAM. Therefore, answers a, b, and d are incorrect.

For more information, see Chapter 11 of *MCSE NT Server 4 in the Enterprise Exam Cram.*

## Question 49

Answers a and c are correct. To add a Windows NT Workstation computer to the domain, that computer must have a computer account. A computer account can be created before you add the computer or during the addition if you have a user account with administrative privileges. You do not need a domain user account or administrative rights to the workstation in this situation. Therefore, answers b and d are incorrect.

For more information, see Chapter 5 of *MCSE NT Server 4 in the Enterprise Exam Cram*.

## Question 50

Answer b is correct. The Domain Admins global group is added to the Administrators local group on every Windows NT computer in the domain. Answer a is incorrect because there's no Backup Operators global group. Answers c and d would also work, but they involve more work than is necessary.

For more information, see Chapter 4 of *MCSE NT Server 4 in the Enterprise Exam Cram*.

## Question 51

Answers a and b are correct. This situation will allow the use of both disk mirroring and disk duplexing. A stripe set without parity is not a fault-tolerant configuration. Therefore, answer c is incorrect. Because the Windows NT system partition cannot be part of a stripe set with parity (which requires three drives), answer d is incorrect.

For more information, see Chapter 6 of *MCSE NT Server 4 in the Enterprise Exam Cram*.

## Question 52

Answers b and e are correct. The frame type is a configuration parameter for NWLink, and it's not provided by a DHCP server. The location of the LMHOSTS file is dependant on the client for a Windows NT client; it's found in the \winnt\system32\drivers\etc folder. The LMHOSTS file location is not provided by a DHCP server. DHCP provides TCP/IP configuration information to DHCP-enabled clients. This information can include an IP address, a subnet mask, a default gateway, WINS server addresses, and DNS server address. Therefore, answers a, c, and d are incorrect

For more information, see Chapter 8 of *MCSE NT Server 4 in the Enterprise Exam Cram*.

## Question 53

Answer c is correct. The **/sos** switch enables Ntldr to display file names as they're loaded. The **/basevideo** switch boots Windows NT in VGA mode. Therefore, answer a is incorrect. The **/NoSerialMice** switch keeps Windows NT from testing COM ports for serial mice. Therefore, answer b is incorrect. The **/Drivers** switch does not exist. Therefore, answer d is incorrect.

For more information, see Chapter 15 of *MCSE NT Server 4 in the Enterprise Exam Cram.*

## Question 54

Answer c is correct. Task Manager will show you the current state of the computer. This includes current memory and CPU utilization, open applications, and running processes. Network Monitor is used to capture network traffic. Therefore, answer a is incorrect. Performance Monitor can also provide you with the current CPU usage, but it involves more work than is needed. Therefore, answer b is incorrect. Server Manager is used for numerous tasks, such as domain synchronization, domain controller promotion, and computer account creation. Therefore, answer d is incorrect.

For more information, see chapters 11 and 15 of *MCSE NT Server 4 in the Enterprise Exam Cram.*

## Question 55

Answer b is correct. As a general rule, you should have one BDC installed for every 2,000 users. Because the recommended number of BDCs is three, answers a, c, and d are incorrect.

For more information, see Chapter 5 of *MCSE NT Server 4 in the Enterprise Exam Cram.*

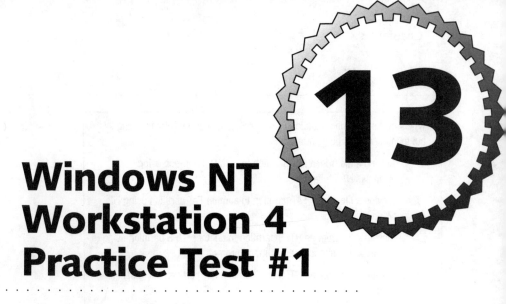

# Windows NT Workstation 4 Practice Test #1

## Question 1

An installation of Windows NT Workstation has three network protocols installed: TCP/IP, NWLink, and NetBEUI. All three are required for some activity on the network. Which protocol should be attached in priority over the others on the network adapter to provide the best network performance?

- ○ a. TCP/IP
- ○ b. NWLink
- ○ c. NetBEUI
- ○ d. The fastest protocol
- ○ e. The protocol used most often

## Question 2

Which of the following tools can be used to create a complete backup of the Registry? [Check all correct answers]

- ❑ a. Windows NT Backup
- ❑ b. Updating the ERD
- ❑ c. Disk Administrator
- ❑ d. REGEDIT
- ❑ e. System applet

# Question 3

Which of the following situations would result in security settings being lost but long file names being retained?

○ a. Moving a file from a FAT partition to an NTFS partition using Windows NT Explorer

○ b. Moving a file from a FAT partition to another FAT partition using File Manager

○ c. Moving a file from an NTFS partition to another NTFS partition using the **move** command at a command prompt

○ d. Moving a file from an NTFS partition to a FAT partition using My Computer

○ e. Moving a file from an NTFS partition to another NTFS partition using a Windows 3.x application

# Question 4

Your Windows NT Workstation machine is a member of a peer workgroup with three other systems. Your system is the only one connected to the Internet. You want to restrict the avenues by which a hacker can gain access to the network over the Internet link. Which of the following actions can be taken to reduce the risk of external attack on any member of the workgroup? [Check all correct answers]

❑ a. Disable the Server service.

❑ b. Disable the Workstation service.

❑ c. Set your subnet mask to 0.0.0.0.

❑ d. Set your IP address to 127.0.0.1.

❑ e. Disable IP forwarding.

❑ f. Unbind all unneeded services.

# Question 5

After using a third-party disk defragmentation tool to organize your boot and system partitions, the Windows NT Workstation system will no longer boot. In fact, it will not even display the boot menu. Which of the following actions should be performed first to attempt to restore the system to normal operation?

○ a.  Reinstall Windows NT Workstation.

○ b.  Use the Last Known Good Configuration.

○ c.  Use the ERD repair process.

○ d.  Use Disk Administrator to restore the configurations of the damaged partitions.

# Question 6

Which of the following utilities can be used to send print jobs to Unix-hosted printers?

○ a.  LPR

○ b.  Spooler service

○ c.  Print Manager

○ d.  Network Neighborhood

# Question 7

A Windows NT Workstation data entry system is used by six different people during the week. The users are allowed to use the Internet to perform research relevant to their data entry, and can send and receive email. Access to the Internet and the data-entry database is granted by the domain when the user logs in. The Web browser settings, email, and other environmental configurations unique to each user need to be retained. What's the minimum number and type of unique user accounts required to maintain these profiles?

○ a.  Six local user accounts

○ b.  Six local accounts and six domain user accounts

○ c.  One domain user account

○ d.  Six domain user accounts

# Question 8

You need to install Windows NT Workstation on a computer from a network share of the distribution files. The computer is already attached to the network using an MS-DOS-based network client. Which of the following actions must you perform to initiate the installation properly?

○ a. Connect to the correct network share and launch WINNT32.

○ b. Reformat the hard drive and boot using the three setup floppies.

○ c. Connect to the correct network share and issue the command **WINNT /OX**.

○ d. Connect to the correct network share and launch WINNT.

# Question 9

You suspect files from your Windows NT Workstation are being copied by someone from the network. You suspect this because you've found printed copies of your confidential files on the printer and in the print room's trash can. You need to determine who is copying your files. Which of the following audit events on the file objects themselves must you track to learn who is copying your files?

○ a. **Read**

○ b. **Execute**

○ c. **Write**

○ d. **Delete**

# Question 10

Mark needs to review the company purchase order forms, which reside in \\fileserver\documents\PO. Mark is a member of the Users, Accounting, and Sales groups. These groups have the following security settings:

| Group | Documents Share | PO Subfolder |
| --- | --- | --- |
| Users | No Access | None specified |
| Accounting | Change | Change |
| Sales | Change | Read |

When Mark attempts to access the correct file, what level of access does he have?

○ a.  Read

○ b.  Change

○ c.  Full Control

○ d.  No Access

# Question 11

If a print server is properly configured to keep the level of administrative tasks to an absolute minimum, when the printer driver is updated on the print server, what other systems on the network require manual updates as well? [Check all correct answers]

❑ a.  MS-DOS

❑ b.  Windows NT Workstation

❑ c.  Windows 95

❑ d.  Windows For Workgroups 3.11

## Question 12

As a system administrator, which of the following are valid changes you can make to the processing activity of Windows NT Workstation? [Check all correct answers]

❑ a. Increase the foreground priority to +3.

❑ b. Launch applications with the **START** command with realtime priority.

❑ c. Force Win32 applications into cooperative multitasking.

❑ d. Launch a Win16 application so that it's preemptively multitasked.

## Question 13

Your boss recently purchased an AS/400 to host your dynamic, multirelational database. Which protocol must be installed on your Windows NT Workstation system to enable communication with this new network member?

○ a. SNMP

○ b. AppleTalk

○ c. DLC

○ d. DHCP

○ e. Visual Basic

## Question 14

DEC Alpha servers can be used to host Windows NT Workstation. Which installation method is supported by this platform?

○ a. Local CD-ROM

○ b. Pulling files from a network share

○ c. An automated install over a network

○ d. An all-floppy installation

# Question 15

Your Windows NT Workstation will be a TCP/IP network client, and will be connected to the Internet via a modem. Which IP address should be used to configure the network interface card?

○ a.  The IP address of the ISP's router

○ b.  The IP address assigned to you by the network administrator

○ c.  The ISP's dynamically assigned IP address

○ d.  127.0.0.1

# Question 16

You've been assigned the task of testing Windows NT Workstation 4.0 against the existing network structure and distributed applications of your organization. Unfortunately, you only have your existing Windows NT Workstation 3.51 system to work with. How can you deploy Windows NT Workstation 4.0 on your system without damaging your Windows NT Workstation 3.51 environment?

○ a.  Perform an upgrade installation.

○ b.  Format the hard drives and start the installation with the three boot floppies.

○ c.  Install into a different %systemroot% directory.

○ d.  Perform a repair installation.

# Question 17

Which one of the following actions will result in a shared resource becoming more secure but still accessible to authorized users?

○ a.  Grant Administrators Full Control access

○ b.  Set the Everyone group to No Access

○ c.  Grant Domain Users Change access

○ d.  Remove the Everyone group from the permissions list

# Question 18

Which built-in Windows NT Workstation groups have the ability to share resources by default? [Check all correct answers]

❑ a. Server Operators

❑ b. Account Operators

❑ c. Print Operators

❑ d. Backup Operators

❑ e. Users

# Question 19

You need to create a volume for storing data files. Initially, you need 3GB of space, but eventually the volume must hold over 14GB of data. Your system currently has two hard drives—one with 1GB of free space and the second with 5GB of free space. Which of the following drive configurations is best suited for your current and future storage needs on Windows NT Workstation?

○ a. Disk duplexing

○ b. Volume set

○ c. Stripe set with parity

○ d. Disk mirroring

○ e. Stripe set without parity

# Question 20

How can you configure your notebook that hosts Windows NT Workstation to make a secure connection with your office LAN over the Internet?

○ a. Create a single DUN entry to dial up the LAN's RAS server.

○ b. Create a DUN entry to connect to a local ISP; then create a DUN entry to connect to the LAN's RAS server using PPTP.

○ c. Create a single DUN entry to connect to a local ISP using PPTP.

○ d. Create a single DUN entry to connect to a local ISP and set the IP address of the modem to the address that would be assigned by the LAN.

# Question 21

If your Windows NT Workstation is to be a member of a network where routing is used, which IP configuration items must be defined to allow communications outside your subnet? [Check all correct answers]

❑ a.  Subnet mask

❑ b.  DNS server

❑ c.  IP address

❑ d.  Default gateway

# Question 22

A new color slide printer has been added to the office LAN. It has been shared so that members of various departments can print presentation slides as necessary. However, after the first week, you discover over 100 discarded slides in the trash can with nonbusiness-related data on them. You need to find out which users are wasting the expensive media used by the slide printer. You open the Properties for the logical printer and enable auditing on the **Print** event for the Everyone group. After a few days, you discover more discarded slides in the trash and decide to check the Event Viewer Security log for recorded activity. But nothing is recorded in the Security log regarding printing. What could be the cause?

○ a.  The users printing the slides are not members of the audited group.

○ b.  File and Object Access was not selected as an audit event type to monitor through User Manager.

○ c.  Users have deleted their audit events from the Event Viewer.

○ d.  Users have not logged out and logged back on since the print audit was started.

## Question 23

While working on sales documents from a remote system connected to the office LAN over a PPTP connection, your hotel room's power flickers. This causes your computer to lose its phone connection. You decide to reboot the computer. Once rebooted, you launch the editing tool and use the File menu to select the last document you were working on. When you attempt to re-open this document, which resides on the office LAN, what happens?

○ a. An error is given stating that the file is unavailable.

○ b. A copy of the file maintained in the network cache is opened.

○ c. A connection is automatically reestablished to pull the document from the LAN.

○ d. You're instructed to reestablish the network link before opening the file.

## Question 24

The application subsystem that supports Windows 16-bit applications under Windows NT Workstation requires which other two subsystems to function? [Check two answers]

❑ a. Windows on Windows (WOW)

❑ b. Windows 32-bit (Win32)

❑ c. POSIX

❑ d. Virtual DOS Machine (VDM)

❑ e. OS/2

## Question 25

The policies defined through the User Manager include which of the following? [Check all correct answers]

❑ a. Audit

❑ b. Security

❑ c. Account

❑ d. User Rights

❑ e. System

# Question 26

The ERD repair process—initialized by selecting R from the menu offered during the initialization of the Windows NT installation procedure—is capable of correcting which of the following problems? [Check all correct answers]

❑ a. Corrupt NTOSKRNL

❑ b. Unable to locate Master Boot Record

❑ c. Corrupt SAM database

❑ d. NTLDR not found

❑ e. Boot sector corruption

❑ f. Multipartition volume failure

# Question 27

Which of the following is the correct command for redirecting a printer port to a network printer share?

○ a. **LPT1>\\SERVER\SHARE**

○ b. **NET USE \\SERVER\SHARE LPT1**

○ c. **NET USE LPT1:\\SERVER\SHARE**

○ d. **NET PRINT LPT1:\\SERVER\SHARE**

# Question 28

Your Windows NT Workstation system has a thrashing hard drive. You suspect it's due to too much paging occurring. What can you do to the system to reduce paging, stop the hard drive from thrashing, and improve the system performance?

○ a. Increase the size of the paging file.

○ b. Move the paging file to the boot partition.

○ c. Add more RAM to the computer.

○ d. Add more L2 cache.

○ e. Spread the paging file across several physical drives.

# Question 29

Your system has three SCSI hard drives. You're using an older SCSI card that does not have an onboard BIOS. The system originally had Windows 95 installed on the first drive, with the second drive used to store data. You installed Windows NT Workstation so that it would be hosted by the third drive in a multiboot configuration. All three drives have only a single partition. Which ARC name appears in the BOOT.INI file for the operating system line labeled "Windows NT Workstation Version 4.00 [VGA mode]"?

○ a. multi(0)disk(0)rdisk(2)partition(1)

○ b. scsi(0)disk(2)rdisk(0)partition(1)

○ c. scsi(0)disk(1)rdisk(0)partition(1)

○ d. multi(0)disk(2)rdisk(0)partition(1)

○ e. scsi(0)disk(2)rdisk(0)partition(0)

# Question 30

Windows 16-bit applications launched in separate memory spaces are capable of exchanging or sharing which of the following items? [Check all correct answers]

❏ a. Memory address space

❏ b. Message queue

❏ c. VDM

❏ d. OLE data

❏ e. Nothing

# Question 31

While using Performance Monitor, you notice several counters that display a value of zero (0) either all the time or sporadically when monitored. What can account for these readings? [Check all correct answers]

❏ a. These are actual readings of no activity

❏ b. Inoperative counters/objects

❏ c. The same counter from two systems is read simultaneously

❏ d. The termination of a monitored process

❏ e. Measurement reading errors

❏ f. Negative differential values

❏ g. Extended counters are used in conjunction with built-in counters

# Question 32

You've been assigned the task of installing Windows NT Workstation on 15 identical computers and setting up all the standard applications used by your organization. You plan on automating the task of installing Windows NT using an answer file and uniqueness database file. Which of the following actions can be used to automate the installation of the applications?

○ a. Use **sysdiff /snap** on a base system, install all the applications, and then use **sysdiff /diff** to create a difference data file. Then apply this difference file to all other systems.

○ b. Add the application installation to the uniqueness database file.

○ c. Create a template machine with all applications installed and duplicate its System32 directory and its Registry to all other systems.

○ d. Application installation cannot be automated.

# Question 33

In order to print to a TCP/IP network-attached print device using the TCP/IP Print service, which of the following items must be available? [Check all correct answers]

❑ a. The DLC protocol

❑ b. The HPMON utility

❑ c. The IP address of the device

❑ d. LPR

❑ e. The printer's name

# Question 34

Which Windows NT Workstation tool can be used to create a roaming user profile (in other words, which tool transforms an existing local profile into a network share stored profile that can be used as a roaming profile)?

○ a. REGEDIT

○ b. User Manager

○ c. Services applet

○ d. Server Manager

○ e. System applet

# Question 35

You've tried to print the same document several times with no printed materials appearing at the printer. You view the print queue for the printer and see all the submitted print jobs still there. You attempt to delete the print jobs, but you're unable to. What's causing this problem and how can it best be corrected?

○ a. The printer driver has failed. Delete and reinstall the printer.

○ b. The printing subsystem is corrupted. Reinstall Windows NT Workstation.

○ c. The spooler is hung. Stop and restart the Spooler service.

○ d. The spool files are corrupted. Delete the files from the spool folder on the print server.

# Question 36

You've just installed a new hard drive in your system. Which of the following provides the best order in which to create a shared volume?

○ a. Format, create partition, assign drive letter, save configuration, share, set permissions

○ b. Assign drive letter, create partition, format, share, set permissions, save configuration

○ c. Create partition, format, assign drive letter, save configuration, set permissions, share

○ d. Create partition, save configuration, format, assign drive letter, share, set permissions

# Question 37

As a member of a peer workgroup, which of the following are true for Windows NT Workstation systems? [Check all correct answers]

❑ a. Share-level security is used.

❑ b. A domain controller is required.

❑ c. Suitable for 10 users/computers.

❑ d. There's no central control.

❑ e. User accounts must be created on each member.

❑ f. Roaming profiles are supported.

# Question 38

A Windows NT Workstation system can participate in the browser service in which of the following capacities? [Check all correct answers]

❑ a. Potential Browser

❑ b. Master Browser

❑ c. Backup Browser

❑ d. Nonbrowser

# Question 39

A Windows NT Workstation machine with all three networking protocols installed will use which protocol when connecting to a Windows NT Server RAS server over a dial-up connection?

○ a. SLIP

○ b. NetBEUI

○ c. TCP/IP

○ d. NWLink

○ e. The one bound first to the modem interface on the Windows NT Workstation system

○ f. The first protocol in common between the two systems

# Question 40

Windows NT Workstation is configured so that any member of any built-in group can log on locally by default.

○ a. True

○ b. False

## Question 41

If a Windows NT Workstation system is disconnected from the network to which it's normally attached, can users still log onto the local system?

○ a.  Yes, the client maintains a cache of the logon security database.

○ b.  Yes, the client hosts local accounts that can be used.

○ c.  No, without the network domain controller, no access to the local client can be obtained.

○ d.  No, for a domain member, local accounts are deactivated.

## Question 42

After Windows NT Workstation has been installed, what step must be taken, and where, to enable Windows NT Backup to be used to perform data protection activities?

○ a.  Backup Operators need to be granted access to the file system though Windows NT Explorer.

○ b.  The tape device driver needs to be installed through the Tape Devices applet.

○ c.  The Backup service must be set to launch automatically through the Services applet.

○ d.  An ERD must be created using the **rdisk /s** command at a command prompt.

## Question 43

On a Windows NT workstation, it's possible to reboot the system without logging in.

○ a.  True

○ b.  False

# Question 44

Through which applet or utility can the location of a memory dump file be defined that's used in the event of a STOP error?

○ a.  Network

○ b.  Server Manager

○ c.  Services

○ d.  User Manager

○ e.  System

○ f.  Dr. Watson

○ g.  Task Manager

# Question 45

From a Windows NT Workstation client using Client Services for NetWare, which of the following NetWare command-line utilities can be used? [Check all correct answers]

❏ a.  attach

❏ b.  capture

❏ c.  syscon

❏ d.  logout

❏ e.  slist

## Question 46

You're a member of the Sales, Events, and Managers groups. The Human Resources shared directory named VACFORM, which contains the vacation request forms, has the following permissions:

- Sales: Read
- Events: Read
- Managers: Change

What level of access do you have for this share?

○ a.  No Access

○ b.  Read

○ c.  Change

○ d.  Full Control

## Question 47

Which of the following statements describe the function of the **/OX** switch when used as a command-line parameter for either WINNT.EXE or WINNT32.EXE?

○ a.  It starts the installation without boot floppies.

○ b.  It defines an alternative source directory.

○ c.  It creates the three setup floppies.

○ d.  It uses a uniqueness database file to guide the install.

## Question 48

A boot disk can be created so that a Windows NT system can be booted if the system partition fails but the boot partition is intact. If the host computer employs a SCSI drive controller that does not have onboard BIOS, which file must be present on the boot floppy that's not required otherwise?

○ a.  NTDETECT.COM

○ b.  BOOT.INI

○ c.  NTLDR

○ d.  WINA20.386

○ e.  NTBOOTDD.SYS

# Question 49

You need to upgrade a Windows NT Workstation 3.51 system to 4.0. The data drives are formatted with HPFS. Which tool can be used to transform these into NTFS volumes?

○ a.  The CONVERT.EXE tool from Windows NT Workstation 4.0

○ b.  The CONVERT.EXE tool from Windows NT Workstation 3.51

○ c.  Windows Explorer from Windows NT Workstation 4.0

○ d.  Disk Administrator from Windows NT Workstation 3.51

# Question 50

Which of the following is a configurable option of Windows NT Workstation? [Check all correct answers]

❑ a.  Disk quota

❑ b.  Logon hours

❑ c.  Warning message at logon

❑ d.  Inactivity timeout

❑ e.  Auto logon

❑ f.  Password-protected screensaver

# Question 51

The VGA Mode selection offered in the boot menu launches Windows NT with which two ARC name command-line parameters? [Check two answers]

❑ a.  **/noserialmice**

❑ b.  **/basevideo**

❑ c.  **/sos**

❑ d.  **/vga**

❑ e.  **/nodebug**

# Question 52

Your Windows NT Workstation system is a DHCP client on a Microsoft domain network. Due to network congestion, your system and the DHCP server failed to communicate properly, and your IP address lease has expired. What's the easiest way to restore network communications to your client now that network traffic has subsided?

- ○ a. Reboot the client.
- ○ b. Reboot the DHCP server.
- ○ c. Issue a **ipconfig /renew** command.
- ○ d. Change your TCP/IP properties to a static address.

# Question 53

You delete the AcctRep user account through User Manager. You immediately realize you deleted the wrong account. After you re-create the account exactly as it existed before, what is true about the access this newly created account has?

- ○ a. It assumes the access permissions of the old account.
- ○ b. It assumes only those access permissions of the old account that were stored in the SAM database.
- ○ c. It has the default access of members of the Users group.
- ○ d. It has access that's independent of the original account.

# Question 54

Where is information recorded about the function of and activities occurring over RAS that can be used to troubleshoot connection problems? [Check all correct answers]

- ❏ a. Registry keys
- ❏ b. DEVICE.LOG
- ❏ c. Dr. Watson
- ❏ d. Event Viewer
- ❏ e. Windows NT Diagnostics
- ❏ f. MODEMLOG.TXT

# Question 55

Your Windows NT Workstation notebook computer has both a modem and a network interface PC card. The modem is used to dial into the office LAN or the Internet while travelling. The modem is attached to a short-wave phone so you can make a connection anywhere. The NIC is used to connect to the office LAN while at work. The office policy does not allow modem connections from clients while logged into the network. What's the best way to configure your system so you won't make modem connections while connected to the network?

O a.  Remove the modem PC card when at work.

O b.  No special configuration is necessary because Windows NT cannot have a network connection and a RAS connection open simultaneously.

O c.  Turn the Plug and Play service to manual through the Services applet.

O d.  Create two hardware profiles: one using the NIC and one using the modem.

# Windows NT Workstation 4 Answer Key #1

| | | | |
|---|---|---|---|
| 1. e | 15. b | 29. b | 43. a |
| 2. a, d | 16. c | 30. e | 44. e |
| 3. d | 17. d | 31. a, b, d, e, f | 45. c, e |
| 4. a, e, f | 18. a, c | 32. a | 46. c |
| 5. c | 19. b | 33. c, e | 47. c |
| 6. a | 20. b | 34. e | 48. e |
| 7. d | 21. a, c, d | 35. c | 49. b |
| 8. d | 22. b | 36. d | 50. c, e, f |
| 9. a | 23. c | 37. c, d, e | 51. b, c |
| 10. d | 24. b, d | 38. a, b, c, d | 52. c |
| 11. a, d | 25. a, c, d | 39. f | 53. d |
| 12. b, d | 26. a, d, e | 40. a | 54. b, d, f |
| 13. c | 27. c | 41. b | 55. d |
| 14. a | 28. c | 42. b | |

# Question 1

Answer e is correct. The protocol used most often should be bound in priority over all others in order to provide the best network performance. TCP/IP, NWLink, or NetBEUI may have been the correct protocol to bind first, but the question did not provide enough information to determine which protocol is used most often. Therefore, answers a, b, and c are incorrect. The fastest protocol bound in priority will not necessarily provide the best performance, especially if it isn't the most used protocol, because the system waits until the first bound protocol times out before trying the next. Therefore, answer d is incorrect.

For more information, see Chapter 9 of *MCSE NT Workstation 4 Exam Cram.*

# Question 2

Answers a and d are correct. Windows NT Backup and REGEDIT are the only tools in this list that can create a complete backup of the Registry. The ERD does not contain all of the Registry—it only contains the System, Security/SAM, and Software hives. Therefore, answer b is incorrect. Disk Administrator can only back up the HKEY_LOCAL_MACHINE\SYSTEM key. Therefore, answer c is incorrect. The System applet cannot back up any part of the Registry. Therefore, answer e is incorrect.

For more information, see Chapter 18 of *MCSE NT Workstation 4 Exam Cram.*

# Question 3

Answer d is correct. Moving a file from an NTFS partition to a FAT partition using My Computer would result in a loss of security settings but the retention of the LFN. Moving a file from a FAT partition to an NTFS partition using Windows NT Explorer would retain the LFN, but because no security settings exist under FAT, there are none to lose. Therefore, answer a is incorrect. Moving a file from a FAT partition to another FAT partition using File Manager will retain the LFN, but because no security settings exist under FAT, there are none to lose. Therefore, answer b is incorrect. Moving a file from an NTFS partition to another NTFS partition using the **move** command at a command prompt will retain both the security settings and the LFN. Therefore, answer c is incorrect. Moving a file from an NTFS partition to another NTFS partition using a Windows 3.x application will retain the security settings but lose the LFN. Therefore, answer e is incorrect.

For more information, see chapters 6 and 7 of *MCSE NT Workstation 4 Exam Cram.*

# Question 4

Answers a, e, and f are correct. Disabling the Server service, disabling IP forwarding, and unbinding all unneeded services are the three actions from this list that will help prevent external attacks. The Workstation service must be active to access resources on the peer workgroup or the Internet. Therefore, answer b is incorrect. Setting your subnet to 0.0.0.0 will prevent you from communicating with the peer workgroup and the Internet. Therefore, answer c is incorrect. Setting your IP address to 127.0.0.1 will prevent you from communicating with other devices because it's the loopback address—your communications will not be transmitted by your NIC. Therefore, answer d is incorrect.

For more information, see Chapter 9 of *MCSE NT Workstation 4 Exam Cram*.

# Question 5

Answer c is correct. For the situation described in this question, the *best* first step is to use the ERD repair process. Reinstalling Windows NT is not the best first step and should only be performed as a last resort. Therefore, answer a is incorrect. The LKGC cannot be used because it isn't offered until after the boot menu, which is not being accessed in this situation. Therefore, answer b is incorrect. The Disk Administrator cannot be used because it requires Windows NT to be booted, which cannot occur in this situation. Therefore, answer d is incorrect.

For more information, see Chapter 18 of *MCSE NT Workstation 4 Exam Cram*.

# Question 6

Answer a is correct. LPR is the client utility used to send print jobs to LPD printers (typically Unix-hosted printers). The spooler service cannot be used by users to send print jobs to printers—it's used by the Windows NT print system to store print jobs on a hard drive before sending them to the printer. Therefore, answer b is incorrect. Print Manager is not a utility found in Windows NT Workstation 4.0—it's a Windows NT Workstation 3.51 utility. In addition, Print Manager is not LPR capable, so it cannot be used to send print jobs to Unix-hosted printers. Therefore, answer c is incorrect. Network Neighborhood cannot be used to send print jobs to Unix-hosted printers because it isn't LPR compliant. Therefore, answer d is incorrect.

For more information, see chapters 10 and 14 of *MCSE NT Workstation 4 Exam Cram*.

## Question 7

Answer d is correct. Six domain user accounts is the minimum number of accounts necessary to properly maintain separate profiles. Six local user accounts may maintain local profiles, but the users will be unable to access the domain where their work is performed. Therefore, answer a is incorrect. Having both local and domain user accounts adds no additional capabilities but rather increases the administrative overhead, because the local accounts are useless. Therefore, answer b is incorrect. Having only one domain user account will not retain separate profiles for each user. Therefore, answer c is incorrect.

For more information, see Chapter 5 of *MCSE NT Workstation 4 Exam Cram.*

## Question 8

Answer d is correct. To perform the installation in this situation, you have to connect to the correct network share and launch WINNT. WINNT32 cannot be launched from MS-DOS; it can only be launched from Windows NT. Therefore, answer a is incorrect. The three setup floppies cannot be used to install from a network share. Also, by formatting the drive, you destroy the only means by which you can access the network and, in turn, the distribution files. Therefore, answer b is incorrect. The WINNT /OX command will create the three boot floppies and then reboot the system using the floppies, but the boot floppies cannot be used to perform a network installation. Therefore, answer c is incorrect.

For more information, see Chapter 3 of *MCSE NT Workstation 4 Exam Cram.*

## Question 9

Answer a is correct. The copy action is a read action, which you need to audit the **Read** event. **Execute, Write,** and **Delete** are not associated with the copy action. Therefore, answers b, c, and d are incorrect.

For more information, see Chapter 4 of *MCSE NT Workstation 4 Exam Cram.*

## Question 10

Answer d is correct. Mark has No Access, because he's a member of the Users group; therefore, he's unable to access the file. The Sales group has Read access, but Mark is also a member of the Users group, which has No Access. Therefore, answer a is incorrect. The Accounting group has Change access, but Mark is also a member of the Users group, which has No Access. Therefore, answer b is incorrect. No group has Full Access. Therefore, answer c is incorrect.

For more information, see Chapter 7 of *MCSE NT Workstation 4 Exam Cram.*

# Question 11

Answers a and d are correct. MS-DOS and WFW 3.11 require manual local installations of updated drivers. Windows NT and Windows 95 can pull the new drivers from the print server when it's properly configured. Therefore, answers b and c are incorrect.

For more information, see Chapter 14 of *MCSE NT Workstation 4 Exam Cram.*

# Question 12

Answers b and d are correct. Launching an application with realtime priority and a Win16 application to be preemptively multitasked are both possible. The former requires administration-level privileges, whereas the latter is done by launching the Win16 application in a separate memory space (that is, it's launched in its own VDM, separate from all other processes). The foreground priority increase is 0, 1, or 2. Therefore, answer a is incorrect. Win32 applications cannot be launched as cooperatively multitasked. Only Win16 applications are launched cooperatively multitasked. Therefore, answer c is correct.

For more information, see Chapter 15 of *MCSE NT Workstation 4 Exam Cram.*

# Question 13

Answer c is correct. DLC is used to communicate with IBM mainframes and network-attached printers. SNMP is used to remotely monitor network events and activities, not to provide mainframe communications. Therefore, answer a is incorrect. AppleTalk is used to provide communications with Macintosh clients. Therefore, answer b is incorrect. DHCP is used to dynamically assign IP information to clients joining the network, not to provide communications with mainframes. Therefore, answer d is incorrect. Visual Basic is a programming language, not a protocol. Therefore, answer e is incorrect.

For more information, see Chapter 14 of *MCSE NT Workstation 4 Exam Cram.*

# Question 14

Answer a is correct. RISC systems (which a DEC Alpha is) can only install Windows NT Workstation from a local CD-ROM. RISC systems do not support network installations of any kind. Therefore, answers b and c are incorrect. Microsoft does not offer an all-floppy installation method for Windows NT. Therefore, answer d is incorrect.

For more information, see Chapter 3 of *MCSE NT Workstation 4 Exam Cram.*

## Question 15

Answer b is correct. The NIC should be configured with the IP address assigned to you by the network administrator. Using the IP address of the ISP's router will not allow you to communicate with the network because it will not be in the correct subnet. Moreover, that address is not a valid address to be used by a private network because it has been assigned to the ISP. Therefore, answer a is incorrect. The IP address dynamically assigned to you by the ISP is only used by the modem interface; it should not be used to reconfigure the NIC. Therefore, answer c is incorrect. Using 127.0.0.1, the loopback address, will prevent your network traffic from being transmitted by the NIC to the network. Therefore, answer d is incorrect.

For more information, see Chapter 10 of *MCSE NT Workstation 4 Exam Cram*.

## Question 16

Answer c is correct. Only installing into a different %systemroot% directory will allow you to install Windows NT Workstation 4.0 while leaving Windows NT Workstation 3.51 intact. Performing an upgrade installation will overwrite Windows NT Workstation 3.51. Therefore, answer a is incorrect. Formatting the hard drives will destroy Windows NT Workstation 3.51. Therefore, answer b is incorrect. Performing a repair installation is not really an option—it's called the repair process, and it will not install Windows NT Workstation 4.0 but will attempt to repair the existing system. Therefore, answer d is incorrect.

For more information, see Chapter 3 of *MCSE NT Workstation 4 Exam Cram*.

## Question 17

Answer d is correct. Removing the Everyone group from the permissions list is the only action in this list that actually increases the security of the share. Granting Administrators Full Control does not add any security to the share. Therefore, answer a is incorrect. Setting the Everyone group to No Access increases security but prevents anyone from accessing the resource. Therefore, answer b is incorrect. Granting Domain Users Change access does not add any security to the share. Therefore, answer c is incorrect.

For more information, see Chapter 7 of *MCSE NT Workstation 4 Exam Cram*.

# Question 18

Answers a and c are correct. Server Operators and Print Operators have the ability to share resources. Server Operators can share either folders or printers, whereas Print Operators are limited to sharing printers. Account Operators, Backup Operators, and Users do not have the ability to share resources. Therefore, answers b, d, and e are incorrect.

For more information, see Chapter 4 of *MCSE NT Workstation 4 Exam Cram*.

# Question 19

Answer b is correct. A volume set is the best drive configuration for this situation because additional drives will need to be added to the system, and the volume storing data will need to be expanded by adding new partitions of space. Windows NT Workstation does not support fault-tolerant drive structures, so disk duplexing, stripe set with parity, and disk mirroring are not true options. Therefore, answers a, c, and d are incorrect. A stripe set without parity is not expandable. Therefore, answer e is incorrect.

For more information, see Chapter 6 of *MCSE NT Workstation 4 Exam Cram*.

# Question 20

Answer b is correct. To connect to your office LAN over the Internet, you must use two DUN entries: one that connects to an ISP and another to connect to the LAN over the Internet using PPTP. (PPTP creates an encrypted communication link between you and the LAN.) Dialing up the LAN directly does not employ the Internet. Therefore, answer a is incorrect. Just connecting to the ISP will not connect you to the LAN. Also, a connection with an ISP is either PPP or SLIP, not PPTP (even though only PPP can support a PPTP connection). Therefore, answer c is incorrect. Using the LAN's IP addresses for the ISP connection will prevent communications from occurring with the ISP. Therefore, answer d is incorrect.

For more information, see Chapter 13 of *MCSE NT Workstation 4 Exam Cram*.

# Question 21

Answers a, c, and d are correct. The subnet mask and IP address must be defined to enable communication on an IP network. Also, to enable communication outside your subnet, you need a default gateway. A DNS server is not a required item for IP communication. Therefore, answer b is incorrect.

For more information, see Chapter 10 of *MCSE NT Workstation 4 Exam Cram*.

## Question 22

Answer b is correct. If the File and Object Access event type is not enabled, no print-related audit events will appear in the Security log. All users are members of the Everyone group. Therefore, answer a is incorrect. Users do not have access to the Security log, so they cannot manipulate its contents. Therefore, answer c is incorrect. Audit event changes are not dependant on logons for initialization. Therefore, answer d is incorrect.

For more information, see Chapter 7 of *MCSE NT Workstation 4 Exam Cram*.

## Question 23

Answer c is correct. Windows NT remembers the network paths used to access resources. It will use the RAS autodial feature to reconnect to the office network to obtain the file from its original location. An error message will only appear if RAS fails to reestablish a connection, and it will not state that the file is unavailable. Therefore, answer a is incorrect. Windows NT does not have a network cache that files can be pulled from. Therefore, answer b is incorrect. Windows NT handles the reconnection to the LAN automatically, so you'll not be instructed to manually reconnect. Therefore, answer d is incorrect.

For more information, see Chapter 13 of *MCSE NT Workstation 4 Exam Cram*.

## Question 24

Answers b and d are correct. Win16 applications require Win32 and VDM. WOW is the actual subsystem that supports Win16 applications; it's not one of the two subsystem required by it. Therefore, answer a is incorrect. POSIX and OS/2 subsystems are not related to or required by Win16. Therefore, answers c and e are incorrect.

For more information, see Chapter 16 of *MCSE NT Workstation 4 Exam Cram*.

## Question 25

Answers a, c, and d are correct. The User Manager's Policy menu is used to access and define the Audit, Account, and User Rights policies. A Security policy is an overarching term used to describe any configuration that can improve security. Therefore, answer b is incorrect. A System policy is a set of Registry settings imposed on a user, group, or computer basis, as defined with the System Policy Editor. Therefore, answer e is incorrect.

For more information, see Chapter 4 of *MCSE NT Workstation 4 Exam Cram*.

## Question 26

Answers a, d, and e are correct. The ERD repair process is capable of repairing NTOSKRNL, replacing the NTLDR, and repairing the boot sector. The ERD repair process cannot repair the MBR, replace the SAM, or restore drive configurations. Therefore, answers b, c, and f are incorrect.

For more information, see Chapter 18 of *MCSE NT Workstation 4 Exam Cram*.

## Question 27

Answer c is correct. **NET USE LPT1:\\SERVER\SHARE** is the correct syntax for redirecting a printer port to a network printer share. The other options are invalid constructions. Therefore, answers a, b, and d are incorrect.

For more information, see Chapter 14 of *MCSE NT Workstation 4 Exam Cram*.

## Question 28

Answer c is correct. Adding more RAM will reduce paging, stop or reduce drive thrashing, and improve system performance. Increasing the size of the paging file will not reduce paging, stop thrashing, or improve system performance. Therefore, answer a is incorrect. Moving the paging file to the boot partition will not reduce paging, stop thrashing, or improve system performance—in fact, it will probably increase them. Therefore, answer b is incorrect. Adding L2 cache may improve system performance, but it will be unnoticeable because it will not reduce paging or stop thrashing. Therefore, answer d is incorrect. Spreading the paging file across multiple drives will not reduce paging or improve system performance, but it might reduce drive thrashing. Therefore, answer e is incorrect.

For more information, see Chapter 15 of *MCSE NT Workstation 4 Exam Cram*.

## Question 29

Answer b is correct. The ARC name in the BOOT.INI file is the boot partition for Windows NT Workstation, which is SCSI(0)DISK(2)RDISK(0) PARTITION(1) for this system. The non-BIOS SCSI card will use SCSI(), and because it's the first and only card, it takes the number zero. The host drive is the third one in the chain, hence DISK(2) is used. RDISK(0) is left at zero because it isn't used. Finally, because there's only a single partition, PARTITION(1) is used. MULTI is used on non-SCSI controllers and on SCSI controllers without BIOS support. Therefore, answers a and d are incorrect. DISK(1) is the system partition host. Therefore, answer c is incorrect. PARTITION(0) is an invalid construction. Therefore, answer e is incorrect.

For more information, see Chapter 6 of *MCSE NT Workstation 4 Exam Cram.*

## Question 30

Answer e is correct. Win16 applications launched in separate memory spaces can share or exchange nothing. Only Win16 applications launched in the same memory space can share or exchange memory address space, message queue, VDM, and OLE data. Therefore, answers a, b, c, and d are incorrect.

For more information, see Chapter 16 of *MCSE NT Workstation 4 Exam Cram.*

## Question 31

Answers a, b, d, e, and f are correct. Zero values appear when no measurable activity is occurring, with inoperative counters/objects, when a monitored process is terminated, when reading errors occur, and with negative differential values. Reading counters from multiple systems and using extended counters do not cause zero values. Therefore, answers c and g are incorrect.

For more information, see Chapter 15 of *MCSE NT Workstation 4 Exam Cram.*

## Question 32

Answer a is correct. The sysdiff utility is the key to performing application installations automatically by duplicating the changes made to a base system. The UDF cannot be used to install applications. Therefore, answer b is incorrect. Copying the System32 directory and the Registry will not only *not* install the applications but will render the destination system unusable. Therefore, answer c is incorrect. The sysdiff utility can be used to automate application installations. Therefore, answer d is incorrect.

For more information, see Chapter 3 of *MCSE NT Workstation 4 Exam Cram.*

## Question 33

Answer c and e are correct. To print to a TCP/IP network-attached printer through the TCP/IP Printing service, you only need to know the IP address and printer name of the device. The DLC protocol, HPMON utility, and LPR need not be present. Therefore, answers a, b, and d are incorrect.

For more information, see Chapter 14 of *MCSE NT Workstation 4 Exam Cram.*

# Question 34

Answer e is correct. The System applet is used to create roaming profiles. REGEDIT, the User Manager, and the Services applet are not used to create roaming profiles. Therefore, answers a, b, and c are incorrect. The User Manager For Domains from Windows NT Server must be used to define the location of a user's profile when it isn't local. The Server Manager is a Windows NT Server tool, but it doesn't create roaming profiles. Therefore, answer d is incorrect.

For more information, see Chapter 5 of *MCSE NT Workstation 4 Exam Cram.*

# Question 35

Answer c is correct. The spooler is hung, and it must be stopped and restarted. A failed print driver would not prevent you from deleting submitted jobs. Therefore, answer a is incorrect. A corrupt printing subsystem is a possible cause, but the resolution option here is not the *best* first step. Therefore, answer b is incorrect. If the spool files are corrupted, print jobs would not be accepted by the print server. Just deleting the spool files would not restart the system properly—the Spooler service would still need to be restarted. Therefore, answer d is incorrect.

For more information, see Chapter 14 of *MCSE NT Workstation 4 Exam Cram.*

# Question 36

Answer d is correct. The correct order is create partition, save configuration, format, assign drive letter, share, set permissions. None of the other answers provide the best order in which to create a shared volume. Therefore, answers a, b, and c are incorrect.

For more information, see Chapter 6 of *MCSE NT Workstation 4 Exam Cram.*

# Question 37

Answers c, d, and e are correct. A workgroup is suitable for 10 users/computers and has no central control, and user accounts must be created on each member. Windows NT does not offer share-level security. Therefore, answer a is incorrect. A domain controller is not used in a workgroup. Therefore, answer b is incorrect. Roaming profiles are not supported because user accounts are not the same from system to system. Therefore, answer f is incorrect.

For more information, see Chapter 12 of *MCSE NT Workstation 4 Exam Cram.*

## Question 38

Answers a, b, c, and d are correct. A Windows NT Workstation system can be any of these.

For more information, see Chapter 12 of *MCSE NT Workstation 4 Exam Cram*.

## Question 39

Answer f is correct. The first protocol in common between the two systems will be used over the RAS link. The protocol bound first to the inbound RAS port on the Windows NT Server is tested first, then the second bound protocol, and so on. SLIP cannot be used to connect to Windows NT Server systems, and it's not a networking protocol. Therefore, answer a is incorrect. NetBEUI, TCP/IP, and NWLink are possible solutions, but the question does not provide enough information to determine which of these protocols both systems have in common. Therefore, answers b, c, and d are incorrect. The dial-up client's binding order is not the determining factor in establishing the protocol to be used over the RAS connection. Therefore, answer e is incorrect.

For more information, see Chapter 13 of *MCSE NT Workstation 4 Exam Cram*.

## Question 40

Answer a is correct. This is a true statement. Windows NT Workstation is a user-focused desktop operating system.

For more information, see Chapter 4 of *MCSE NT Workstation 4 Exam Cram*.

## Question 41

Answer b is correct. The client system can host its own local accounts; these can be employed by users to gain access to local resources. The client does not maintain a cache of the security database. Therefore, answer a is incorrect. The client requires a domain controller to log into the domain but not to log on local accounts. Therefore, answer c is incorrect. Local accounts are not deactivated when the client is a domain member. Therefore, answer d is incorrect.

For more information, see Chapter 4 of *MCSE NT Workstation 4 Exam Cram*.

## Question 42

Answer b is correct. The tape device driver needs to be installed through the Tape Devices applet. The Backup Operators group has access to all files by default. Therefore, answer a is incorrect. There is no Backup service that can be launched automatically. Therefore, answer c is incorrect. Updating the ERD is a good idea, but it's not a requirement for using Windows NT Backup. Therefore, answer d is incorrect.

For more information, see Chapter 7 of *MCSE NT Workstation 4 Exam Cram.*

## Question 43

Answer a is correct. This is a true statement. The Shut Down button is active on the logon window displayed after the Ctrl+Alt+Del key sequence by default.

For more information, see Chapter 8 of *MCSE NT Workstation 4 Exam Cram.*

## Question 44

Answer e is correct. The System applet's Startup/Shutdown tab offers this configuration setting. The Network applet, Services applet, User Manager, Dr. Watson, and Task Manager do not offer a STOP error memory dump file configuration setting. Therefore, answers a, c, d, f, and g are incorrect. The Server Manager is a Windows NT Server utility, and it does not offer this setting either. Therefore, answer b is incorrect.

For more information, see Chapter 18 of *MCSE NT Workstation 4 Exam Cram.*

## Question 45

Answers c and e are correct. Both syscon and slist can be used from Windows NT Workstation. The attach, capture, and logout utilities are not supported through CSNW. Therefore, answers a, b, and d are incorrect.

For more information, see Chapter 11 of *MCSE NT Workstation 4 Exam Cram.*

## Question 46

Answer c is correct. You have Change access because access levels are cumulative. None of the other answers provide the correct cumulative permission. Therefore, answers a, b, and d are incorrect.

For more information, see Chapter 7 of *MCSE NT Workstation 4 Exam Cram.*

## Question 47

Answer c is correct. The /OX switch is used to create the setup floppies. The /B switch is used to perform the install without boot floppies. Therefore, answer a is incorrect. The /S switch is used to define an alternate source path. Therefore, answer b is incorrect. The /UDF switch is used to define a UDF for an automated installation. Therefore, answer d is incorrect.

For more information, see Chapter 3 of *MCSE NT Workstation 4 Exam Cram*.

## Question 48

Answer e is correct. NTBOOTDD.SYS is the driver for SCSI translation required for non-BIOS controllers. The other four files are always found on a boot disk for Windows NT. Therefore, answers a, b, c, and d are incorrect.

For more information, see Chapter 17 of *MCSE NT Workstation 4 Exam Cram*.

## Question 49

Answer b is correct. The CONVERT.EXE tool from Windows NT Workstation 3.51 is the only tool in this list that can convert HPFS to NTFS. Windows NT Workstation 4.0 has absolutely no support for HPFS. Therefore, answers a and c are incorrect. The Disk Administrator from Windows NT Workstation 3.51 does not offer a conversion function. Therefore, answer d is incorrect.

For more information, see Chapter 6 of *MCSE NT Workstation 4 Exam Cram*.

## Question 50

Answers c, e, and f are correct. Windows NT Workstation offers a warning message at logon, auto logon, and password-protected screensavers. Windows NT does not offer a disk quota and an inactivity timeout. Therefore, answers a and d are incorrect. Windows NT Server offers logon hours. Therefore, answer b is incorrect.

For more information, see Chapter 8 of *MCSE NT Workstation 4 Exam Cram*.

## Question 51

Answers b and c are correct. The parameters /basevideo and /sos are present on the VGA Mode line by default. The parameters /noserialmice and /nodebug are not present on the VGA Mode line by default. Therefore, answers a and e are incorrect. The parameter /vga is not a valid parameter. Therefore, answer d is incorrect.

For more information, see Chapter 18 of *MCSE NT Workstation 4 Exam Cram.*

## Question 52

Answer c is correct. The **ipconfig /renew** command provides the easiest way to restore network communications, assuming network congestion has ceased. Rebooting the client is not the easiest solution because it forces you to stop work while the system reboots. (However, it will request a new lease from the DHCP server.) Therefore, answer a is incorrect. Rebooting the DHCP server is not a wise option because it takes the vital system offline, may cause other lease duration problems, and may cause other services to go offline as well while the machine reboots. Therefore, answer b is incorrect. Changing your TCP/IP properties to a static address requires a static address, will remove you from being a DHCP client, and still requires a reboot. Therefore, answer d is incorrect.

For more information, see Chapter 10 of *MCSE NT Workstation 4 Exam Cram.*

## Question 53

Answer d is correct. The new account has access independent of the original account. The new account has a new SID and is therefore a unique account unassociated with the old account. Once an account is deleted, it's gone. The new account does not assume the access permissions of the old account—it has a new SID and is a different user as far as Windows NT is concerned. Therefore, answers a and b are incorrect. The new account would only have the access of the members of the Users group if it was a member of the Users group itself. This might not have been a feature of the original account re-created in the new account. Therefore, answer c is incorrect.

For more information, see Chapter 4 of *MCSE NT Workstation 4 Exam Cram.*

## Question 54

Answers b, d, and f are correct. DEVICE.LOG, the Event Viewer, and MODEMLOG.TXT can be useful troubleshooting resources because they record information about RAS activities. Registry keys do not maintain RAS activity information. Therefore, answer a is incorrect. Dr. Watson doesn't track RAS events; it focuses on applications. Therefore, answer c is incorrect. Windows NT Diagnostics provides no useful RAS-related information. Therefore, answer e is incorrect.

For more information, see Chapter 13 of *MCSE NT Workstation 4 Exam Cram.*

## Question 55

Answer d is correct. Creating two hardware profiles is the best method of resolving this issue. Removing the modem is not only a hassle, it can result in a damaged or lost card, it opens up the possibility of leaving the modem behind when travelling, and it does not employ the built-in solution of hardware profiles. Therefore, answer a is incorrect. Windows NT can support both network and RAS connections simultaneously. Therefore, answer b is incorrect. The Plug and Play service (if installed) does not need to be set to manual to handle this situation. Therefore, answer c is incorrect.

For more information, see Chapter 5 of *MCSE NT Workstation 4 Exam Cram*.

# Windows NT Workstation 4 Practice Test #2

## Question 1

You need to specify unique memory configurations for an MS-DOS application. How would you accomplish this under Windows NT Workstation? [Check all correct answers]

❑ a. Create a shortcut to the DOS executable and edit the properties of the shortcut.

❑ b. Change the settings in the CONFIG.NT file.

❑ c. Use the VDM Manager from the Control Panel.

❑ d. Using the Environment tab in the System applet, add or modify environment variables.

❑ e. Alter the parameters in the AUTOEXEC.NT file.

## Question 2

After you've altered several values in the Registry, your system will not boot past the blue screen displaying the version and build of the installed operating system. What's the best action you can take to restore Windows NT Workstation to a bootable state?

○ a. Use the ERD repair process.

○ b. Use REGEDT32's Undo option.

○ c. Hold down Ctrl while booting.

○ d. Use the Last Known Good Configuration option.

# Question 3

The Windows NT FAT file system supports long file names, 4GB partitions, and unlimited files in its root directory.

○ a. True

○ b. False

# Question 4

Your company policy requires callback security on all RAS connections. You and several other workers often telecommute. Instead of using a single RAS server connection point, each of you dials into a modem attached directly to your office LAN desktop, which is a Windows NT Workstation system. Which of the following options offers the best security?

○ a. Set Callback to No Call Back.

○ b. Enable the Capture Caller ID feature.

○ c. Set Callback to Set By Caller.

○ d. Set Callback to Roaming.

○ e. Set Callback to Preset To and define your home number.

# Question 5

Under which of the following conditions would you want to perform an up-grade installation of Windows NT Workstation instead of a full new install? [Check all correct answers]

❏ a. When you want to retain the existing installed applications

❏ b. When you want to repair a minor Registry problem

❏ c. When you want to change the SID

❏ d. When a defective driver is being used by the system core

❏ e. When you want to retain your local profile

# Question 6

What's the proper Registry change to the WinLogon key to prevent Windows NT Workstation machines from being shut down without a user first logging onto the system?

- ○ a.  Change the Registry value of **ShutdownWithoutLogon** from 1 to 0.
- ○ b.  Change the Registry value of **ShowLogonShutdown** from 1 to 0.
- ○ c.  Use the System applet to change the Shutdown Without Logon setting from Yes to No.
- ○ d.  Change the Registry value of **ShutdownBeforeLogon** from 1 to 0.

# Question 7

Which of the following pieces of information are displayed by Task Manager? [Check all correct answers]

- ❑ a.  The size of the kernel in memory
- ❑ b.  The size of the paging file
- ❑ c.  The number of active threads
- ❑ d.  The peak memory usage

# Question 8

Your Windows NT Workstation machine is the print server for a three-device printer pool. One of the printers experiences a paper jam in the middle of an eight-page document. What happens to that print job?

- ○ a.  It's automatically rerouted to one of the other online printers.
- ○ b.  It's automatically canceled and removed from the print queue.
- ○ c.  It's automatically held in the print queue until the paper jam is cleared; then it continues to print on the original printer.
- ○ d.  It's automatically respooled to disk and an error message is sent to a Print Operator.

# Question 9

Your Windows NT Workstation system is experiencing long delays when reading or writing files. You don't notice any other strange behavior. Which type of counters should you watch to determine whether a bottleneck is causing the problem?

○ a. Physical disk object counters

○ b. Logical disk object counters

○ c. Memory object counters

○ d. Server object counters

○ e. System object counters

# Question 10

The office security policy prevents network clients from using a modem. All communications must be handled through the LAN's RAS server, fax service, or Internet proxy. However, your network client is a notebook computer that you take home and on the road when traveling. While out of the office, you need to connect to the office LAN and ISPs to perform work tasks. What can you do to allow network-only access while at the office but enable the modem while away?

○ a. Create two local user accounts—one for home, the other for the office.

○ b. Create two computer system policies—one for home, the other for the office.

○ c. Create two local user profiles—one for home, the other for the office.

○ d. Create two hardware profiles—one for home, the other for the office.

# Question 11

The System: Processor Queue Length Performance Monitor counter can be used to detect which type of bottleneck?

○ a. RAM

○ b. Disk

○ c. CPU

○ d. Network

# Question 12

On a network that has no external communications and that's a single subnet, which components must be defined for a Windows NT Workstation machine in order to enable TCP/IP communications? [Check all correct answers]

❑ a.  DNS server

❑ b.  IP address

❑ c.  Default gateway

❑ d.  WINS server

❑ e.  Subnet mask

# Question 13

A standard local user on a Windows NT Workstation system who's a member of the Users group is able to launch applications using the **START** command at which priority levels? [Check all correct answers]

❑ a.  High (13)

❑ b.  Pause (0)

❑ c.  Normal (8)

❑ d.  System (27)

❑ e.  Realtime (24)

❑ f.  Low (4)

❑ g.  Kernel (31)

# Question 14

The ERD repair process can perform which of the following functions on a Windows NT Workstation system? [Check all correct answers]

❑ a.  Repair the startup environment

❑ b.  Restore the security database

❑ c.  Replace the entire Registry

❑ d.  Inspect the boot sector

❑ e.  Inspect the ACLs of NTFS volumes

# Question 15

Your office has a Windows NT Server network that uses NWLink as its primary networking protocol. You create a computer account for a new client through the Server Manager on the PDC. After configuring the client system with Windows NT Workstation and installing NWLink, you add it to the network by removing a fully functional Windows 95 system from the network and connecting the new system in its place. After booting, you discover that the client is unable to communicate over the network. What's the most likely reason for this?

- ○ a. A protocol mismatch
- ○ b. A memory conflict
- ○ c. A bad cable
- ○ d. The wrong frame type

# Question 16

You've just purchased a new computer system from a custom computer shop. All of the computer's components are listed on the Windows NT HCL. However, the SCSI drive controller is listed as having downloadable drivers. Which process must you employ to ensure a successful installation of Windows NT Workstation on this system?

- ○ a. After the install, use the SCSI Adapters applet to install the drivers.
- ○ b. Skip the autodrive detection and install the drivers manually during setup.
- ○ c. Copy the drivers to the third setup floppy so that the setup process will use them automatically.
- ○ d. Install normally. The setup process will use generic drivers.

# Question 17

Where would you enable the PPP.LOG file so that you can use its contents to troubleshoot RAS connections?

- ○ a. In the Server Manager
- ○ b. Through the Modems applet
- ○ c. In the Registry
- ○ d. Through the Event Viewer

# Question 18

A drive failure causes a corruption of the SYSTEM key in your Windows NT Workstation Registry. Luckily you have a three-day-old copy of the SYSTEM key on a floppy. Which of the following methods is the best choice for restoring this key after you replace the failed hard drive?

○ a.  User Manager

○ b.  Server Manager

○ c.  Windows NT Diagnostics

○ d.  Disk Administrator

○ e.  ERD repair process

# Question 19

Which of the following components is required when sharing a local printer from a Windows NT Workstation system?

○ a.  Workstation service

○ b.  AppleTalk

○ c.  DLC

○ d.  Server service

○ e.  TCP/IP Printing service

# Question 20

Your Windows NT Workstation system has an ISDN connection to the Internet and is connected to the office network. No one else on the network needs to gain access to the Internet. Your boss is concerned about Internet hackers gaining access to the network via your ISDN connection. What single step can you take to eliminate this threat?

○ a.  Remove TCP/IP from the network.

○ b.  Remove the Workstation service from your system.

○ c.  Use 0.0.0.0 as your subnet mask.

○ d.  Set your gateway address to 127.0.0.1.

○ e.  Disable IP forwarding on your system.

# Question 21

A file named "Sales Records from 1999.xls" has the following security settings:

- Everyone: Read
- Sales: Change
- Managers: Full Control

This file is moved to a FAT partition on the same Windows NT Workstation system. What are its resultant properties?

○ a. Same permissions; 8.3 file name

○ b. All permissions are Change; same file name

○ c. All permissions are Read; 8.3 file name

○ d. All permissions are lost; same file name

# Question 22

What's the correct command-line syntax for launching an installation from a network share that employs a UDF script named PENT3.TXT from the fifth system and an answer file named SPECS1.TXT from a system booted using a Network Client Administrator MS-DOS client disk?

○ a. **winnt /b /u:pent3.txt /udf:5, specs1.txt**

○ b. **winnt32 /b /u:specs1.txt /udf:5, pent3.txt**

○ c. **winnt /b /u:specs1.txt /udf:5, pent3.txt**

○ d. **winnt /b /u:specs1.txt /udf:pent3.txt, 5**

# Question 23

You need to retain the desktop environments for several different users who share the same three Windows NT Workstation computers to interact with network resources. How can you accomplish this?

○ a. Use local profiles.

○ b. Use a single mandatory profile.

○ c. Use a single roaming profile.

○ d. Use roaming profiles.

# Question 24

What must be altered in a DUN phonebook entry when you're connecting to a Unix dial-up server instead of a Windows NT Server RAS dial-up server?

○ a. The dial-up server type

○ b. The Accept Microsoft Encrypted Authentication option

○ c. Whether to use a terminal window

○ d. The logon script

# Question 25

Which of the following statements are true in regard to the Windows NT Workstation 4.0 paging file? [Check all correct answers]

❑ a. A paging file is never required on the boot partition.

❑ b. The paging file can be hosted by an HPFS partition.

❑ c. The paging file can be split across several physical drives.

❑ d. The default size of the paging file is the same as physical RAM.

❑ e. The system must be rebooted to employ changes to the Virtual Memory dialog box.

# Question 26

Why might all 16-bit Windows applications fail when just one of them has a problem?

○ a. They all use thunking.

○ b. They use 16-bit code.

○ c. They have only a single message queue.

○ d. They use 8.3 file names.

○ e. They all share a single memory space.

# Question 27

Your computer has a single 3GB hard drive. If you have a single 75MB partition formatted with FAT and hosting MS-DOS, which of the following installation methods will not experience an error?

○ a. A network install

○ b. Using the three setup floppies

○ c. Executing **winnt /b** from the CD-ROM

○ d. Copying the i386 directory to the FAT partition

# Question 28

Which Performance Monitor counter should you watch to determine whether excessive disk thrashing is due to a memory shortage?

○ a. Processor: % Processor Time

○ b. Memory: Pages/Thread

○ c. Memory: Pages/Second

○ d. LogicalDisk: Avg. Disk Bytes/Transfer

# Question 29

A multiboot system hosts both MS-DOS and Windows NT Workstation. When the system is powered up, it boots directly into Windows NT Workstation without displaying the boot menu. Why?

○ a. Installing MS-DOS overwrites the Windows NT files in the system partition.

○ b. NTLDR is missing.

○ c. The timeout value in the BOOT.INI file is set to 0.

○ d. The multiboot option in the System applet is not checked.

# Question 30

Which of the following audit event types enabled through the User Manager should be selected to monitor your system for an application with memory activities that cause other applications to fail?

- ○ a. Application Activity
- ○ b. Process Tracking
- ○ c. Security Policy Changes
- ○ d. Restart, Shutdown, and System
- ○ e. File and Object Access

# Question 31

The MarketDocs network share has the following permissions:

- Administrators: Full Control
- Users: none defined
- Managers: Change
- Marketing: Read
- Sales: No Access

Bob is a member of the Users, Managers, and Marketing groups. Which type of access does he enjoy for this share?

- ○ a. No Access
- ○ b. Read
- ○ c. Change
- ○ d. Full Control

## Question 32

Members of which of the following groups can log onto a Windows NT Workstation system by default?

- ○ a. Backup Operators, Power Users, and Users
- ○ b. Power Users, Users, and Guests
- ○ c. Backup Operators, Power Users, Users, Guests, and Everyone
- ○ d. Users only
- ○ e. Administrators, Backup Operators, Power Users, Users, Guests, and Everyone

## Question 33

You want to build a boot floppy to use in the event of a system partition failure. Your Intel system only hosts Windows NT Workstation and uses EIDE drives. Which of the following files should be placed on this floppy? [Check all correct answers]

- ❑ a. BOOTSECT.DOS
- ❑ b. OSLOADER.EXE
- ❑ c. NTBOOTDD.SYS
- ❑ d. BOOT.INI
- ❑ e. NTOSKRNL.EXE
- ❑ f. NTLDR

## Question 34

Where should the static name resolution files be placed to maximize the lookup performance for RAS clients?

- ○ a. HOSTS should be stored on the RAS server, and LMHOSTS should be stored on the RAS clients.
- ○ b. Both HOSTS and LMHOSTS should be stored on the RAS server.
- ○ c. HOSTS should be stored on the RAS clients, and LMHOSTS should be stored on the RAS server.
- ○ d. Both HOSTS and LMHOSTS should be stored on the RAS clients.

# Question 35

Which of the following Windows NT Workstation applets and/or utilities are involved in transforming a local profile into a roaming profile? [Check all correct answers]

- ❑ a.  Network applet
- ❑ b.  System applet
- ❑ c.  Regional Settings applet
- ❑ d.  Server Manager
- ❑ e.  User Manager

# Question 36

Which of the following files is associated with a mandatory profile?

- ○ a.  CONFIG.NT
- ○ b.  NTCONFIG.POL
- ○ c.  NTUSER.MAN
- ○ d.  SYSTEM.INI

# Question 37

After you've physically connected a new HP network printer to a network cable and properly set the printer's internal features, what's the next step in installing the network-attached printer?

- ○ a.  Install PostScript on your Windows NT Workstation print server.
- ○ b.  Install DLC on your Windows NT Workstation print server.
- ○ c.  Install TCP/IP Printing on your Windows NT Workstation print server.
- ○ d.  Install NetBEUI on your Windows NT Workstation print server.

# Question 38

Your Windows NT Workstation system hosts two 6GB hard drives on the same ATI drive controller. The second drive has two partitions of 2GB each. The second of these partitions hosts the main Windows NT Workstation directory and related system files. Using Disk Administrator, you create two 1GB partitions using the remaining space on the second partition. A message is displayed stating you need to change the ARC name in the BOOT.INI file. Which of the following is the most likely ARC name to reflect the change suggested by the message?

○ a. multi(0)disk(0)rdisk(1)partition(2)

○ b. multi(0)disk(0)rdisk(2)partition(2)

○ c. multi(0)disk(0)rdisk(1)partition(4)

○ d. multi(0)disk(0)rdisk(3)partition(4)

# Question 39

The Windows NT Workstation Disk Administrator can be used to create which of the following disk configurations? [Check all correct answers]

❏ a. Duplexed drives

❏ b. Stripe sets with parity

❏ c. Volume sets

❏ d. Standalone partitions

❏ e. Stripe sets

❏ f. RAID 2

# Question 40

If your Windows NT Workstation system hosts the same protocols (TCP/IP, NWLink, and NetBEUI) as the Windows NT Server RAS system you're dialing into, how can you guarantee you'll establish a connection that supports Winsock?

○ a. Instruct the Windows NT Server administrator to bind TCP/IP in priority to the RAS port.

○ b. Remove all non-TCP/IP protocols from the client.

○ c. Bind TCP/IP in priority to the RAS port on the client.

○ d. No action is required because TCP/IP is the only protocol supported over RAS connections.

# Question 41

Which of the following utilities can you use to obtain information about the operational status of the CPU? [Check all correct answers]

☐ a.  Network Monitor

☐ b.  Task Manager

☐ c.  Windows NT Diagnostics

☐ d.  Performance Monitor

# Question 42

What's the best file system to use on partitions larger than 400MB?

○ a.  FAT

○ b.  NTFS

○ c.  HPFS

○ d.  NFS

# Question 43

How can you most effectively and efficiently make backups of your data files on a weekly basis?

○ a.  Use the System applet to schedule weekly backups.

○ b.  Manually execute a backup through Windows NT Backup each week.

○ c.  Use Windows NT Backup's Schedule command from the Options menu to schedule automatic weekly backup operations.

○ d.  Use the Scheduler service to launch weekly backup operations.

## Question 44

How can you determine whether a scheduled NTBACKUP operation completed successfully?

○ a. Check the Server Manger history list.

○ b. View the User Manager's action record.

○ c. View the backup log created by NTBACKUP.

○ d. Examine the Registry.

○ e. View the applications log through the Event Viewer.

## Question 45

For a Windows NT Workstation system to provide IP forwarding, which condition must be met?

○ a. The NetBIOS interface must be disabled.

○ b. A HOSTS file must be present.

○ c. The routing table must include 127.0.0.1.

○ d. Two or more network interfaces must be present.

○ e. The Server service must be removed.

## Question 46

Windows NT Workstation supports which of the following types of applications? [Check all correct answers]

❑ a. Windows 3.x

❑ b. OS/2 Warp

❑ c. Solaris

❑ d. Windows 95

❑ e. POSIX

# Question 47

Which of the following components are required to support Windows 3.1 applications? [Check all correct answers]

- ❑ a.  WOW
- ❑ b.  POSIX
- ❑ c.  VDM
- ❑ d.  RPC
- ❑ e.  Win32

# Question 48

RAS connections do not support NetBEUI connections because the NetBEUI protocol cannot be routed.

- ○ a.  True
- ○ b.  False

# Question 49

Your computer system hosts both MS-DOS and Windows NT Workstation. You've been assigned the responsibility of evaluating several Plug and Play devices. Therefore, you must remove Windows NT Workstation from your system so you can install Windows 98. Which of the following methods will result in a system without Windows NT? [Check all correct answers]

- ❑ a.  Perform an upgrade install of Windows 98 over Windows NT.
- ❑ b.  Use the Remove OS option from the Add/Remove Programs applet.
- ❑ c.  Use the three setup floppies to boot and delete the NTFS partition hosting Windows NT.
- ❑ d.  From DOS, delete the Windows NT boot files and the Windows NT directories.
- ❑ e.  Use the DOS FDISK tool to remove NTFS volumes from the extended partition.

# Question 50

A Windows NT Workstation system can act as a Master Browser for an entire domain.

○ a. True

○ b. False

# Question 51

Your Windows NT Workstation system is using a NetWare-hosted print device. You're gaining access to NetWare resources through CSNW. How can you configure the system to notify you when your documents are actually printed?

○ a. Enable the Print Notification option through the local Windows NT logical printer.

○ b. Enable the Notify When Printed option through CSNW.

○ c. Enable the Notify Client option through printcon on the NetWare server.

○ d. Watch the Alert view of Performance Monitor.

# Question 52

Which of the following commands, when issued from a command prompt, will update your Emergency Repair Disk?

○ a. **erdupd /s**

○ b. **rdisk /s**

○ c. **regedit /erd**

○ d. **net erd /update**

# Question 53

Which of the following statements is true about static name resolution files?

○ a.  The LMHOSTS file maps hostnames to IP addresses, whereas the HOSTS file maps ARC names to NetBIOS names.

○ b.  The HOSTS file maps hostnames to IP addresses, whereas the LMHOSTS file maps NetBIOS names to FQDNs.

○ c.  The LMHOSTS file maps MAC addresses to IP addresses, whereas the HOSTS file maps IP addresses to NetBIOS names.

○ d.  The HOSTS file maps hostnames to IP addresses, whereas the LMHOSTS file maps IP addresses to NetBIOS names.

# Question 54

To use a SCSI tape device with NTBACKUP, what must be done? [Check all correct answers]

❑ a.  Ensure the drive controller is properly installed.

❑ b.  Enable the SCSI Tape Services through the Services applet.

❑ c.  Add the device through Tape Devices.

❑ d.  Install the device drivers through the Devices applet.

# Question 55

What is DHCP used for on a network hosting Windows NT Workstation clients?

○ a.  To maintain a routing table

○ b.  To assign IP addresses

○ c.  To maintain a relationship between IP addresses and NetBIOS names

○ d.  To redirect network requests

# 16

# Windows NT Workstation 4 Answer Key #2

| | | | |
|---|---|---|---|
| 1. a, b, e | 15. d | 29. c | 43. d |
| 2. d | 16. b | 30. b | 44. c |
| 3. b | 17. c | 31. c | 45. d |
| 4. e | 18. d | 32. e | 46. a, d, e |
| 5. a, b, d, e | 19. d | 33. d, f | 47. a, c, e |
| 6. a | 20. e | 34. d | 48. b |
| 7. a, c, d | 21. d | 35. b | 49. c, d |
| 8. c | 22. c | 36. c | 50. a |
| 9. b | 23. d | 37. b | 51. b |
| 10. d | 24. b | 38. c | 52. b |
| 11. c | 25. c, e | 39. c, d, e | 53. d |
| 12. b, e | 26. e | 40. c | 54. a, c |
| 13. a, c, f | 27. b | 41. b, d | 55. b |
| 14. a, b, d | 28. c | 42. b | |

# Question 1

Answers a, b, and e are correct. You can specify unique memory configurations for an MS-DOS application by creating a shortcut to the MS-DOS executable and editing the properties of the shortcut. This creates a PIF (Program Information File). By altering an MS-DOS executable's PIF file, you can modify the DOS VDM environment. By editing the CONFIG.NT file, the runtime environment for all VDMs may be changed, as is the case with the DOS CONFIG.SYS file. By editing the AUTOEXEC.NT file, the runtime environment for all VDMs may be changed, as is the case with the DOS AUTOEXEC.BAT file. There is no VDM Manager utility in Windows NT. Therefore, answer c is incorrect. The environment variables in the Environment tab in the System applet do not affect VDMs. Therefore, answer d is incorrect.

For more information, see Chapter 16 of *MCSE NT Workstation 4 Exam Cram*.

# Question 2

Answer d is correct. The LKGC is the most likely option for restoring the system to a bootable state. The ERD repair process may not restore the portion of the Registry you altered, so it's not the best first action. Therefore, answer a is incorrect. REGEDT32 does not have an Undo option. What's more, you would need to be able to boot the system to use this tool anyway. Therefore, answer b is incorrect. Holding down the Ctrl key while booting will not change how the system boots. Therefore, answer c is incorrect.

For more information, see Chapter 18 of *MCSE NT Workstation 4 Exam Cram*.

# Question 3

Answer b is correct. This is a false statement. Windows NT's FAT file system has a 512-file limit in its root directory.

For more information, see Chapter 6 of *MCSE NT Workstation 4 Exam Cram*.

# Question 4

Answer e is correct. The only option in this list that offers true callback security is setting Callback to Preset To and defining a specific number. Setting Callback to No Call Back is against company policy and offers no security. Therefore, answer a is incorrect. There is no Capture Caller ID feature in Windows NT's built-in RAS. Therefore, answer b is incorrect. Setting Callback to Set By Caller is not secure. Therefore, answer c is incorrect. There is no Roaming feature in Windows NT's built-in RAS. Therefore, answer d is incorrect.

For more information, see Chapter 13 of *MCSE NT Workstation 4 Exam Cram*.

## Question 5

Answers a, b, d, and e are correct. An upgrade install will retain applications, repair the Registry, replace drivers, and retain local profiles. A new install is required to change the SID. Therefore, answer c is incorrect.

For more information, see Chapter 3 of *MCSE NT Workstation 4 Exam Cram*.

## Question 6

Answer a is correct. Changing the Registry value of **ShutdownWithoutLogon** from 1 to 0 is the proper action. **ShowLogonShutdown** and **Shutdown-BeforeLogon** are not valid Registry values. Therefore, answers b and d are incorrect. The System applet does not offer a Shutdown Without Logon setting. Therefore, answer c is incorrect.

For more information, see Chapter 8 of *MCSE NT Workstation 4 Exam Cram*.

## Question 7

Answers a, c, and d are correct. The Task Manager displays the peak memory usage, kernel size, and active threads. The Task Manager does not display the size of the paging file. Therefore, answer b is incorrect.

For more information, see Chapter 15 of *MCSE NT Workstation 4 Exam Cram*.

## Question 8

Answer c is correct. The print job remains in the queue and waits for the print jam to be cleared. Once the jam is cleared, the job will continue to print. In most cases, the page of the document that jammed will need to be sent again manually. The document will not be rerouted to another printer, removed from the print queue, or respooled to disk. Therefore, answers a, b, and d are incorrect.

For more information, see Chapter 14 of *MCSE NT Workstation 4 Exam Cram*.

## Question 9

Answer b is correct. Logical disk object counters are the best choice here—they can provide data about disk space usage and about read/write activities. This is just what's needed to attack the reported problem. Although using physical disk counters may appear to be an attractive solution, storing files requires writing to a particular partition. Physical disk counters are helpful in resolving hardware problems, but not necessarily when dealing with read/write activities or delays. Therefore, answer a is incorrect. Because the system is behaving normally, it's unlikely that system, server, and memory object counters will help in resolving what's apparently a storage device problem. Therefore, answers c, d, and e are incorrect.

For more information, see Chapter 15 of *MCSE NT Workstation 4 Exam Cram*.

## Question 10

Answer d is correct. Separate hardware profiles may indeed be established for networked use and detached use. The modem can be disabled in the office hardware profile, whereas the network card can be disabled in the "away" hardware profile. This is the right approach to take. Multiple user accounts, computer policies, and user profiles will not offer a solution. Therefore, answers a, b, and c are incorrect.

For more information, see Chapter 5 of *MCSE NT Workstation 4 Exam Cram*.

## Question 11

Answer c is correct. The System: Processor Queue Length is often used to detect CPU bottlenecks. RAM, disk, and network bottleneck detection does not employ this counter. Therefore, answers a, b, and d are incorrect.

For more information, see Chapter 15 of *MCSE NT Workstation 4 Exam Cram*.

## Question 12

Answers b and e are correct. Only the IP address and subnet mask must be defined. Neither a DNS server nor a WINS server are required. Therefore, answers a and d are incorrect. The default gateway is not required because no routing is occurring on this network. Therefore, answer c is incorrect.

For more information, see Chapter 10 of *MCSE NT Workstation 4 Exam Cram*.

## Question 13

Answers a, c, and f are correct. A non-administrator can launch applications using the **START** command with priorities of Low, Normal, and High. Pause, System, and Kernel are invalid options. Therefore, answers b, d, and g are incorrect. Realtime can only be used by administrators. Therefore, answer e is incorrect.

For more information, see Chapter 15 of *MCSE NT Workstation 4 Exam Cram*.

## Question 14

Answers a, b, and d are correct. The ERD repair process can repair the startup environment, restore the security database, and repair the boot sector (as well as verify system files). The entire Registry is not stored on the ERD, so it cannot be replaced on the system. Therefore, answer c is incorrect. The ERD repair process does not inspect the ACLs of NTFS volumes. Therefore, answer e is incorrect.

For more information, see Chapter 18 of *MCSE NT Workstation 4 Exam Cram*.

## Question 15

Answer d is correct. The most likely cause is that the wrong frame type was defined for the NWLink protocol. A protocol mismatch would only occur if both the client and the network were not using the same protocol, but, in this case, they're both using NWLink. Therefore, answer a is incorrect. A memory conflict is very rare in Windows NT—an IRQ conflict is more likely. Therefore, answer b is incorrect. A bad cable is not a probable cause because a Windows 95 system was just on the same connection and it was fully functional. Therefore, answer c is incorrect.

For more information, see Chapter 11 of *MCSE NT Workstation 4 Exam Cram*.

## Question 16

Answer b is correct. The proper action is to skip the autodrive detection and install the drivers manually during setup. Installing the drivers through the SCSI Adapters applet is only an option when the drive controller is not the host of the boot and system partitions. Therefore, answer a is incorrect. Copying the driver to the third setup floppy will not add the driver to the install list. Therefore, answer c is incorrect. The generic drivers typically do not function on devices where a downloadable driver is indicated on the HCL. Therefore, answer d is incorrect.

For more information, see Chapter 3 of *MCSE NT Workstation 4 Exam Cram*.

# Question 17

Answer c is correct. The PPP.LOG file is enabled through the Registry. The Server Manager does not offer any RAS-related controls. Therefore, answer a is incorrect. The Modems applet can only be used to enable a device log. Therefore, answer b is incorrect. The Event Viewer does not offer RAS-specific log access. Therefore, answer d is incorrect.

For more information, see Chapter 13 of *MCSE NT Workstation 4 Exam Cram*.

# Question 18

Answer d is correct. Disk Administrator is the best tool from this list for restoring the SYSTEM key. User Manager, Server Manager, and Windows NT Diagnostics do not offer Registry repair options. Therefore, answers a, b, and c are incorrect. The ERD repair process requires an ERD, which this scenario does not offer (just a copy of the SYSTEM key is not enough). Therefore, answer e is incorrect.

For more information, see Chapter 18 of *MCSE NT Workstation 4 Exam Cram*.

# Question 19

Answer d is correct. The Server service is the only listed component involved in the basic function of sharing a local printer. The Workstation service is only required to access network resources, not to offer them. Therefore, answer a is incorrect. AppleTalk is not supported by Windows NT Workstation; it's only available through Windows NT Server's Services for Macintosh. Therefore, answer b is incorrect. DLC is only needed when Windows NT is a print server for a network-attached printer. Therefore, answer c is incorrect. The TCP/IP Printing service is only required when LPD/LPR access to the printer is required. Therefore, answer e is incorrect.

For more information, see Chapter 14 of *MCSE NT Workstation 4 Exam Cram*.

# Question 20

Answer e is correct. The single action you should take is disabling IP forwarding. Removing TCP/IP from the network is unnecessary and a lot of work. Therefore, answer a is incorrect. The Workstation service is required to access network resources; it does not affect the ability of outside users to compromise your system. Therefore, answer b is incorrect. A subnet mask of 0.0.0.0 is invalid. Therefore, answer c is incorrect. A gateway address of 127.0.0.1 is useless. What's more, this situation did not indicate that routing was being used. Therefore, answer d is incorrect.

For more information, see Chapter 10 of *MCSE NT Workstation 4 Exam Cram*.

## Question 21

Answer d is correct. The process of moving a file from one partition to another essentially copies the file to the new partition and deletes the original. A copied file always assumes the permissions of its new container, but that does not come into effect here because FAT partitions do not have file-level permissions, so all permissions are lost. Also, Windows NT's FAT supports LFNs, so the file name is retained. Therefore, answers a, b, and c are incorrect.

For more information, see Chapter 6 of *MCSE NT Workstation 4 Exam Cram*.

## Question 22

Answer c is correct. The proper syntax is **winnt /b /u:specs1.txt /udf:5, pent3.txt**. The syntax **winnt /b /u:pent3.txt /udf:5, specs1.txt** has the UDF and answer files reversed. Therefore, answer a is incorrect. Winnt32 cannot be used from MS-DOS. Therefore, answer b is incorrect. The syntax **winnt /b /u:specs1.txt/ udf:pent3.txt, 5** has the UDF file name and the ID reversed. Therefore, answer d is incorrect.

For more information, see Chapter 3 of *MCSE NT Workstation 4 Exam Cram*.

## Question 23

Answer d is correct. Using roaming profiles is the only real way to maintain each user's environmental settings on all three computers. Local profiles will not allow the users to have the same configuration on each system. Therefore, answer a is incorrect. Mandatory profiles will not allow users to retain their own settings. Therefore, answer b is incorrect. A single roaming profile will not allow users to maintain separate and distinct environments. Therefore, answer c is incorrect.

For more information, see Chapter 5 of *MCSE NT Workstation 4 Exam Cram*.

## Question 24

Answer b is correct. You must change the authentication and encryption policy to accept clear text or CHAP, because Unix servers do not support MS-CHAP. The dial-up server type does not need to be changed if a PPP connection is being made. Therefore, answer a is incorrect. Terminal window settings do not need to be changed. Therefore, answer c is incorrect. Using a logon script is not a required change. Therefore, answer d is incorrect.

For more information, see Chapter 13 of *MCSE NT Workstation 4 Exam Cram*.

## Question 25

Answers c and e are correct. The statements "The paging file can be split across several physical drives" and "The system must be rebooted to employ changes to the Virtual Memory dialog box" are true. When STOP error actions are defined on the Startup/Shutdown tab of the System applet, a 2MB paging file is required on the boot partition. Therefore, answer a is incorrect. HPFS is not supported by Windows NT Workstation 4.0. Therefore, answer b is incorrect. The default size of the paging file is 12MB larger than the physical RAM. Therefore, answer d is incorrect.

For more information, see Chapter 15 of *MCSE NT Workstation 4 Exam Cram*.

## Question 26

Answer e is correct. Using a single memory space is the downfall of Win16 applications. Thunking, 16-bit code, and 8.3 file names are not inherently faulty. Therefore, answers a, b, and d are incorrect. A single message queue can cause some difficulties, but it's not usually the culprit in this situation. Therefore, answer c is incorrect.

For more information, see Chapter 16 of *MCSE NT Workstation 4 Exam Cram*.

## Question 27

Answer b is correct. The three-setup-floppy installation method creates the destination partition before it copies the necessary installation files. A network install process and installing from the CD-ROM both copy the 120MB of data to a formatted drive before rebooting to start the actual installation. With a 75MB partition (with several megabytes being used for DOS), you'll encounter an error. Therefore, answers a and c are incorrect. Copying the i386 directory manually will cause an error due to insufficient space. Therefore, answer d is incorrect.

For more information, see Chapter 3 of *MCSE NT Workstation 4 Exam Cram*.

## Question 28

Answer c is correct. The Memory: Pages/Second counter should be watched to decide whether you need more RAM to reduce disk thrashing. If you need to find out the percentage of elapsed time a processor is busy, you would look at % Processor Time. Therefore, answer a is incorrect. There is no counter named Pages/Thread. Therefore, answer b is incorrect. The LogicalDisk: Avg. Disk

Bytes/Transfer counter indicates the amount of bytes transferred to and from a disk—it does not relate to memory. Therefore, answer d is incorrect.

For more information, see Chapter 15 of *MCSE NT Workstation 4 Exam Cram*.

## Question 29

Answer c is correct. The timeout value in the BOOT.INI file is set to 0. If the system partition files were overwritten, Windows NT would not boot. Therefore, answer a is incorrect. If NTLDR were missing, Windows NT would not boot. Therefore, answer b is incorrect. There is no multiboot option. Therefore, answer d is incorrect.

For more information, see Chapter 3 of *MCSE NT Workstation 4 Exam Cram*.

## Question 30

Answer b is correct. Process Tracking tracks threads and processes, including applications. Application Activity is not a valid selection. Therefore, answer a is incorrect. Security Policy Changes tracks modifications to security and policies. Therefore, answer c is incorrect. Restart, Shutdown, and System tracks system restarts. Therefore, answer d is incorrect. File and Object Access is for tracking NTFS objects such as files and printers. Therefore, answer e is incorrect.

For more information, see Chapter 15 of *MCSE NT Workstation 4 Exam Cram*.

## Question 31

Answer c is correct. Bob has Change access to this share due to the combined levels of Managers and Marketing. The Users nondefined level has no effect. Therefore, answers a, b, and d are incorrect.

For more information, see chapters 4 and 7 of *MCSE NT Workstation 4 Exam Cram*.

## Question 32

Answer e is correct. Because Windows NT Workstation is aimed at end users, it's open to nearly all users—it permits members of Administrators, Backup Operators, Power Users, Users, Guests, and Everyone to log on locally. Therefore, answers a, b, c, and d are incorrect.

For more information, see Chapter 4 of *MCSE NT Workstation 4 Exam Cram*.

# Question 33

Answers d and f are correct. The files that always appear in the system partition on a PC running Windows NT are BOOT.INI, NTLDR, and NTDETECT.COM (not listed). BOOTSECT.DOS is only required on multi-boot systems with non-Windows NT operating systems. Therefore, answer a is incorrect. OSLOADER.EXE is only used on RISC systems. Therefore, answer b is incorrect. NTBOOTDD.SYS is only required on systems using SCSI drive controllers without BIOS support. Therefore, answer c is incorrect. NTOSKRNL.EXE is found on the boot partition and should not be on the boot floppy. Therefore, answer e is incorrect.

For more information, see Chapter 17 of *MCSE NT Workstation 4 Exam Cram*.

# Question 34

Answer d is correct. The fastest lookup time occurs when both HOSTS and LMHOSTS files are stored on the local hard drive of each RAS client, because no WAN traffic needs to occur to resolve a resource location. Storing these files somewhere other than on the client increases the lookup time. Therefore, answers a, b, and c are incorrect.

For more information, see Chapters 10 and 13 of *MCSE NT Workstation 4 Exam Cram*.

# Question 35

Answer b is correct. Only the System applet from Windows NT Workstation is involved in transforming a local profile into a roaming profile. The Network and Regional Settings applets are not involved. Therefore, answers a and c are incorrect. Server Manager is a Windows NT Server utility and is not involved. Therefore, answer d is incorrect. The User Manager is not able to make the necessary domain changes, so the User Manager For Domains from Windows NT Server must be used. Therefore, answer e is incorrect.

For more information, see Chapter 5 of *MCSE NT Workstation 4 Exam Cram*.

# Question 36

Answer c is correct. NTUSER.MAN is associated with mandatory profiles. CONFIG.NT is used to define the environment of VDMs. Therefore, answer a is incorrect. NTCONFIG.POL is the system policies file. Therefore, answer b is incorrect. SYSTEM.INI is a backward-compatible file for Windows 95 and Windows 3.x applications. Therefore, answer d is incorrect.

For more information, see Chapter 5 of *MCSE NT Workstation 4 Exam Cram*.

## Question 37

Answer b is correct. Installing DLC is the next step. PostScript is not an installation module—it's a setting on an existing logical printer. Therefore, answer a is incorrect. TCP/IP Printing is only used in conjunction with Unix or other TCP/IP-only print servers or clients using LPR/LPD. Therefore, answer c is incorrect. NetBEUI is not a required protocol for network-attached printers. Therefore, answer d is incorrect.

For more information, see Chapter 14 of *MCSE NT Workstation 4 Exam Cram*.

## Question 38

Answer c is correct. The ARC name multi(0)disk(0)rdisk(1)partition(4) is the most likely one to reflect the suggested change. In most cases, adding new partitions to a drive pushes the partition number of the boot partition up. The ARC name multi(0)disk(0)rdisk(1)partition(2) is the original ARC name. Therefore, answer a is incorrect. RDISK(2) indicates a third hard drive. Therefore, answer b is incorrect. RDISK(3) indicates a fourth hard drive. Therefore, answer d is incorrect.

For more information, see Chapter 17 of *MCSE NT Workstation 4 Exam Cram*.

## Question 39

Answers c, d, and e are correct. The Windows NT Workstation Disk Administrator can be used to create volume sets, standalone partitions, and stripe sets. The Windows NT Workstation Disk Administrator cannot be used to create duplexed drives, stripe sets with parity, and RAID 2 configurations (mirroring or duplexing), because they're not supported by Windows NT Workstation. Therefore, answers a, b, and f are incorrect.

For more information, see Chapter 6 of *MCSE NT Workstation 4 Exam Cram*.

## Question 40

Answer c is correct. Binding TCP/IP in priority to the RAS port on the client is the only way to ensure this protocol will be used over the RAS connection. Binding TCP/IP first on the RAS server will not guarantee its use because the binding order of the client is used. Therefore, answer a is incorrect. Uninstalling protocols is an unnecessary operation. Therefore, answer b is incorrect. The near random binding order of the protocols on the client does not guarantee which one will be used, so some action must be taken. Therefore, answer d is incorrect.

For more information, see Chapter 13 of *MCSE NT Workstation 4 Exam Cram*.

## Question 41

Answers b and d are correct. The Task Manager and Performance Monitor can be used to obtain CPU status. Network Monitor and Windows NT Diagnostics do not offer insight into the operational status of the CPU. Therefore, answers a and c are incorrect.

For more information, see Chapter 15 of *MCSE NT Workstation 4 Exam Cram*.

## Question 42

Answer b is correct. NTFS offers better performance than FAT on partitions 400MB and larger. FAT only offers better performance than NTFS on partitions smaller than 200MB. Therefore, answer a is incorrect. HPFS and NFS are not supported by Windows NT. Therefore, answers c and d are incorrect.

For more information, see Chapter 6 of *MCSE NT Workstation 4 Exam Cram*.

## Question 43

Answer d is correct. The Scheduler service must be employed using the AT command to launch weekly backup operations automatically. The System applet cannot schedule events. Therefore, answer a is incorrect. Manual execution of the backup is not the most efficient solution. Therefore, answer b is incorrect. Windows NT Backup does not have its own built-in Schedule command or capability. Therefore, answer c is incorrect.

For more information, see Chapter 7 of *MCSE NT Workstation 4 Exam Cram*.

## Question 44

Answer c is correct. The only way to verify the completion of a backup is to check the backup log created by NTBACKUP. The Server Manager does not offer a history list. What's more, it's a Windows NT Server utility. Therefore, answer a is incorrect. The User Manager does not offer an action record. Therefore, answer b is incorrect. The Registry does not contain backup status information. Therefore, answer d is incorrect. Although the applications log in

Event Viewer will indicate when NTBACKUP started and finished, it won't show anything about completion status. Therefore, answer e is incorrect.

For more information, see Chapter 7 of *MCSE NT Workstation 4 Exam Cram*.

## Question 45

Answer d is correct. IP forwarding requires two or more network interfaces. The NetBIOS interface is not associated with IP forwarding. Therefore, answer a is incorrect. The HOSTS file is not associated with IP forwarding. Therefore, answer b is incorrect. The routing table's inclusion of the loopback address does not affect IP forwarding. Therefore, answer c is incorrect. The Server service is not associated with IP forwarding. Therefore, answer e is incorrect.

For more information, see chapters 9 and 10 of *MCSE NT Workstation 4 Exam Cram*.

## Question 46

Answers a, d, and e are correct. Windows NT Workstation supports MS-DOS, Win16, Win32, POSIX.1, and OS/2 v.1 applications. Windows NT does not support OS/2 Warp and Solaris applications. Therefore, answers b and c are incorrect.

For more information, see Chapter 16 of *MCSE NT Workstation 4 Exam Cram*.

## Question 47

Answers a, c, and e are correct. A Windows 3.1 or Win16 application runs in the WOW (Windows On Windows) environment, which itself requires a VDM (Virtual DOS Machine), which in turn requires the Win32 subsystem. POSIX is not required for hosting Win16 applications. Therefore, answer b is incorrect. RPC is not employed by the Win16 subsystem. Therefore, answer d is incorrect.

For more information, see Chapter 16 of *MCSE NT Workstation 4 Exam Cram*.

## Question 48

Answer b is correct. This is a false statement. RAS connections can support NetBEUI in spite of it not being a routable protocol.

For more information, see Chapter 13 of *MCSE NT Workstation 4 Exam Cram*.

## Question 49

Answers c and d are correct. Removing Windows NT can be accomplished in two basic ways. If FAT volumes host Windows NT, you can delete all the Windows NT files from DOS. If NTFS is used, you can employ the three setup floppies to remove the NTFS partitions. Windows 98 does not provide an upgrade path from Windows NT Workstation. Therefore, answer a is incorrect. There is no Remove OS option. Therefore, answer b is incorrect. The DOS FDISK tool cannot even see NTFS volumes in an extended partition. Therefore, answer e is incorrect.

For more information, see Chapter 3 of *MCSE NT Workstation 4 Exam Cram*.

## Question 50

Answer a is correct. This is a true statement. Although in most cases a Windows NT Server system will win the Browser election, Windows NT Workstation machine is capable of being the Master Browser.

For more information, see Chapter 12 of *MCSE NT Workstation 4 Exam Cram*.

## Question 51

Answer b is correct. Enabling the CSNW Notify When Printed option is the proper action. Logical printers do not offer this option. Therefore, answer a is incorrect. Printcon is a print utility that's native to NetWare and cannot be used for this purpose. Therefore, answer c is incorrect. The Alert view will not show the completion of print jobs. Therefore, answer d is incorrect.

For more information, see chapters 11 and 14 of *MCSE NT Workstation 4 Exam Cram*.

## Question 52

Answer b is correct. Only **rdisk /s** will update the ERD. The others are invalid constructions. Therefore, answers a, c, and d are incorrect.

For more information, see Chapter 18 of *MCSE NT Workstation 4 Exam Cram*.

## Question 53

Answer d is correct. The HOSTS file indeed maps hostnames to IP addresses, and LMHOSTS maps IP addresses to NetBIOS names. Therefore, answers a, b, and c are incorrect.

For more information, see Chapter 10 of *MCSE NT Workstation 4 Exam Cram*.

## Question 54

Answers a and c are correct. To use a SCSI tape drive, you need to ensure the drive controller is properly installed through the SCSI applet and install the device through Tape Devices applet. There is no SCSI Tape Services. Therefore, answer b is incorrect. Drivers are not installed through the Devices applet. Therefore, answer d is incorrect.

For more information, see chapters 5 and 7 of *MCSE NT Workstation 4 Exam Cram.*

## Question 55

Answer b is correct. DHCP is used to dynamically assign IP addresses and other TCP/IP settings to clients. The routing table is maintained manually by the **ROUTE** command or dynamically by RIP. Therefore, answer a is incorrect. WINS maintains a relationship between IP addresses and NetBIOS names. Therefore, answer c is incorrect. Network requests are redirected by redirectors such as logical printers connected to network printer shares or mapped drive letters connected to network shares. Therefore, answer d is incorrect.

For more information, see Chapter 10 of *MCSE NT Workstation 4 Exam Cram.*

# CERTIFIED CRAMMER SOCIETY

PHI SLAMMA CRAMMA

A breed apart, a cut above the rest—a true professional. Highly skilled and superbly trained, certified IT professionals are unquestionably the world's most elite computer experts. In an effort to appropriately recognize this privileged crowd, The Coriolis Group is proud to introduce the Certified Crammer Society. If you are a certified IT professional, it is our pleasure to invite you to become a Certified Crammer Society member.

Membership is free to all certified professionals and benefits include a membership kit that contains your official membership card and official Certified Crammer Society blue denim ball cap emblazoned with the Certified Crammer Society crest—proudly displaying the Crammer motto "Phi Slamma Cramma"—and featuring a genuine leather bill. The kit also includes your password to the Certified Crammers-Only Web site containing monthly discreet messages designed to provide you with advance notification about certification testing information, special book excerpts, and inside industry news not found anywhere else; monthly Crammers-Only discounts on selected Coriolis titles; *Ask the Series Editor* Q and A column; cool contests with great prizes; and more.

## GUIDELINES FOR MEMBERSHIP

Registration is free to professionals certified in Microsoft, A+, or Oracle DBA. Coming soon: Sun Java, Novell, and Cisco. Send or email your contact information and proof of your certification (test scores, membership card, or official letter) to:

Certified Crammer Society Membership Chairperson
**THE CORIOLIS GROUP, LLC**
14455 North Hayden Road, Suite 220, Scottsdale, Arizona 85260-6949
Fax: 480.483.0193 • Email: ccs@coriolis.com

## APPLICATION

Name:

Society Alias:

Choose a secret code name to correspond with us and other Crammer Society members. Please use no more than eight characters.

Address:

Email:

*Coriolis introduces*

# EXAM CRAM INSIDER™

A FREE ONLINE NEWSLETTER

Stay current with the latest certification information. Just email us to receive the latest in certification and training news for Microsoft, Java, Novell, A+, and more! Read e-letters from the Publisher of the Exam Cram series, Keith Weiskamp, and Exam Cram Series Editor, Ed Tittel, about future trends in IT training and education. Access valuable insider information on exam updates, new testing procedures, sample chapters, and links to other useful, online sites. Take a look at the featured program of the month, and who's in the news today. We pack all this and more into our *Exam Cram Insider* online newsletter to make sure *you* pass your next test!

To sign up for our twice monthly newsletter, go to www.coriolis.com and click on the sign up sheet, or email us at eci@coriolis.com and put "subscribe insider" in the body of the message.

EXAM CRAM INSIDER – Another reason Exam Cram is *The Smartest Way To Get Certified.™* And it's <u>free</u>!

# CORIOLIS HELP CENTER

Here at The Coriolis Group, we strive to provide the finest customer service in the technical education industry. We're committed to helping you reach your certification goals by assisting you in the following areas.

## Talk to the Authors

We'd like to hear from you! Please refer to the "How to Use This Book" section in the "Introduction" of every Exam Cram guide for our authors' individual email addresses.

## Web Page Information

The Certification Insider Press Web page provides a host of valuable information that's only a click away. For information in the following areas, please visit us at:
**www.coriolis.com/cip/default.cfm**

- Titles and other products
- Book content updates
- Roadmap to Certification Success guide
- New Adaptive Testing changes
- New Exam Cram Live! seminars
- New Certified Crammer Society details
- Sample chapters and tables of contents
- Manuscript solicitation
- Special programs and events

## Contact Us by Email

Important addresses you may use to reach us at The Coriolis Group.

### eci@coriolis.com

To subscribe to our FREE, bi-monthly on-line newsletter, *Exam Cram Insider*. Keep up to date with the certification scene. Included in each *Insider* are certification articles, program updates, new exam information, hints and tips, sample chapters, and more.

### techsupport@coriolis.com

**For technical questions and problems with CD-ROMs.** Products broken, battered, or blown-up? Just need some installation advice? Contact us here.

### ccs@coriolis.com

**To obtain membership information for the** *Certified Crammer Society*, **an exclusive club for the certified professional.** Get in on members-only discounts, special information, expert advice, contests, cool prizes, and free stuff for the certified professional. Membership is FREE. Contact us and get enrolled today!

### cipq@coriolis.com

**For book content questions and feedback about our titles, drop us a line.** This is the good, the bad, and the questions address. Our customers are the best judges of our products. Let us know what you like, what we could do better, or what question you may have about any content. Testimonials are always welcome here, and if you send us a story about how an Exam Cram guide has helped you ace a test, we'll give you an official Certification Insider Press T-shirt.

### custserv@coriolis.com

**For solutions to problems concerning an order for any of our products.** Our staff will promptly and courteously address the problem. Taking the exams is difficult enough. We want to make acquiring our study guides as easy as possible.

## Book Orders & Shipping Information

### orders@coriolis.com

To place an order by email or to check on the status of an order already placed.

### coriolis.com/bookstore/default.cfm

To place an order through our online bookstore.

### 1.800.410.0192

To place an order by phone or to check on an order already placed.

# What's On The CD-ROM

The *MCSE Core Four Practice Tests Exam Cram*'s companion CD-ROM contains four practice exams, one on each of the Core Four topics. These exams are built using an interactive adaptive format that allows you to practice in an exam environment similar to Microsoft's own testing format.

## System Requirements

### Software

➤ Your operating system must be Windows 95/98 or NT 4.

➤ Internet Explorer or Netscape Navigator with Java capabilities is needed to complete the projects included in this book. (The software is not provided on this CD-ROM.)

### Hardware

➤ Minimum of a 486/66 MHz processor is recommended.

➤ 16MB RAM is the minimum requirement.